Nicaragua

WORLD BIBLIOGRAPHICAL SERIES

General Editors:
Robert L. Collison (Editor-in-chief)
Sheila R. Herstein
Louis J. Reith
Hans H. Wellisch

VOLUMES IN THE SERIES

VOLUME 44

Nicaragua

Ralph Lee Woodward, Jr.
Compiler
Edited by Sheila R. Herstein

CLIO PRESS
OXFORD, ENGLAND · SANTA BARBARA, CALIFORNIA

British Library Cataloguing in Publication Data

Woodward, Ralph Lee
Nicaragua. – (World bibliographical series; 44)
1. Nicaragua – Bibliography
I. Title   II. Series
016.97285   Z1481

ISBN 0-903450-79-8

Clio Press Ltd.,
55 St. Thomas' St.,
Oxford OX1 1JG

ABC-Clio Information Services,
Riviera Campus, 2040 Alameda Padre Serra,
Santa Barbara, Ca. 93103, USA

Designed by Bernard Crossland
Computer typeset by Peter Peregrinus Ltd.
Printed and bound in Great Britain by
Antony Rowe Ltd., Chippenham

THE WORLD BIBLIOGRAPHICAL SERIES

This series will eventually cover every country in the world, each in a separate volume comprising annotated entries on works dealing with its history, geography, economy and politics; and with its people, their culture, customs, religion and social organization. Attention will also be paid to current living conditions – housing, education, newspapers, clothing, etc. – that are all too often ignored in standard bibliographies; and to those particular aspects relevant to individual countries. Each volume seeks to achieve, by use of careful selectivity and critical assessment of the literature, an expression of the country and an appreciation of its nature and national aspirations, to guide the reader towards an understanding of its importance. The keynote of the series is to provide, in a uniform format, an interpretation of each country that will express its culture, its place in the world, and the qualities and background that make it unique.

SERIES EDITORS

Robert L. Collison (Editor-in-chief) is Professor Emeritus, Library and Information Studies, University of California, Los Angeles, and is currently the President of the Society of Indexers. Following the war, he served as Reference Librarian for the City of Westminster and later became Librarian to the BBC. During his fifty years as a professional librarian in England and the USA, he has written more than twenty works on bibliography, librarianship, indexing and related subjects.

Sheila R. Herstein is Reference Librarian and Library Instruction Coordinator at the City College of the City University of New York. She has extensive bibliographic experience and described her innovations in the field of bibliographic instruction in 'Team teaching and bibliographic instruction', *The Bookmark*, Autumn 1979. In addition, Doctor Herstein co-authored a basic annotated bibliography in history for Funk & Wagnalls *New encyclopedia*, and for several years reviewed books for *Library Journal*.

Louis J. Reith is librarian with the Franciscan Institute, St. Bonaventure University, New York. He received his PhD from Stanford University, California, and later studied at Eberhard-Karls-Universität, Tübingen. In addition to his activities as a librarian, Dr. Reith is a specialist on 16th-century German history and the Reformation and has published many articles and papers in both German and English. He was also editor of the *American Society for Reformation Research Newsletter*.

Hans H. Wellisch is Associate Professor at the College of Library and Information Services, University of Maryland, and a member of the American Society of Indexers and the International Federation for Documentation. He is the author of numerous articles and several books on indexing and abstracting, and has also published *Indexing and abstracting: an international bibliography*. He also contributes frequently to *Journal of the American Society for Information Science, Library Quarterly,* and *The Indexer*.

For
Xavier and Anne

Contents

Contents

Contents

Introduction

The Central American Republic of Nicaragua is presently undergoing the most revolutionary transformation in its history. Nicaragua is a country whose progress has often been shaped by natural disaster, violence, civil war and revolution. The present upheaval seeks to restructure the country in order to provide social justice and economic equality for a population which has long been downtrodden and exploited by an extremely durable élite. The resilience of this élite, from which many of the Sandinista leaders themselves come, has made this revolution distinctly different from other social revolutions of 20th-century Latin America. The Central American states have much in common, yet Nicaragua has often stood out as an exception. Today, once more, Nicaragua stands alone in Central America, embarked on a path toward socialism feared by the governing élites of all of her sister states on the isthmus.

Although in area (55,000 square miles) Nicaragua is the largest state in Central America, it ranks fourth, behind Guatemala, El Salvador and Honduras, in population. Most of the population, however, is concentrated in the western region along the Pacific coast, where the climate is drier and more comfortable than in the steaming lowlands of the Caribbean watershed of the isthmus. The country has great geographical diversity, but the most striking features are the volcanoes rising along the spine of the highlands that parallel the Pacific shore throughout Central America. Another notable feature of Nicaragua's geography, however, is the break there in this mountain chain, a break that made Nicaragua one of the most probable sites for an interoceanic canal. Moreover, it has meant that unlike most of the major cities of Central America, which are in the highlands, Nicaragua's population centres — Granada, León and Managua — are all located near sea-level.

Before the arrival of the Spaniards, the area of the present-day Republic of Nicaragua represented the southern frontier of Mayan and Nahua culture. Several large tribes, at varying stages of civilization, inhabited the region. Although the archaeology of this area is less spectacular than in the centres of Mesoamerican culture to the north, there remain many stone monuments and other evidence of these peoples. In addition to the influence from the north, pre-Columbian Nicaragua also had important ties with South American tribes and thus was part of a land-bridge between the Americas.

The arrival of an expedition from Panama under Francisco Hernández de Córdoba in 1524 sent deep shock waves through the Indian communities of Nicaragua. Initial contact with the Spaniards had been friendly, and Spanish priests baptized thousands of Indians residing on the shores of the great Lake Nicaragua. Córdoba founded the towns of Granada on Lake Nicaragua and León on Lake Managua. The early days of Spanish rule were under the direction of the ruthless governor of Panama, Pedro Arías de Avila (Pedrarias Dávila), who himself came to Nicaragua as governor of the new colony in 1526. The Spanish settlers quickly divided up the lands and enslaved the Indians of the Pacific watershed. Bitter struggles among the conquistadores led to civil war and violence. Between war and the diseases which the Spaniards brought from Europe (smallpox, plague, syphillis, etc.), much of the Indian population perished. Yet since the Spaniards brought few of their women to Nicaragua, race mixture occurred frequently and the mestizo became the racial majority of modern Nicaragua.

The turbulent and violent early days of Nicaraguan history were followed by reorganization of the colony within the Kingdom of Guatemala, with its capital at Guatemala City. While Nicaragua produced some indigo and other export products, most of the colonists settled into a subsistence pattern, or raised cattle which they drove along the rude *camino real* to markets in El Salvador and Guatemala, where export agriculture developed to a somewhat higher degree. To the southeast, Costa Rica developed slowly as a dependency of Nicaragua. Thus, a measure of interdependence developed among the Central American provinces. Within Nicaragua a landholding élite developed around Granada. It would become a citadel of traditional conservatism. León also developed a creole élite, but that city became more associated with the development of the bureaucracy of the colonial government. When the volcano Momotombo erupted and buried it in 1610, the city was rebuilt several miles to the west, where it grew once more to rival Granada. At the close of the colonial period it was the focus of strong Liberal sentiment and the site of the only university in Central America outside the capital city of Guatemala.

Independence from Spain, declared in 1821, came without the devastating wars that scarred much of Latin America, but it ushered in a period of intense conflict between Conservative Granada and Liberal

León. Civil war for most of the next forty years left the country exhausted politically and devastated economically. The United Provinces of Central America had disintegrated by 1840 and the five states became sovereign republics. Plans for an interoceanic canal fuelled Nicaraguan optimism, but the Anglo-American rivalry for control of such a route contributed to further disruption of the country. On the Caribbean shore the British followed an aggressive policy which 17th-century buccaneers had begun. A British protectorate over the Miskito Indians left an English-speaking legacy there to the present day.

United States interest in the isthmus accelerated following its acquisition of the Pacific coast of North America. After 1848 Nicaragua was on the main route to the California gold-fields, as Cornelius Vanderbilt developed a prosperous isthmian transit company. Then came one of Nicaragua's most traumatic experiences, the invasion by the filibuster William Walker, who in 1855 brought a small band of adventurers from California to aid the Liberals. Within a year he had made himself president of the country. Walker's rule was short-lived, however, and a combined Central American force, with British aid, defeated the Tennesseean the following year.

The Walker episode discredited the Liberals in Nicaragua and ushered in more than thirty years of comparative peace and stability under the Conservatives. This delayed the 'Liberal Reform' which after 1860 swept over the rest of Central America. José Santos Zelaya finally overcame the Conservatives in 1893 and launched a Liberal dictatorship in Nicaragua. Zelaya promoted economic development, emphasizing export production as had Liberals elsewhere on the isthmus, but he also put the country deeply in debt and encountered growing opposition from both the Conservatives and certain foreign economic interests. His enemies forced him from power in 1909, but turmoil followed, leading to a US intervention that put the country under the control of North American Marines in collaboration with the Conservative Party.

The US occupation lasted until 1925, but no sooner had the Marines departed than renewed Conservative-Liberal conflict brought them back in 1926. An agreement with the Liberal General José M. Moncada provided for US supervision of elections, but in effect allowed the Liberals to retain power, an arrangement more consistent with US support generally of the Liberal Party in Central America. One Liberal general, however, Augusto César Sandino, refused to recognize the agreement and launched a guerrilla struggle against the US military presence. The Marines finally departed in 1933, but not before establishing a powerful National Guard that would dominate the country for the next half-century under the leadership of Anastasio Somoza García and his sons. Sandino himself was treacherously murdered at the hands of the Guard, becoming a martyr to the cause of anti-imperialism. His legendary struggle against the Marines served as a popular cloak for the movement that ultimately ended the Somoza dynasty in 1979.

Under the Somozas, Nicaragua made some economic gains, but the country became notorious for its political repression. Moreover, the economic gains were largely confined to a tiny élite and small middle class. Thus Nicaragua was ripe for a major social revolution. The earthquake that destroyed much of Managua in 1972 signalled the beginning of the end for the Somoza régime. The breakdown in the social and economic order, an increase in crime, and the blatant misappropriation of international relief funds by the Somozas brought widespread opposition to the régime from within the middle and upper classes.

All efforts to effect a peaceful termination of the dictatorship failed. Meanwhile, the Frente Sandinista de Liberación Nacional (FSLN) developed among university students and labour leaders and began to carry out terrorist and guerrilla attacks against the government. Its successes were unimpressive, however, until after the assassination of Pedro Joaquín Chamorro, the popular editor of *La Prensa*, the country's leading newspaper and legal voice of opposition to the Somozas. This brutal act, for which the public blamed the government, ignited a general insurrection in support of the Sandinistas. In the devastating war that followed, much of the republic's productive assets were destroyed before the dictator finally fled on 19 July 1979.

The Sandinistas quickly seized control and, with significant aid from Cuba and the eastern bloc, built a strong political and military machine dedicated to the socialization of the country and to promoting a more equitable society. They had notable success in education, health care and other social areas, while the task of reconstructing the shattered economy remained immense. The Sandinistas created a huge military establishment with aid from the socialist countries, ostensibly for their own defence but causing nervousness to their neighbours and the United States. At the time of writing, the future of the Sandinista revolution is still uncertain. The private sector remains important within the country and the Sandinista government continues to seek peaceful means of carrying forth the revolution, while fearing intervention from the USA or its Central American client states.

The revolution has attracted substantial attention and there is a growing volume of publication on various aspects of its progress. In general, however, serious writing on Nicaragua has been very limited in most fields and available works in English are scarce. Only in a few areas where there has been notable attention directed toward Nicaragua in the English-speaking world is there extensive publication. Such topics include efforts to construct an interoceanic canal through Nicaragua, the William Walker episode, the United States occupation of Nicaragua during the first third of this century, and the present Sandinista revolution.

This bibliography seeks to identify the principal works in each field, emphasizing works in English when available, but necessarily including many works in Spanish. The volume is primarily concerned with published books, but a considerable number of periodical articles have also been cited either because of their quality or because of the absence or rarity of books on the subject. In addition, several doctoral dissertations and a few masters theses have been listed, since they often represent the most penetrating research on specific subjects and in most cases they are readily available through University Microfilms International in Ann Arbor, Michigan, USA. The bibliography is not intended as a comprehensive list of all publications on Nicaragua, but primarily as a guide to the most significant publications in each field, with annotations that should help the reader to identify both the scope and utility of individual items.

Within each section, items are arranged alphabetically by title, the only exception being in the section on travel accounts where they are listed in chronological order to facilitate the finding of works dealing with specific periods. Following the main entries in each section are cross-references to related works in other sections of the volume. An index enables easy location of specific authors, titles and subjects.

The initial section, 'The Country and Its People', is concerned with general works that introduce the reader to the country as a whole. The Sandinista revolution has so changed conditions in Nicaragua, however, that none of the former guides to the country are especially useful today. Nor has any new guide been published that will satisfy all of the needs of the newcomer to Nicaragua or the student wishing to get a general idea of the country. A new edition of the *Area handbook for Nicaragua* is therefore eagerly awaited. In the meantime, a number of the items listed in this section will provide some information, along with various pamphlets periodically issued by the new government and usually available at Nicaraguan consulates. A subsection on current events lists a number of specialized newsletters that do provide up-to-date coverage of events in Nicaragua. More general news publications, notably the *Economist* (London) and the *New York Times*, have also provided considerable coverage of Nicaragua since the fall of Somoza.

General geographies of Nicaragua are limited to works in Spanish, but West and Augelli's work on *Middle America* provides an adequate introductory description of the country. Special mention should also be made of David Radell's excellent *Historical geography of western Nicaragua*, one of the most useful works ever written on the country. Works on the violent geology of Nicaragua, which are limited, are also included in the geography section, as are works on climate, maps, atlases and gazetteers, tourism and travel guides, and sailing directions and cruising guides.

Nicaragua has attracted a remarkable number of interesting and informative accounts by foreign travellers and residents, thirty-seven of which have been selected for inclusion here. Most are in English, and date mainly from the 19th century when the English and North American public eagerly read of the travels of their countrymen to exotic lands in the tropics. Although each of those selected has its own peculiar value, special attention is called to the accounts of Gage, Stephens, Baily, Squier, Scherzer, Stout, Boyle, Belt and Thompson. A further source of mid-19th-century impressions of Nicaragua, not listed in this bibliography, can be found in California travel accounts, for Nicaragua was on the route of many of the '49ers.

Although many of the travellers' accounts comment on Nicaragua's varied and exotic flora and fauna, scientific writing in this area has not been very extensive. Lake Nicaragua's unique freshwater sharks have attracted some attention, along with other fish. The works of Jaime Villa are especially noteworthy, as is the lovely volume by Thomas Thorson on Nicaraguan lake fishes.

The archaeology of Nicaragua is less spectacular than that of its Mayan neighbours, but there are some notable ruins and monuments to earlier peoples. The items listed in this bibliography reflect a growing awareness of the region, and the works of Lothrop, Healy and Stone are useful introductions to the area and its literature.

The large number of entries on historical works included in this volume does not so much reflect the field of the compiler as it does the volume of publication on Nicaraguan history. Apart from a number of useful works on Central American history, several works dealing specifically with Nicaragua deserve mention. There is no adequate general history of the country in any language, although Meyer's *Historical dictionary* is a handy reference work. MacLeod, Sherman and Wortman all help to place Nicaragua in the perspective of colonial Central America, but those who can read French should not overlook Romero-Vargas' important thesis on the 18th century. The 19th century has attracted a great deal of historical writing, especially on the Anglo-American rivalry and the William Walker episode. Likewise, the period of the US occupation of Nicaragua in the early 20th century prompted much comment and documentation, both on the intervention itself and on Sandino's struggle against the Marines. Among the works covering the Somoza period, Millett's *Guardians of the dynasty* stands out as definitive. The Sandinista revolution has spawned a number of informative books and more can be expected, but most of those published to date are listed in the section on politics.

Information on Nicaragua's population draws principally on Nicaraguan census publications or United Nations works. Interpretive research and writing largely remains to be done in this area. Anthropologists have taken an interest in the Nicaraguan population, however, and the section entitled 'Nationalities and Minorities' includes a number of excellent studies. Mary Helms has spearheaded serious consideration of Nicaragua as a 'frontier' of Mesoamerica, while a number of other studies focus on various communities of the Caribbean coastal region. There is little published material in English on Nicaraguan folklore, but there are several works in Spanish listed.

Religion has always played a major role in Nicaraguan life, and it is of vital importance today. Although publication in English on this important topic is limited, the section on religion lists a variety of works dealing both with the traditional Roman Catholic Church and with the theology of liberation which is so important in the revolution. There are also some works dealing with the unique role of Protestantism in Nicaragua.

There is need for more research on the sociology of Nicaragua, accounting for the relatively few works in the 'Social Conditions' section. There are a few provocative articles on the revolution, especially in the subsection on social structure. There is also a dearth of information on the specifics of social services and health care in the new Nicaragua.

Nicaragua has a sordid record respecting human rights, but the new government has made an effort to improve the situation. As the reports in the 'Human Rights' section indicate, however, there is still room for further advance. It should be noted that there are two commissions for monitoring human rights violations in Nicaragua. The Permanent Commission on Human Rights in Nicaragua (CPDHN), formed to protest at violations of human rights under the Somoza dictatorship, has continued to operate independently under the Sandinistas. A second Commission on Human Rights is operating as an organ of the Sandinista government, and understandably has painted a rosier picture.

Politics is another area upon which there has been considerable publication both at the polemic and scholarly levels. Fifty-seven items have been included, with a sizeable number dealing with the Sandinista revolution. Among the works on the revolution, especially noteworthy are those of Booth, Walker, Weber, Gorman and Black.

Nicaragua's foreign relations have been most important with the other Central American states, Great Britain or the United States, and most of the sixty-one items in this section deal with those topics. Some works dealing with the Central American Common Market are found in the subsection on Nicaragua's relations with the other Central American states, while others will be found in the sections on economics and trade.

Works dealing with the legal system and government administration are limited, especially items in English. However, some information can be gleaned from the relevant sections.

There are a variety of statistical sources for Nicaragua, and although there are comparatively few main entries listed in this section, particular attention is directed to the large number of cross-references listed here, since most of the statistical sources are listed primarily under their respective topical headings.

Economics has occupied the attention of a considerable volume of work, with widely varying views on progress under the Somozas and in the Central American integration movement. With the related sections on trade and commerce, industry and mining, forestry, agriculture, transport and communications and labour, there is considerable information available, especially if the reader knows some Spanish. Many of the works relating to Nicaragua's efforts to develop an interoceanic route are found in the section on transport and communications.

Although the need is great, there as yet has been little attention to the environment in Nicaragua. The cross-references in this section, however, point to some additional works dealing with ecology and the environment.

Although publication in English is limited, there has been considerable concern for cultural affairs in Nicaragua. As Charles Stansifer has pointed out in *Cultural policy in the old and the new Nicaragua*, the Granada élite took great pains to preserve Nicaraguan culture during the Somoza years, and the Sandinista government has a strong commitment to developing the arts and sciences in the new Nicaragua. A section of this bibliography is devoted to educational developments, but there is little on science and technology, reflecting Nicaragua's underdeveloped condition. Literature, on the other hand, has long been of great importance in the country. Poetry is especially popular and is found everywhere. This bibliography only scratches the surface of the voluminous output of Nicaraguan poetry, and has largely been confined to Nicaraguan literature translated into English. Several bibliographies and anthologies are cited, however, to assist the reader wishing to pursue Nicaragua's rich literary tradition further. White's new anthology of Nicaraguan poets is especially recommended as an introduction. There has been considerable attention to the language of Nicaraguans, both in terms of Nicaraguan Spanish and Indian dialects, the work of Carlos Mantica being especially noteworthy. There are also some notable developments in the visual and performing arts, but relatively little has found its way into printed materials.

Nicaragua is not blessed with major libraries or archives, nor with adequate guides to those there are. Major earthquakes in 1931 and 1972, as well as other natural disasters and frequent civil war, have been hard on public depositories of records and printed matter. The Banco Central has Nicaragua's largest library and collects works on all subjects. It is open to the public and it also carries on extensive bibliographical services. The National Library (Biblioteca Nacional Rubén Darío) has recently been given a new home in the Complejo Eduardo Contreras in Managua. There are a number of important specialized libraries in the country, most notably that of the Instituto Centroamericano de Administración de Empresas (INCAE) on economics and business. University libraries in Nicaragua are of some consequence, but are less important than the libraries mentioned above. As elsewhere in Central America, some of the most important collections in the country are in private libraries. More detailed description of libraries and archives in Nicaragua will be found in Grieb's *Research guide to Central America and the Caribbean.*

Publishing is dealt with in several sections. There are three daily newspapers in Managua and a number of other news and literary publications. Special mention should be made of the Ministry of Culture publication *Nicarauac*, and also of the most important independent cultural reviews, *Revista del Pensamiento Centroamericano* and *El Pez y la Serpiente.*

The section on bibliographies includes a number of general Latin American bibliographies, but does not include such general bibliographical tools as the *Readers guide to periodical literature, Bibliographical index,* etc. Although many are published obscurely, there has been considerable publication on Nicaraguan bibliography, owing principally to the work of René Rodríguez Masís at the Biblioteca of the Banco Central and Jorge Eduardo Arellano, director of the Instituto de Estudio del Sandinismo. Most of the bibliographies are listed in their respective topical sections, but are also cross-referenced. It is the intention of this volume to provide a bibliographical tool for those interested in learning more about Nicaragua. It is not by any means a

Introduction

comprehensive listing, and the serious researcher will need to consult the more specialized bibliographies listed here. Much of the research on Nicaragua is in obscure journals and in theses and dissertations. These cannot all be listed in this volume, but the bibliographies of the Banco Central and others listed here should lead the reader to those sources. In most areas it will not be possible to delve deeply into Nicaragua's development without a reading knowledge of Spanish, but it is hoped that this bibliography may make some contribution to a better understanding of the country's people and institutions.

Acknowledgements
Completion of this bibliography would have been impossible without the assistance of a great many people. Among those to whom the author is most grateful are Xavier Zavala Cuadra and his staff at the Centro de Investigaciones y Activadades Culturales in Managua; René Rodríguez Masís and his staff at the Library of the Banco Central de Nicaragua; Pablo Antonio Cuadra and Roberto Cardenal at *La Prensa* (Managua); Thomas Niehaus and his staff, especially Martha Robertson, at the Latin American Library, and Barbara Everet, Cristina Fowler and other staff members in the Howard-Tilton Library of Tulane University; Jorge Eduardo Arellano at the Instituto de Estudio del Sandinismo in Managua; Thomas Bloch at the Library of the Instituto Centroamericano de Administración de Empresas in Managua; Richard E. Greenleaf, director of the Center for Latin American Studies at Tulane University; Charles L. Stansifer, director of the Center for Latin American Studies at the University of Kansas; Norma Piacun and James O'Meara of the Tulane Computer Laboratory; Sheila R. Herstein, deputy chief, Reference Division of the Library of the City College of the City University of New York; staff members of the Louisiana State University Library at Baton Rouge, the Latin American Collection of the University of Texas at Austin, and the Library of Congress; and my beloved wife, Sue McGrady Woodward. Their assistance and advice contributed enormously to the quality of the work, but the compiler must retain full

Introduction

responsibility for any omissions or errors which it may contain. Preparation of this bibliography was also assisted by grants from the Tulane University Council on Research and Center for Latin American Studies.

New Orleans
January 1983

The Country and Its People

General

1 Adorable Nicaragua.
René Moser, Raymond Pons. Boulogne, France: Delroisse [1976]. 180p.

A collection of striking colour photos by Moser accompanied by a text by Pons, former French ambassador to Nicaragua, on the country's history, antiquities, geography, climate, wildlife, culture, social services, tourist attractions, folklore and economy. These descriptions, in French, English, Spanish and German, are quite brief, the principal value of the work being the photos.

2 Area handbook for Nicaragua.
John Morris Ryan (and others), prepared for the Foreign Area Studies of the American University by Johnson Research Associates. Washington, DC: US Government Printing Office, 1970. 391p. maps. bibliog. charts.

This reference work has lost much of its former value as a guide to Nicaragua because of the major changes that have occurred as a result of the Sandinista revolution. The work nevertheless remains useful on some aspects of the country's development, and certainly as a description of pre-revolutionary Nicaragua. Successive chapters deal with the physical environment, history, population, ethnic groups, social structure, family life, living conditions, education, artistic and intellectual expression, religion, political system, foreign relations, economy, agriculture, industry, labour, trade, public order and safety, and the armed forces. A new edition, edited by James D. Rudolph, and entitled *Nicaragua, a country study*, is scheduled for publication soon by the American University in Washington, DC.

3 **The Caribbean Year Book.**
Edited by Colin Rickards. Toronto: Caribook, 1980. 50th ed.
922p.

Published annually, formerly under the title *The West Indies and Caribbean Year Book*, this valuable guide provides basic data on all the countries of the Caribbean Basin. In the 1979-80 edition (50th), Nicaragua is dealt with on p. 530-49, with sections on its history, geography, population, culture, government, public and social services, communications, natural resources, industries, finance, trade, and tourist facilities, with a business directory appended. Considerable statistical data is included, but much of this information is outdated and a more current edition has not yet been published.

4 **Central America, lands seeking unity.**
Charles Paul May. Camden, New Jersey: Thomas Nelson & Sons, 1966. 224p. maps. bibliog. (World Neighbor Books).

An historical and geographical overview for children, containing background information on other subjects. It is simplistic and inaccurate in places, but at least this illustrated work provides a vigorous and interesting introduction to the region for young people.

5 **The Central American republics.**
Franklin D. Parker. New York: Oxford University Press, 1964. 348p.

Although now somewhat dated, this general reference work still has broad utility for basic information on each of the Central American republics. It includes a perceptive history of the region and much useful data on a broad range of topics for the individual states.

6 **Centro América 1982, Análisis Económicos y Políticos Sobre la Región.** (Central America 1982, economic and political analyses of the region.)
Guatemala City: División de Estudios Económicos, Inforpress Centroamericana, 1982. 302p. maps.

An annual publication prepared by the publishers of *Central America Report* (q.v.) and *Inforpress Centroamericana* (q.v.), this statistical and analytic survey of Central America provides a great deal of information on the region as a whole and on each state. It focuses especially on economic information for 1981 and preceding years, and is also useful for details on the political structure and personnel of each state. Although expensive (US$75 to subscribers to *Inforpress Centroamericana* or the *Latin American Research Review*, $125 to non-subscribers), its objective and comprehensive coverage makes it a most valuable reference volume and a must for libraries serious about Central America.

7 **Centro América, subdesarrollo y dependencia.** (Central America, underdevelopment and dependency.)
Mario Monteforte Toledo. Mexico City: Universidad Nacional Autónoma de México, 1972. maps. bibliog.

A major socio-economic study of Central America. Successive chapters survey geography, demography, health, agriculture, industry, the integration movement, foreign domination and dependence, politics, labour, the military, the Church, and the tradition of violence.

8 **Datos básicos sobre Nicaragua.** (Basic data on Nicaragua.)
Frente Sandinista de Liberación Nacional. Managua:
Secretaría Nacional de Propaganda, 1980. 40p.

This little booklet contains only basic statistical data on the Nicaraguan population, economic activity, employment, agriculture, industrial production, trade and education for the years 1976-79. It does, however, provide a useful introduction to the country.

9 **Dollars and dictators, a guide to Central America.**
Albuquerque, New Mexico: Resource Center, 1982. 272p.

A profile of each Central American country, with a thorough examination of US foreign aid there and a detailed account of US business and military activity.

10 **Latin American Perspectives.**
Riverside, California: Latin American Perspectives, 1974- .
quarterly.

This quarterly review contains frequent and perceptive coverage of Nicaragua by distinguished Latin American authors. The journal focuses on the struggle between capitalism and socialism in Latin America. Of particular interest are nos. 25-26 (vol. 7, nos. 2-3, spring-summer 1980) dedicated to 'Central America: the strong men are shaking', and no. 29 (vol. 8, no. 1, spring 1981) on 'Revolutionary Nicaragua'.

11 **Nicaragua: dictatorship and revolution.**
Jan Karmali, Hugh O'Shaughnessy, Andrew
Pollak. London: Latin America Bureau, 1979. 50p. map.
bibliog. (Latin America Bureau Special Brief).

A very convenient booklet listing basic data, political parties, unions and principal government officials of the country following the Sandinista triumph. It includes a political chronology (1821-1979) and a brief, although not altogether reliable, history of the country, especially since 1933. Appendixes contain basic documents of the Sandinista régime.

12 **Nicaragua, patria libre.** (Nicaragua, free country.)
Casa de las Américas, vol. 20, no. 117 (Nov.-Dec. 1979).
238p. map.

This entire issue of *Casa de las Américas* is dedicated to Nicaragua. It contains a speech by Fidel Castro, poetry, a brief history of Nicaragua by Sergio Ramírez, a series of articles on various aspects of Nicaraguan history and the Sandinista revolution, eye-witness accounts of the war, book reviews and interviews with Daniel Ortega, Humberto Ortega and Luis Carrión. The volume has a decidedly Marxist tone and lacks objectivity, but it also portrays much of the enthusiasm of the new Nicaragua. It documents the close relationship between revolutionary Cuba and the Sandinistas.

13 **Nicaragua: summary of the current situation.**
Bank of London and South America Review, vol. 16, no. 1
(Feb. 1982), p. 24-27.

A succinct and objective overview of recent developments in Nicaragua. The
Bank of London and South America Review periodically contains useful summary
analyses of the situation in Nicaragua.

14 **Nicaragua, tierra de maravillas.** (Nicaragua, land of marvels.)
Edited by Paco Gallegos. Managua: Cámara Nacional de
Comercio y Industrias de Managua, 1964. 443p. maps.

This work's present value is as a record of Managua before the devastating
earthquake of 1972. It contains many colour photos of the principal buildings,
along with descriptions and lists of principal business and public offices, doctors,
lawyers and other professionals. The work covers not only Managua, but each of
the Nicaraguan departments, and despite its date its comprehensiveness makes it
still of some use as a guide to the country on matters other than politics and
current events. The text in this work is in both English and Spanish.

15 **Now we can speak: a journey through the new Nicaragua.**
Frances Moore Lappe, Joseph Collins. San Francisco:
Institute for Food and Development Policy, 1982. 120p.

Vivid descriptions of contemporary Nicaragua are presented through thirty-eight
photographs and discussions with Nicaraguans from all walks of life. The work
offers a very favourable view of Nicaragua under Sandinista rule.

16 **Sandino's dream was Somoza's nightmare and our hope.**
Managua: Agencia Nueva Nicaragua, 1982. 286p.

The title on the cover of this work is 'What the present U.S. administration
doesn't want you to know about Nicaragua'. In consecutive chapters it discusses
the Sandinista viewpoint on the philosophy and politics of the Nicaraguan government, the economic situation, the land reform and food production programmes,
health, housing, education and other social services, government structure, international relations, human rights, the military, popular organizations, the media,
religion and the Caribbean coast problem. Appendixes, p. 207-86, reproduce key
documents of the revolution. The volume is strongly hostile to the United States
and to all groups not enthusiastically supporting the Sandinista government.

17 **South American Handbook.**
London: Rand McNally, 1981. 58th ed. 1,343p. (title varies
slightly).

Despite its title, the *South American Handbook* covers all of Latin America and
the Caribbean and is one of the best available guides to basic data on the entire
region. First published in 1921, and annually since 1924, it devotes only twenty
pages exclusively to Nicaragua, but is a handy reference item for historical,
geographical, economic and statistical data as well as a practical guide to hotels,
currency exchange and other introductory information. It is especially recommended to travellers who may be going through several Latin American countries.

18 **This is Nicaragua.**
Maureen Tweedy. Ipswich, England: East Anglian
Magazine, 1953. 116p.
A brief history of Nicaragua followed by the author's impressions and photographs, providing a guide to the country. Although now thirty years old, this delightful guidebook still conveys much of the feeling of the country and some of its out-of-the-way places. A final chapter relates 'Indian stories, legends, potions and philtres'.

Monografías Departmentales. (Departmental monographs.)
See item no. 37.

The key to the Pacific: the Nicaragua canal.
See item no. 550.

Current events

19 **Central America Report.**
Guatemala City: Inforpress Centroamericana, 1974- . weekly.
A very informative and objective review of economics and politics. Normally runs to eight pages. Substantial coverage of Nicaragua.

20 **Envio.** (Mailing.)
Edited by Alvaro Argüello H., SJ. Managua: Instituto
Histórico Centroamericano, Universidad Centroamericana
(PO Box A-194), 1981- . monthly.
A very informative newsletter, published in Spanish, English, or German (subscribers should indicate their preference), containing articles on and analyses of the situation in Nicaragua. Particular attention is devoted to revolutionary progress and the role of the Church, but all kinds of subjects are dealt with in this perceptive newsletter.

21 **Inforpress Centroamericana.** (Central American Information
Press.)
Guatemala City: Inforpress Centroamericana, 1972- . weekly.
A sixteen-page weekly report on political and economic events in all the Central American countries, with frequent special in-depth economic reports. More detailed than *Central America Report* which is also published by Inforpress (see above), *Inforpress Centroamericana* is published in Spanish only.

22 **Latin America.**
New York: Facts on File, 1973-79. annual.
Issued annually for the years 1972-78, with varying annual editors, these volumes provide a summary of the principal news stories for the past year. Useful for reviewing recent events or updating. Organized by country. Unfortunately, this series was not continued after the 1978 edition, but see the entry below.

The Country and Its People. Current events

23 **Latin America.**
Edited by Jon D. Cozean. Washington, DC; Harpers Ferry, West Virginia: Stryker-Post Publications, 1967-. annual. (World Today Series).

Although the review of the past year's events is less complete in this series than in the Facts on File series of the same title (see above), this series includes basic data on each Latin American country, making it a useful reference. Organized by country.

24 **Latin America Regional Reports: Caribbean.**
London: Latin American Newsletters, 1979- . c. 10 per year.

Succeeds earlier publications by the same publisher: *Latin America* (1967-77), *Latin American Economic Report* (1973-79), and *Latin American Political Report* (1977-79). Published about ten times per year, this newsletter provides excellent summary news coverage of Nicaragua and the region. See also, by the same publisher, *Latin America Weekly Report* (1979-present), which also has frequent coverage of Nicaragua. To a substantial degree, these two newsletters duplicate each other.

25 **Mesoamérica.**
Edited by Fred B. Morris. San José: Institute for Central American Studies, 1982- . monthly. in English.

A very competent and objective review of events in Central America, with both commentary and factual reporting. Includes both political and economic coverage.

26 **La Nación Internacional, Edición Centroamericana.** (The International Nation, Central American edition.) Edited by Marcel Angulo de Castro. San José: La Nación, 1982- . weekly.

A review of Central American news, published by one of the leading Costa Rican dailies. Tends to support US policy in Central America.

27 **Nicaraguan Perspectives.**
Berkeley, California: Nicaraguan Information Center, 1981- .

Informative articles on contemporary Nicaragua, sympathetic to the Sandinista revolution. Five issues had appeared by late 1982.

28 **Por el Rescate de la Revolución Democrática Nicaragüense.** (For the rescue of the Nicaraguan democratic revolution.) Movimiento Democrático Nicaragüense. San José: MDN, 1982- . weekly.

An anti-Sandinista journal published by the Nicaraguan Democratic Movement (MDN), representing Nicaraguan exiles opposing the Sandinista government.

Geography

General surveys

29 **Geografía ilustrada de Nicaragua, con un apéndice sobre el reciente terremoto de Managua.** (Illustrated geography of Nicaragua, with an appendix on the recent earthquake in Managua.)
Jaime Incer Barquero. Managua: Recalde, 1973. 255p.
A useful textbook addition to Incer's more substantial 1970 *Nueva geografía de Nicaragua* (q.v.), with much statistical information and a detailed description of the 1972 earthquake destruction.

30 **A land of lakes and volcanoes.**
Luis Marden. *National Geographic Magazine*, vol. 85 (Aug. 1944), p. 161-92. map.
A richly illustrated feature on Nicaragua in the mid-1940s. See also treatments of Nicaragua in the *National Geographic*, vol. 1 (Oct. 1889), p. 315-35; vol. 10 (July 1899), p. 247-66; vol. 12 (Jan. 1901), p. 22-32; vol. 20 (Dec. 1909), p. 1,102-15; vol. 51 (March 1927), p. 370-78; vol. 61 (May 1932), p. 593-627; and vol. 161 (July 1981), p. 58-61.

31 **Middle America, its lands and peoples.**
Robert C. West, John P. Augelli. Englewood Cliffs, New Jersey: Prentice Hall, 1976. 2nd ed. 494p. maps. bibliog.
This is the standard geography of the Middle American region: Mexico, Central America and the Caribbean. Coverage of Nicaragua is not extensive, but it is very well done. See especially p. 438-48, although general characteristics are dealt with in other sections as well.

32 **Notas geográficas y económicas sobre la República de Nicaragua.** (Geographical and economic notes on the Republic of Nicaragua.)
Pablo Levy. [Managua]: Fondo de Promoción Cultural, Banco de América, 1976. 527p. map. (Colección Cultural, Serie Geografía y Naturaleza, no. 1).

This excellent survey of Nicaraguan geography and economy was published originally in Nicaragua in 1871 and then in Paris in 1873 (also in Spanish). It contains a great deal of statistical and descriptive material on the people and production of Nicaragua in the 1860s as well as commentary on its history and politics. A fine map of the country is also included. Levy provides detailed information on the country's economy, immigration, geography, population, ethnic groups, etc. It is one of the major foreign impressions of the country published in the 19th century.

33 **Nueva geografía de Nicaragua: ensayo preliminar.** (New geography of Nicaragua: preliminary essay.)
Jaime Incer Barquero. Managua: Recalde, 1970. 582p. maps. bibliog.

A detailed geographic description of Nicaragua, with broad coverage of geologic development, climate, regional descriptions, population and economic characteristics. Essentially supersedes the standard school geography of Nicaragua by Francisco Terán and Jaime Incer, *Geografía de Nicaragua* (Managua: Banco Central de Nicaragua, 1964).

34 **The state of Nicaragua of the Greater Republic of Central America.**
Gustavo Niederlein. Philadelphia: Philadelphia Commercial Museum, 1898. 93p. map.

Although fairly brief, this monograph gives a great deal of specific data, much of it statistical, based on observation pursued in 1897-98. It treats the topography, geology, mineral wealth and soils, climates, flora and fauna, population, agriculture, commerce, industry, finance, and political situation. A valuable source for this period.

Exposición sumaria de viajes y trabajos geográficos sobre Nicaragua durante el siglo XIX. (Summary description of travels and geographic works on Nicaragua during the 19th century.)
See item no. 69.

The states of Central America: their geography, topography, climate, population, resources, production, commerce, political organization, aborigines, etc., etc., comprising chapters on Honduras, San Salvador, Nicaragua, Costa Rica, Guatemala, Belize, the Bay Islands, the Mosquito Shore, and the Honduras Inter-Oceanic Railway.
See item no. 83.

Central American jungles.
See item no. 103.

Revista de la Academia de Geografía e Historia de Nicaragua.
(Nicaraguan Academy of Geography and History review.)
See item no. 155.

Estructuras socioeconómicas, poder y estado en Nicaragua, de 1821 a 1875. (Socio-economic structures, power and the state in Nicaragua, 1821-1875.)
See item no. 189.

Handbook of Middle American Indians.
See item no. 266.

Man, crops and pests in Central America.
See item no. 532.

Report of the Nicaraguan Canal Commission, 1897-1899.
See item no. 557.

Regional geography

35 **La costa atlántica de Nicaragua.** (The Nicaraguan Atlantic coast.)
Managua: Biblioteca y Servicios de Información, Banco Central de Nicaragua, 1980. 6p. (Bibliografía Corta no. 18).
A selection of sixty-nine books and articles dealing with Nicaragua's Caribbean shore. See also René Rodríguez Masís, *Selección de la obra 'La costa atlántica de Nicaragua'* (q.v.).

36 **An historical geography of western Nicaragua: the spheres of influence of León, Granada and Managua, 1519-1965.**
David R. Radell. PhD dissertation, University of California, Berkeley, 1969. 295p. (Available from University Microfilms, Ann Arbor, Michigan, order no. 70-6196).
An excellent historical geography of the part of Nicaragua where most of the population resides. This work concentrates on the the rivalry among the three main cities of the country and offers one of the best general histories of Nicaraguan development from the colonial period to the present.

37 **Monografías Departmentales.** (Departmental monographs.)
Julián Guerrero, Lola Soriano. Managua, 1964-75. 14 vols.
A very valuable collection of monographs on each of the Nicaraguan departments except Zelaya and Río San Juan. Each volume includes a survey of statistical and geographical data, with a short historical sketch. The individual volumes are: 1. *Boaco* (1964). 47p.; 2. *Carazo* (1964). 124p.; 3. *Chinandega* (1964). 220p.; 4. *Chontales* (1969). 259p.; 5. *Estelí* (1967). 215p.; 6. *Granada* (1975). 544p.; 7. *Jinotega* (1966). 190p.; 8. *León* (1968). 322p.; 9. *Madriz* (1974). 186p.; 10. *Managua* (1964). 284p.; 11. *Masaya* (1965). 241p.; 12. *Matagalpa* (1967). 290p.; 13. *Nueva Segovia* (1969). 311p.; 14. *Rivas* (1966). 293p.

38 **La Mosquitia en la revolución.** (Mosquitia in the revolution.)
Edited by Jaime Wheelock Román. Managua: Centro de
Investigaciones y Estudios Para la Reforma Agraria, 1981.
308p. maps. bibliog. (Colección Blas Real Espinales).
Studies carried out by the Agrarian Reform Research and Study Centre dealing
with various aspects of Nicaragua's Caribbean coast: history, rural development,
mining and agriculture. Two appendixes provide chronologies of the jurisdictional
and general historical developments of the region. A number of charts, maps and
photos illustrate the text.

Selección de la obra *La costa atlántica de Nicaragua.* (Selection from
the work *The Atlantic coast of Nicaragua.*)
See item no. 702.

Geology and natural resources

39 **Los estudios sobre los recursos naturales en las Américas.
Tomo 1. Estudio preliminar en Guatemala, El Salvador,
Honduras, Nicaragua, Costa Rica, Panamá y Zona del Canal
sobre la situación actual de la investigación y de la
organización relativa al estudio de los recursos naturales.**
(Studies on natural resources in the Americas. Volume 1.
Preliminary study in Guatemala, El Salvador, Honduras,
Nicaragua, Costa Rica, Panama and the Canal Zone on the
present situation in research and relative organization of the
study of natural resources.)
Proyecto 20 del Programa de Cooperación Técnica de la
Organización de Estados Americanos, Centro de
Entrenamiento para la Evaluación de Recursos
Naturales. Mexico City: Instituto Panamericano de
Geografía e Historia, 1953. 446p. maps.
A very thorough survey of the cartography, geology, hydrology, soils, vegetation,
fishing, hunting and organization of each state.

40 **Geophysical investigations of the Nicaragua rise.**
Ben Nnaemeka Nwaochei. PhD dissertation, Rutgers
University, 1981. 87p. bibliog. (Available from University
Microfilms, Ann Arbor, Michigan, order no. 81-15228).
A crustal section across the Nicaragua rise is presented here, deduced from a
combination of seismic refractions, gravity and magnetic data.

41 **Nicaragua: national inventory of physical resources, Central America and Panama.**
US Engineer Agency for Resources Inventories. Washington, DC: US Agency for International Development, Resources Inventory Center, Corps of Engineers, 1966. various paginations. maps. (Publication no. AID/RIC GIPR no. 6).
Published in Spanish and English, thirty-four maps with accompanying tables and text provides basic information on the geography and geology, including water resources and drainage, soils, vegetation, climate, rock types, mineral resources, construction materials, suitability for road construction, population, land use and potential, urban areas, ports, waterways, industries, tourism, education, health, highways, railroads, pipelines, airfields, communications, electric power, geodesy and mapping.

42 **Site and source effects on ground motion in Managua, Nicaragua.**
Jeffrey A. Johnson. PhD dissertation, University of California, Los Angeles, 1975. 144p. bibliog. (Available from University Microfilms, Ann Arbor, Michigan, order no. 75-22634).
Studies local geologic conditions and ground motion at several locations in Managua from a viewpoint of structural engineering.

43 **A study of seismic risk for Nicaragua.**
Haresh C. Shah (and others). Stanford, California: Stanford University, Department of Civil Engineering, John A. Blume Earthquake Engineering Center, 1975. 2 vols. maps. bibliog.
A detailed, technical study of Nicaraguan earthquakes, with particular reference to the 1972 earthquake and procedures for mapping seismic risk, with specific recommendations for the design of structures. See also *Seismic and fault hazard studies for Banco Central de Nicaragua* (Oakland, California: Woodward, Lundgren & Associates, 1975).

44 **Tephra stratigraphy and physical aspects of recent volcanism near Managua, Nicaragua.**
David C. Bice. PhD dissertation, University of California, Berkeley, 1980. 476p. bibliog. (University Microfilms order no. 81-12965).
A technical study that adds significantly to knowledge on the nature of the active volcanism in Nicaragua.

45 **Terremoto '72: elites y pueblo.** (Earthquake '72: élites and the people.)
Francisco Lainez. Managua: Editorial Unión, 1977. 258p.
A thoughtful examination of the effects of the 1972 earthquake on Nicaraguan society. Lainez is critical of the government's handling of the reconstruction effort and of the social injustice that occurred from it. An important work for under-

standing the 1970s in Nicaragua. See also Universidad Nacional Autónoma de Nicaragua, *El terremoto de Managua y sus consecuencias* (The Managua earthquake and its consequences), in *Cuadernos Universitarios* (León, Nicaragua), 2nd series, no. 8 (1973), containing eight essays dealing with the impact on city planning, the economy, education and geological aspects of the disaster.

46 Volcanic history of Nicaragua.
Alexander R. McBirney, Howell Williams. Los Angeles: University of California Press, 1965. 73p.

A concise but very informative survey of the Nicaraguan volcanoes by two of the world's leading volcanologists.

Un pueblo y su conductor, terremoto de Managua 1972. (A people and their leader, the Managua earthquake of 1972.)
See item no. 329.

Guía de recursos básicos contemporáneos para estudios de desarrollo en Nicaragua. (Guide to basic contemporary resources for the study of Nicaraguan development.)
See item no. 685.

Climate

47 Weather and climate of Mexico and Central America.
J. A. Vivo Escoto. In: *Handbook of Middle American Indians*, vol. 1. Edited by Robert Wauchope, Robert West. Austin, Texas: University of Texas Press, 1964, p. 187-215. maps.

Although there is little attention by name specifically to Nicaragua in this article, it provides an excellent overview of climatic conditions in the region, with many maps.

Maps, atlases and gazetteers

48 Central America early maps up to 1860.
K. S. Kapp. North Bend, Ohio: K. S. Kapp Productions, 1974. 64p.+28 plates.

An annotated list of 277 maps of Central America from 1548 to 1860. Annotations indicate location of original maps and distinguishing characteristics as well as later editions. Twenty-eight of the maps are reproduced in black and white plates. The list is arranged chronologically, with an alphabetical index appended.

49 **Mapa de Nicaragua [and] Mapa guía de Managua.** (Map of
   Nicaragua [and] Guide map of Managua.)
   Managua: Instituto Nicaragüense de Turismo, 1980.
   Physical and political 1:1,200,000 map of the republic, with a kilometrage table.
   Based on a 1980 official map of the republic prepared by the Instituto Geográfico
   Nacional, the Ministerio de la Construcción and the Instituto Nicaragüense de
   Turismo. On the reverse is a good 1:25,000 street map of Managua, showing
   travel agencies, hotels, restaurants, bars, banks, shopping centres, diplomatic lega-
   tions, theatres, recreational facilities, hospitals and clinics, government offices,
   airline offices and bus terminals, universities and other points of interest.

50 **Mapa de la República de Nicaragua.** (Map of the Republic of
   Nicaragua.)
   Instituto Geográfico Nacional.   Novara, Italy: Instituto
   Geográfico de Agostini, 1976. scale 1:500,000.
   A plasticized relief map showing principal roads and political divisions, with a
   1:200,000 inset of the region around Managua, including Masaya and Granada.

51 **Nicaragua.**
   Chicago: Rand McNally, Texaco, 1978. 44x61cm. scale
   1:1,140,480.
   A detailed road map, with relief shown. Includes inset maps of Granada, León
   and Managua. Text information in both English and Spanish.

52 **Nicaragua: official standard names approved by the United
   States Board on Geographic Names.**
   US Board on Geographic Names.   Washington, DC: Office
   of Geography, Department of the Interior, 1956. 49p.
   (Gazetteer no. 25).
   About 3,800 entries for places and features in Nicaragua, showing their latitude
   and longitude, with cross-references.

53 **Publicaciones y servicios.** (Publications and services.)
   Managua: Ministerio de Planificación, Instituto Nicaragüense
   de Estudios Territoriales [1982]. unpaginated.
   This is the catalogue of map publications of the Instituto Nicaragüense de Estudios Territoriales (INETER), formerly the Instituto Geográfico Nacional. A
   number of high-quality map series are available, including basic five-colour topo-
   graphical maps, scale 1:250,000 (12 maps); scale 1:50,000 (292 maps); and scale
   1:25,000 for the Managua region only. There is also an extensive series of cadas-
   tral maps, radar maps, urban maps, and various thematic maps. INETER is
   located in the Centro Camilo Ortega in Managua.

54 **Red vial de Nicaragua.** (Highway network of Nicaragua.)
   Dirección General de Caminos, Departamento de
   Ingeniería. Managua: Dirección General de Caminos, 1976.
   scale approx. 1:1,750,000.
   General road map of Nicaragua.

Catalog of nautical charts, region 2. Defense Mapping Agency catalog of maps, charts and related products. Part 2 - Hydrographic products, vol. 2. Central and South America and Antarctica.
See item no. 57.

Catalogue of admiralty charts and other hydrographic publications 1982.
See item no. 58.

Guía de recursos básicos contemporáneos para estudios de desarrollo en Nicaragua. (Guide to basic contemporary resources for the study of Nicaraguan development.)
See item no. 685.

A list of books, magazine articles and maps relating to Central America, including the republics of Costa Rica, Guatemala, Honduras, Nicaragua and Salvador, 1800-1900.
See item no. 691.

Tourism and travel guides

55 **Anuario de Turismo, República de Nicaragua.** (Tourism
   annual, Republic of Nicaragua.)
   Managua: Oficina Ejecutiva de Encuestas y Censos, 1975-79.
   annual.
   Published for the years 1974-78, these volumes provide descriptive detail on tourist attractions and statistical information on tourism in Nicaragua.

56 **Fodor's Central America.**
   Edited by Robert C. Fischer (and others). New York: David
   McKay, 1980. 427p. map.
   Coverage on Nicaragua in this otherwise competent tourist guide to Central America is limited to p. 393-417. It provides basic data on the country, including an ample listing of hotels.

South American Handbook.
See item no. 17.

Sailing directions and cruising guides

57 Catalog of nautical charts, region 2. Defense Mapping Agency catalog of maps, charts and related products. Part 2 - Hydrographic products, vol. 2. Central and South America and Antarctica.
US Defense Mapping Agency. Washington, DC: Defense Mapping Agency Office of Distribution Services, 1981. 60p.
A catalogue of available US charts on the Nicaraguan region. For other publications of the Defense Mapping Agency, see *Part 2 - Hydrographic products, vol. 10. Miscellaneous and special purpose navigational charts, sheets, and tables* (Publication 1NA), and *Part 3 - Topographic products, vol. 5. Western hemisphere, large scale and city maps.*

58 Catalogue of admiralty charts and other hydrographic publications 1982.
Taunton, England: Hydrographer of the Navy, 1982. 156p. maps. (Publication no. NP131).
Catalogue to British charts and other publications useful to mariners in Nicaraguan waters. This edition corrected through November 1981. A new edition will be published in 1983. Nicaraguan charts are found in index T, p. 119. See also *The mariner's handbook*, 5th ed. (Hydrographer of the Navy, 1979), containing information on admiralty charts and navigation publications, general navigation, general meteorology, etc.

59 A cruising guide to the Caribbean and the Bahamas, including the north coast of South America, Central America, and Yucatan.
Jerrems C. Hart, William T. Stone. New York: Dodd, Mead, 1976. 578p. bibliog.
The standard yachtsman's guide for cruising Caribbean waters, with some detailed maps and descriptions of Nicaragua's Caribbean coastal regions and harbours. Coverage of the offshore islands is better than the shore coverage, but the Nicaraguan section of this work, found in chapter 17, 'The Panama Canal to Swan Island', is rather skimpy. Although useful in places, it is not a substitute for the following item or for *Sailing directions, en route, for the Caribbean Sea* (q.v.).

60 East coasts of Central America and Gulf of Mexico pilot.
Great Britain. Hydrographer of the Navy. Taunton, England: Hydrographic Department, 1970 (with supplements). (Publication 69A).
Sailing directions covering Nicaragua's Caribbean coast with detailed descriptions of coastal navigational dangers and aids.

Geography. Sailing directions and cruising guides

61 **Pacific coasts of Central America and United States pilot.**
Great Britain. Hydrographer of the Navy. Taunton,
England: Hydrographic Department, 1975 (with supplements).
8th ed. (Publication 8).
Sailing directions covering the Pacific coasts of Panama northward through the
United States, including off-lying islands between latitudes 4°N. and 48°25′N.

62 **Sailing directions, enroute, for the Caribbean Sea.**
US Defense Mapping Agency Hydrographic
Center. Washington, DC: US Government Printing Office,
1976 (with subsequent changes). 467p. maps. bibliog.
(Publication 144). 2nd ed., 1983.
The most recent US guide to waters along the Caribbean coast of Nicaragua,
with information on signals, cautions, regulations, climate, etc. Specific sailing
instructions for this coast are found in sector 12, p. 353-66. Corrections are issued
periodically. These instructions supersede the *Sailing directions for the east coast
of Central America and Mexico, including the north coast of Colombia,* 5th ed.
(USGPO, 1952, with supplements). The earlier instructions, however, include
some detail omitted from the current directions.

63 **Sailing directions, enroute, for the west coasts of Mexico and
Central America, second edition, 1979.**
US Defense Mapping Agency Hydrographic/Topographic
Center. Washington, DC: US Government Printing Office,
1980 (with subsequent changes). 171p. maps. (Publication
153).
The most recent US guide to the Pacific coast of Nicaragua, with information on
signals, cautions, regulations, climate, etc. Specific sailing instructions for the
Nicaraguan coast are found in sector 7, p. 109-115. Corrections are issued period-
ically.

64 **West Indies directory, part VI. The north coast of South
America from Trinidad westward, and the coast to the Bay of
Honduras.**
London: James Imray & Son, 1879. 152p.
These early sailing directions for the Nicaraguan coast now have historical value
for their descriptions. Editions for other years may also be available. These
descriptions provide guidance for navigators and much of the information would
still be applicable a hundred years later, but more reliable recent guides, mentioned above, should be used for safe passage. US Hydrographic Office sailing
directions issued in the early 20th century are also valuable historical sources for
their detailed descriptions. See for example, *Central America and Mexico pilot,
east coast, from Gallinas Point, Colombia, to the Rio Grande* (Washington, DC:
US Government Printing Office, 1920. 2nd ed. 371p. maps).

Travellers' Accounts

65 **Relación breve y verdadera de algunas cosas de las muchas que sucedieron al padre Fray Alonso Ponce en las provincias de la Nueva España, siendo comisario general de aquellas partes.**
(Brief and true account of some things among the many that happened to Friar Alonso Ponce in the provinces of New Spain, he being commissar-general of those parts.)
Alonso Ponce (Alonso de San Juan). Madrid: Viuda de Calero, 1873. 2 vols.

A fascinating 16th-century description of Central America. Nicaraguan observations are found only in volume 1, p. 335-83. There is a separate published index of this rare edition by Raul Guerrero, *Indice clasificado de la Relación breve y verdadera de algunas cosas de las muchas que sucedieron al Padre Fray Alonso Ponce en las provincias de la Neuva España*, Mexico City: Vargas Bea [i.e. Rea], 1949. 86p. (Biblioteca Aportación Histórica). Only 100 copies of this index were published, but it appeared previously in the *Boletín Bibliográfico de Antropología Americana*, vol. 7 (1943), p. 56-84.

66 **The English-American, his travail by sea and land; or a new survey of the West India's, containing a journall of three thousand and three hundred miles within the mainland of America.**
Thomas Gage. London: R. Cotes, 1648. 220p. many subsequent eds.

This is one of the classics of Central American travel literature. Gage was an English friar who had migrated to Spain and then made a journey through Central America. Before returning to England he published this highly critical work on the Spanish Empire. His descriptions are fascinating and very revealing of the social and economic conditions as well as the physical realities of 17th-century Central America. The account includes considerable comment on Nicaragua. A modern biographical recounting of Gage's tale is Norman Newton's *Thomas Gage in Spanish America* (London: Faber & Faber; New York: Barnes & Noble, 1969. 214p.).

67 **Some account of the Mosquito Territory: contained in a memoir written in 1757, while that country was in possession of the British.**
Robert Hodgson. Edinburgh: W. Blackwood, 1822. 2nd ed. 55p.

An important early British account of the Mosquito Coast, with considerable geographical information. It includes (p. 15) a table of the population of the principal settlements on this coast along with much descriptive material on the inhabitants. It emphasizes the potential resources of the place and encourages further British development.

68 **Travels in Central America, 1821-1840.**
Franklin D. Parker. Gainesville, Florida: University of Florida Press, 1970. 340p. map. bibliog.

Using excerpts from the major travellers' accounts of the period, Parker provides a fascinating description of Central American customs, politics, economy and society, with considerable discussion of Nicaragua included. Featured in the volume are the accounts of Orlando Roberts, James Wilson, George Alexander Thompson, Jacob Haefkens, Henry Dunn, James Jackson Jarves, George Washington Montgomery, George Byam, Thomas Young and John Lloyd Stephens.

69 **Exposición sumaria de viajes y trabajos geográficos sobre Nicaragua durante el siglo XIX.** (Summary description of travels and geographic works on Nicaragua during the 19th century.)
Désiré Pector. *Boletín Nicaragüense de Bibliografía y Documentación*, vol. 18 (July-Aug. 1977), p. 66-69.

Brief guide to 19th-century travellers who wrote about Nicaragua. Pector published a considerable amount about Nicaragua near the end of the 19th century. This is drawn from his *Etude économique sur la république de Nicaragua* (Economic study of the Republic of Nicaragua).

70 **Sketch of the Mosquito shore, including the territory of Poyais, description of the country; with some information as to its production, the best mode of culture & c., chiefly intended for settlers.**
Thomas Strangeways. Edinburgh: W. Blackwood, 1822. 355p. map.

Written by Gregor MacGregor's aide-de-camp to attract settlers to his ill-fated Poyais colony on the Honduran Caribbean coast, this is a fascinating description of the flora and fauna, agriculture, production and potential commerce of the whole region. It is particularly detailed on the flora and fauna of the whole Mosquito Coast. It presents an especially favourable view of the region in its efforts to attract immigrants. See also, in the same vein although much briefer, John Wright, *Memoir of the Mosquito Territory, as respecting the voluntary cession of it to the Crown of Great Britain: pointing out some, of the many, advantages to be derived from the occupation of that country; more especially, after our ill success at Buenos-Ayres, as set forth in a memorial presented to the right honourable Lord Castlereagh* (London: J. Hatchard, 1808. 32p.).

71 **Narratives of voyages and excursions on the east coast and in the interior of Central America; describing a journey up the River San Juan and passage across the Lake of Nicaragua to the city of Leon pointing out the advantages of a direct commercial intercourse with the natives.**
Orlando W. Roberts. Edinburgh: Constable, 1827. 302p. map.
A very revealing account of Nicaragua shortly after independence from Spain.

72 **Incidents of travel in Central America, Chiapas and Yucatan.**
John Lloyd Stephens. New York: Dover, 1969. 2 vols.
facsimile reprint of 1st ed., New York, Harper, 1841. 2 vols.
many subsequent eds.
The US government sent John Lloyd Stephens as its envoy to the disintegrating Central American government in 1839. He failed in that task, but succeeded in producing one of the most delightful and informative descriptions of Central America ever written. He travelled widely, commenting on the geography, politics, society, inhabitants, archaeology and economy.

73 **Narrative of a residence on the Mosquito Shore, during the years 1839, 1840 & 1841, with an account of Truxillo and the adjacent islands of Bonacca and Roatan.**
Thomas Young. London: Smith, Elder, 1842. 172p.
A very valuable first-hand description of the Caribbean coast by a British resident. Young makes perceptive comments not only about the situation on the Mosquito Coast, but also about the politics and economy of the country in general.

74 **Der Freistaat Nicaragua in Mittel-Amerika und seine Wichtigkeit für den Welthandel, den Ackerbau und die Colonisation.** (The Republic of Nicaragua in Middle America and its significance for world trade, agriculture and colonization.)
Alexander von Bulow. Berlin: G. Hempel, 1849. 139p. map.
One of the more perceptive accounts of Nicaragua during the stormy mid-19th century. It contains much information on the politics and the economy. A Spanish translation of the chapter on emigration and colonization appeared in the *Revista* of the Nicaraguan Academia de Geografía e Historia, vols. 28-29 (1964), p. 9-30.

75 **Central America.**
John Baily. London: T. Saunders, 1850. 164p. map.
John Baily spent many years in Central America during the first half of the 19th century, and his guide is one of the most useful on the period. It has descriptive chapters on both the State of Nicaragua and the Mosquito Territory, as well as a general chapter on Central American characteristics and physical conditions. It is an important historical source for the mid-19th century and also has an excellent map.

76 **Nicaragua. Nach eigener Anschauung im Jahre 1852 und mit besonderer Beziehung auf die Auswanderung nach den heissen Zonen Amerika's beschrieben.** (Nicaragua. A descriptive view of America's torrid zones in the year 1852, with particular attention to colonization.)
C. F. Reichardt. Braunschweig, Germany: F. Vieweg, 1854. 296p. map.

One of the most careful and important of the 19th-century travel accounts of Nicaragua. Describes the country at a critical time, when it had become a major transit route and shortly before the William Walker episode. Detailed description of Granada and surrounding area, with good coverage of other areas, including the Caribbean coast. Reichardt came to Nicaragua via steamer from New York. His first chapter describes that journey.

77 **Nicaragua, its people, scenery, monuments, resources, conditions and proposed canal.**
Ephraim George Squier. New York: Harper, 1860. rev. ed. 691p. map.

First published in 1852, and issued in 1853 under the title of *Travels in Central America*, this is Squier's principal work on Nicaragua. Squier was the aggressive United States envoy to Central America in the mid-19th century. He provides a great deal of information on a broad range of topics, but his strong anti-British, pro-Liberal and racist biases often colour his statements. Squier published extensively in books and articles on Central America in the 1850s. For a study of Squier's Central American experience, see Charles L. Stansifer, *The Central American career of E. George Squier* (PhD dissertation, Tulane University, 1959), which has also been published in a Spanish version in the *Revista Conservadora del Pensamiento Centroamericano* (vol. 20, no. 98, p. 33-64). See also *Waikna* and *The states of Central America*, both listed below.

78 **Diario de John Hill Wheeler, ministro de los Estados Unidos en Nicaragua, 1854-1857.** (Diary of John Hill Wheeler, United States minister in Nicaragua, 1854-1857.)
Managua: Banco de América, 1974. 171p. (Colección Cultural, Serie Fuentes Históricas).

Diary of the US envoy in Nicaragua during the William Walker invasion. Translated from an unpublished English manuscript in the Library of Congress.

79 **Waikna: adventures on the Mosquito shore, a facsimile of the 1855 edition.**
Samuel A. Bard (*pseud.* for Ephraim George Squier), edited by Daniel E. Alleger. Gainesville, Florida: University of Florida Press, 1965. 366p.

An autobiographical novel. This edition includes an excellent introduction by Alleger, as well as a helpful index.

80 **Repúblicas de Centro América o idea de su historia i de su estado actual.** (The republics of Central America, or an idea of their history and present states.)
Francisco Solano Astaburuaga y Cienfuegos. Santiago de Chile: Imprenta del Ferrocarril, 1857. 116p.

Astaburuaga was the Chilean chargé d'affaires in Central America. He spent most of his time in Costa Rica, but he makes some very perceptive comments on politics and life in Nicaragua.

81 **Travels in the free states of Central America: Nicaragua, Honduras and San Salvador.**
Carl Scherzer. London: Longman, Brown, Green, Longman & Roberts, 1857. 2 vols. maps.

One of the most careful and detailed 19th-century descriptions of Nicaragua is found in vol. 1, p. 1-238. Scherzer describes both the physical and human characteristics, with substantial attention to geography, geology, flora and fauna, political events, social customs, agriculture, trade, religion, etc. Scherzer published a number of other volumes and articles dealing with more specialized scientific data on the region.

82 **Reminiscences of the 'Filibuster' War in Nicaragua.**
Charles W. Doubleday. New York, London: Putnam, 1886. 225p.

A lively account by an American who was already in Nicaragua at the time of William Walker's expedition. Doubleday joined with Walker, but later broke with him over 'ethical issues'. His account is excellent both for his observations of Nicaragua before the invasion and of the Walker episode itself.

83 **The states of Central America: their geography, topography, climate, population, resources, production, commerce, political organization, aborigines, etc., etc., comprising chapters on Honduras, San Salvador, Nicaragua, Costa Rica, Guatemala, Belize, the Bay Islands, the Mosquito Shore, and the Honduras Inter-Oceanic Railway.**
Ephraim George Squier. New York: Harper, 1858. 782p.

Detailed and often strongly opinionated description of Nicaragua by the US envoy to Central America in the middle of the 19th century. This work reflects Squier's ambitious hopes for US development of the region and his compilation of a wide variety of informative data.

84 **Nicaragua: past, present and future; a description of its inhabitants, customs, mines, minerals, early history, modern filibusterism, proposed inter-oceanic canal and manifest destiny.**
Peter F. Stout. Philadelphia: J. E. Potter, 1859. 372p. bibliog.

Stout was a resident of Nicaragua at the time of Walker's invasion. He gives a fairly thorough description not only of the Walker episode, but also of the country in general. He favoured US acquisition of Nicaragua.

85 **Patriots and filibusterers, or incidents of political and exploratory travel.**
Laurence Oliphant. Edinburgh, London: W. Blackwood, 1860. 242p.

The personal recollections of an English traveller who came to Nicaragua to join William Walker's army, but who arrived too late. He is very pro-filibuster and argued that Walker's success would have been beneficial to English commercial interests. Oliphant, who published a number of other volumes on his travels and impressions, also discusses the southern United States in this volume, and their relation to the Walker episode.

86 **A travers l'Amérique Centrale, le Nicaragua et le canal interocéanique.** (Across Central America, Nicaragua and the interoceanic canal.)
Félix Belly. Paris: Librairie de la Suisse Romande, 1867. 2 vols. maps.

Félix Belly was a French agent sent to Central America to negotiate a canal treaty. He spent most of his time in Nicaragua and his detailed and perceptive memoir is one of the more useful and interesting sources of the period. See also Cyril Allen's biography of Belly, *France in Central America: Félix Belly and the Nicaraguan canal* (New York: Pageant, 1966. 163p. bibliog.).

87 **A ride across a continent: a personal narrative of wanderings through Nicaragua and Costa Rica.**
Frederick Boyle. London: R. Bentley, 1868. 2 vols.

An entertaining and informative account by an Englishman, with special interest in history and archaeology. The two volumes deal principally with Nicaragua, through which the author travelled widely. This account is especially useful for its description of life in Nicaraguan mining towns in the 1860s.

88 **Dottings on the roadside, in Panama, Nicaragua, and Mosquito.**
Bedford Clapperton Trevelyan Pim, Berthold Seemann. London: Chapman & Hall, 1869. 468p. maps. bibliog.

Pim was the commander of the British warship *Gorgon*, active on the Central American coast during the 1840s. He received a land grant and contract from Her Majesty's government to build a railroad from the Caribbean coast to Lake

Nicaragua in 1859, and from the Nicaraguan government in 1865. This rambling but fascinating work is in part a history of Mosquitia, but also an account of Pim's travels in Nicaragua. Commander Pim also wrote a book on the Nicaraguan canal project: *The gate of the Pacific* (London: L. Reeve, 1863. 432p.).

89 A naturalist in Nicaragua.
Thomas Belt. London: Edward Bumpus, 1888. 2nd ed. 403p.

First published in London, 1874, Belt's careful observations of flora and fauna make this one of the most important Nicaraguan travel accounts of the 19th century. Belt resided at the gold mines in Chontales and travelled extensively in the forests and savannahs of Nicaragua. The Banco Central de Nicaragua published a Spanish translation of this account in 1976.

90 Las impresiones de un general de las fuerzas confederadas sobre Centroamérica en los años finales del siglo XIX. (The impressions of a Confederate general in Central America in the last years of the 19th century.)
Ralph Lee Woodward, Jr. *Anuario de Estudios Centroamericanos*, vol. 4 (1979), p. 39-66.

Former Confederate general Edward Porter Alexander, named arbiter of the Nicaraguan-Costa Rican boundary dispute at the end of the 19th century, offers some perceptive and interesting impressions of his travels and experiences in the two countries in letters sent back to his wife and daughter in the United States.

91 The Nicaragua canal.
William E. Simmons. New York, London: Harper, 1900. 334p. (1899 edition entitled *Uncle Sam's new waterway*).

A picturesque view of Nicaragua at the turn of the century by a proponent of the Nicaragua canal. Describes people and customs as well as geography, history and government, especially of the region near the proposed canal route. The work's value is much enhanced by about thirty interesting photographs. An appendix includes a US Senate bill to provide for the construction of a canal in Nicaragua by the US government.

92 Ocean to ocean: an account, personal and historical, of Nicaragua and its people.
J. W. G. Walker. Chicago: A. C. McClurg, 1902. 309p.

An important view of Nicaragua at the turn of the century, written by the head of the United States congressional commission that investigated Nicaraguan canal possibilities. See also Walker's official report *Report of the Nicaraguan Canal Commission* (q.v.).

93 Central America and its problems: an account of a journey from the Rio Grande to Panama.
Frederick Palmer. New York: Moffat, Yard; London: T. W. Laurie, 1910. 347p.

Travel description and personal impressions during a 1909 trip through Central America. Comment on political leaders and the people's life-styles, with a little history from standard sources thrown in. Considerable attention to Nicaragua, especially on p. 144-85, but other references scattered throughout the book.

94 On the earthquake line: minor adventures in Central America.
Morley Roberts. London: Arrowsmith, 1924. 310p.

Roberts' geologic discussion of causes of earthquakes is of dubious value, but this work is very useful for its description of life and customs in the rural Nicaraguan area of Cosigüina.

95 Rainbow countries of Central America.
Wallace Thompson. New York: E. P. Dutton, 1926. 284p. map.

A highly descriptive travel account, heavily illustrated. The discussion of Nicaragua on p. 38-65 is principally concerned with the US intervention. Other chapters deal with topical descriptions, and contain much data on mining, agriculture, trade, communications, daily life, human patterns, education, politics, revolution, popular attitudes and daily life not easily found elsewhere.

96 The Central Americans: adventures and impressions between Mexico and Panama.
Arthur J. Ruhl. New York, London: Scribner, 1928. 284p.

This chatty, illustrated account contains a revealing chapter on 'Troubled Nicaragua' (p. 75-132), providing some insight into the country under United States occupation.

97 Our neighbor Nicaragua.
Floyd Cramer. New York: Frederic A. Stokes, 1929. 243p.

As a history of Nicaragua from the Spanish conquest through the Sandino revolt, this strongly opinionated and undocumented work has little value, but it does offer a first-hand picture of the country in the 1920s from a US point of view. It is sharply critical of Sandino and highly laudatory toward the US intervention.

98 I had nine lives: fighting for cash in Mexico and Nicaragua.
Joseph Crad (*pseud.* for Edward Clarence Trelawney-Ansell). London: S. Low, Marston, 1938. 234p.

The personal memoir of a British soldier of fortune who served with Pancho Villa in the Mexican revolution and later with Sandino in Nicaragua. Vivid descriptions of the horrors of these wars.

99 Through unknown Nicaragua; the adventures of a naturalist on a wild-goose chase.
Mervyn G. Palmer. London: Jarrold, 1945. 150p. maps.

A narrative account of a one-man expedition, principally through eastern Nicaragua, with numerous photos and drawings. Palmer comments on the wildlife, plants, people, customs, geography, etc.

100 **Wayfarer in Central America.**
   Tord K. E. Wallstrom, translated by M. A.
   Michel. London: Arthur Barker; New York: Roy
   Publishers, 1955. 192p.
Travel account of a Swedish journalist. Contains some interesting observations on
Somoza's Nicaragua. Wallstrom talked to a lot of ordinary people.

101 **Red rumba: a journey through the Caribbean and Central
   America.**
   Nicholas Wollaston. London: Hodder & Stoughton, 1962.
   231p.
Useful for the author's interviews with ordinary people on a trip through Cuba,
Guatemala, Honduras, Nicaragua, Costa Rica, El Salvador, Panama, Puerto
Rico, Haiti and the Dominican Republic. Nicaragua is covered on p. 138-54.
Wollaston also has a revealing interview with dictator Luís Somoza.

This is Nicaragua.
See item no. 18.

Notas geográficas y económicas sobre la República de Nicaragua.
(Geographical and economic notes on the Republic of Nicaragua.)
See item no. 32.

The state of Nicaragua of the Greater Republic of Central America.
See item no. 34.

Wild life in the interior of Central America.
See item no. 114.

The Kemble papers.
See item no. 173.

Our jungle diplomacy.
See item no. 413.

France in Central America: Félix Belly and the Nicaraguan canal.
See item no. 429.

Agricultural settlement and development in eastern Nicaragua.
See item no. 520.

Flora and Fauna

General

102 **Biologia centrali-americana, zoology, botany and archaeology.**
Edited by Frederick Ducane Goodman, Osbert
Salvin. London: R. J. Porter & Dulau, for the editors,
1879-1915. 63 vols. maps. bibliog.

This is a massive study of the flora and fauna of the region from Mexico through
Panama, containing much information on Nicaragua. Volume 1 (1915) contains
an introduction to the work and outlines its contents. Volumes 2-52 (1879-1915),
prepared by a large number of distinguished scholars, identify 38,637 different
species of the fauna of the Middle American region, of which 19,067 are
described for the first time and 18,051 are illustrated. These volumes contain
1,173 plates, including maps. Volumes 51-57, prepared by W. B. Hemsley, on the
botany of the region, describe 11,626 species, 196 for the first time, with 144
illustrations and 111 plates, including maps. Volumes 58-62, prepared by Alfred
P. Maudslay, deal with the archaeology of the region, and volume 63 contains
archaic Maya inscriptions, collected by J. T. Goodman. The archaeological portion, however, has little to do with Nicaragua. This remarkable collection provides
a solid base for the study of the flora and fauna of Nicaragua, although the
volumes are not, for the most part, organized geographically.

103 **Central American jungles.**
Don Moser. New York: Time-Life Books, 1975. 184p.
(The American Wilderness).

A lavishly illustrated odyssey of Central American flora, fauna and landscape.
Many of the full colour photos are of Nicaraguan scenes.

104 **High jungles and low.**
Archie Carr, illustrations by Lee Adams. Gainesville,
Florida: University of Florida Press, 1953. 226p.
Fascinating account of the author's travels and researches in the jungles of Honduras and Nicaragua in the 1940s. Describes the flora and fauna and their relation to the ecology and the people of the region.

105 **Indice semántico de la flora y fauna nicaragüense.** (Semantic
index to Nicaraguan flora and fauna.)
Alejandro David Bolaños. *Nicaragua Indígena*, no. 47
(1969), p. 71-104.
An alphabetical listing of about 350 species of Nicaraguan flora and fauna with brief descriptions.

**Sketch of the Mosquito shore, including the territory of Poyais,
description of the country; with some information as to its production, the
best mode of culture & c., chiefly intended for settlers.**
See item no. 70.

A naturalist in Nicaragua.
See item no. 89.

**Through unknown Nicaragua; the adventures of a naturalist on a
wild-goose chase.**
See item no. 99.

Flora

106 **L'Amérique Centrale, recherches sur sa flore et sa géographie.
Résultats d'un voyage dans les états de Costa Rica et de
Nicaragua exécuté pendant les années 1846-1848.** (Central
America, research on its flora and its physical geography.
Results of a journey in the states of Costa Rica and
Nicaragua during the years 1846-1848.) Anders S.
Oersted. Copenhagen: B. Luno, for F. S. Muhle, 1863. 18p.
maps.
A major 19th-century work on Nicaraguan flora, done by the Danish scientist A. S. Oersted. Includes twenty-one lovely plates. Earlier, Oersted published several articles on his Central American research, including 'Central America Gesnereceer, et systematisk, plantegeographisk Bidrag til Centralamerikas Flora', in *Kongeligt Dansk Videnskabernes Selskab* (Copenhagen 1859, vol. 5, part 1, p. 75-152. map. 10 plates).

107 **Calendario de frutas y vegetales disponibles en el mercado local.** (List of fruits and vegetables available in the local market.)
Managua: Banco Central de Nicaragua, Departamento de Investigaciones Tecnológicas, 1978. 4th ed. 98p.
Charts and graphs show monthly rises and declines in prices and availability of fruits and vegetables in Managua.

Fauna

108 **Anfibios de Nicaragua: introducción a sus sistemática, vida y costumbres.** (Amphibians of Nicaragua: introduction to their structure, life and habits.)
Jaime Villa. Managua: Instituto Geográfico Nacional, with the Banco Central de Nicaragua, 1972. 216p. maps. bibliog.
First, and as yet the only, volume in a projected series on Nicaraguan amphibians. Heavily illustrated, this work contains a general introduction to the subject, followed by a detailed classification of Nicaraguan caecilians, salamanders and frogs. Villa's bibliography is useful as a guide to the limited periodical literature on the topic.

109 **Birds of tropical America.**
Alexander F. Skutch. Austin, Texas: University of Texas Press, 1983. 320p.
Describes, with beautiful drawings by Dana Gardner and photographs by the author, thirty-four species of tropical Central and South American birds. Painstaking detail on the lives and daily habits of these birds.

110 **Fauna of Middle America.**
L. C. Stuart. In: *Handbook of Middle American Indians*, vol. 1. Edited by Robert Wauchope, Robert West. Austin, Texas: University of Texas Press, 1964, p. 316-62.
An excellent introduction to the fauna of the region including Nicaragua.

111 **Investigations of the ichthyofauna of Nicaraguan lakes.**
Thomas S. Thorson. Lincoln, Nebraska: School of Life Sciences, University of Nebraska, 1976. 663p. bibliog.
A beautifully illustrated guide to Nicaraguan lake fish, partially financed by the Banco Central de Nicaragua. Texts in English and Spanish. This work is an outgrowth of a symposium held during the annual meeting of the American Society of Ichthyologists and Herpetologists in San José, Costa Rica, in 1973. See also Norman H. Jensen, *The reproduction and development of the bull shark, carcharhinus leucas, in the Lake Nicaragua-Rio San Juan system*, PhD dissertation, University of Nebraska, 1972 (University Microfilms order no. 72-31874),

and Kenneth R. McKaye, *Some aspects of the behavior and ecology of the cichlid fishes of Lake Jiloa, Nicaragua*, PhD dissertation, University of California, Berkeley, 1975 (University Microfilms order no. 76-15300).

112 **Peces nicaragüenses de agua dulce.** (Nicaraguan freshwater fish.)
Jaime Villa. Managua: Banco de América, Fondo de Promoción Cultural, 1982. 255p. bibliog. (Colección Cultural, Serie de Geografía y Naturaleza, no. 3).

Introductory chapters discuss Nicaraguan fish and their environment and systems of classification. Subsequently 34 families, 78 genera, and 183 species of Nicaraguan freshwater fish are identified. Illustrated. This handsome work supersedes Villa's earlier *Sinopsis de los peces de Nicaragua; guía para la identificación de los especies de agua dulce* (Synopsis of Nicaraguan fish; guide to the identification of freshwater species), Managua: UNAN (Universidad Autónoma de Nicaragua), Departamento de Biología, 1971 (3rd ed. 132p. bibliog.). Two earlier, but hard to find, studies in English of this topic include Seth Eugene Meek, *Synopses of the fishes of the great lakes of Nicaragua*, Chicago: Field Colombian Museum (Publication no. 121, Zoological Series, vol. 8, no. 4, July 1907. 132p. illus.), and Ignatius Astorqui, SJ, *Fishes from the great lakes of Nicaragua*, MS thesis, University of Miami, Coral Gables, Florida, 1961 (128p., with extensive bibliography). See also Villa's *Lista tentativa de los vertebrados inferiores de Nicaragua* (Tentative list of the lower vertebrates of Nicaragua), Managua: UNAN, 1971 (37p.), a comprehensive list of the freshwater fish, amphibians and reptiles of the country. Professor Villa is presently preparing a revised edition of this paper.

113 **Serpientes venenosas de Nicaragua.** (Venomous snakes of Nicaragua.)
Jaime Villa. Managua: Novedades, 1962. 91p. bibliog.

Describes the fifteen species of venomous snakes in Nicaragua, illustrated with photographs and drawings. A brief section also describes some non-venomous snakes which appear similar to venomous species. A brief final section dispels a number of Nicaraguan myths regarding serpents.

114 **Wild life in the interior of Central America.**
George Byam. London: John W. Parker, 1849. 253p.

An entertaining and informative description of wildlife in Nicaragua by a British officer. Byam also comments on political affairs, but he is primarily occupied with his anecdotal wildlife descriptions.

Archaeology of the Rivas Region, Nicaragua.
See item no. 117.

Caribbean edge, the coming of modern times to isolated people and wildlife.
See item no. 260.

The impact of commercial exploitation on sawfish and shark populations in Lake Nicaragua.
See item no. 567.

Prehistory and
Archaeology

115 **Archaeological researches in Nicaragua.**
John F. Bransford. Washington, DC: Smithsonian
Institution, 1881. 96p. Facsimile ed., Managua: Banco de
América [1974?] (Colección Cultural).
Dr. Bransford came to Nicaragua with a US naval expedition making surveys for
the projected interoceanic canal. The archaeological description, richly illustrated,
is based on his studies on Ometepe Island, Lake Nicaragua, and on a ranch near
Moyogalpa.

116 **Archaeology of lower Central America.**
Samuel K. Lothrop. In: *Handbook of Middle American
Indians*, vol. 4. Edited by Robert Wauchope, G. F. Ekholm,
G. R. Wiley. Austin, Texas: University of Texas Press, 1966,
p. 180-208.
A guide to the state of Nicaraguan archaeology through the 1960s written by one
of the leading specialists in the archaeology of the region.

117 **Archaeology of the Rivas Region, Nicaragua.**
Paul F. Healy. Waterloo, Ontario: Wilfrid Laurier
University, 1980. 382p. bibliog.
A detailed archaeological description on this region of the Pacific coastal plain of
Nicaragua, with descriptions of the pre-Columbian Indians and their ceramics,
artefacts, culture, etc. It also has a discussion of the literature of Nicaraguan
archaeology, p. 31-34, and a very extensive bibliography, p. 347-64. This work
includes a chapter on the fauna of the region by Mary Pohl and Paul F. Healy.

118 **Central America.**
Claude F. Baudez, translated by James Hogarth. Geneva:
Nagel, 1970. 255p. bibliog.
A richly illustrated guide to the archaeology of Central America by a leading
French archaeologist. Nicaragua receives considerable attention, more than in
most archaeologies of Central America which tend to concentrate on the Maya
heritage of upper Central America. Baudez defines Central America as that area
between Guatemala and Colombia, thus excluding Guatemala from this study.

119 **Central American and West Indian archaeology; being an**
   introduction to the archaeology of the states of Nicaragua,
   Costa Rica, Panama and the West Indies.
   Thomas A. Joyce. London: Warner, 1916. 270p. maps.
   bibliographic essay.
One of the first attempts at a comprehensive survey of lower Central American
archaeology, Joyce devotes his first three chapters to Nicaragua and northeastern
Costa Rica. The work is heavily illustrated with photographs and drawings.

120 **Ceramic stratigraphy in southwestern Nicaragua.**
   Albert Holden Norweb. In: *XXXV Congreso Internacional*
   de Americanistas, México, 1962, actas y memorias, vol. 1.
   Mexico City, 1964, p. 551-61. map. bibliog.
An outline of the ceramic sequence of southwestern Nicaragua.

121 **La colección Squier-Zapatera, estudio de estatuaria**
   prehispánica. (The Squier-Zapatera collection, study of
   pre-Columbian statuary.)
   Jorge Eduardo Arellano. Managua [1980?]. 184p. maps.
   bibliog.
A careful, well-documented study of the statuary discovered by E. G. Squier on
the island of Zapatera. This collection is found in the 'Patio de Idolos' of the
Colegio de Centroamérica in Granada, Nicaragua. The work is richly illustrated
with photographs and drawings, and includes in an appendix (p. 163-68) a translation of S. K. Lothrop's 'The stone statues of Nicaragua' (q.v.), Manuel Ignacio
Pérez Alonso's account of his excursion to Zonzapote in May 1942, and a collection of photos by Manuel Otaño.

122 **Excavaciones arqueológicas en El Bosque.** (Archaeological
   excavations at El Bosque.)
   Jorge Espinosa Estrada. Managua: Ministerio de Obras
   Públicas, Instituto Geográfico Nacional, Departamento de
   Antropología e Historia, 1976. 70p. maps. bibliog.
An important monograph on the first palaeo-Indian site found in northern Nicar-
agua, describing what is perhaps one of the oldest archaeological sites in
America, with Carbon-14 readings of 16,000 BC to 30,000 BC.

123 **Geologic observations on the ancient footprints near Managua, Nicaragua.**
Howel Williams. In: *Contributions to American Anthropology and History*, vol. 9, no. 52. Washington, DC: Carnegie Institution, 1952, p. 1-31. maps. bibliog. (Publication no. 596).

A detailed description of the ancient footprints around Managua, especially those at Acahualinca (El Cauce) and El Recreo, adding geologic analysis to archaeological findings and concluding that the prints are between 2,000 and 5,000 years old. This revises earlier claims by some archaeologists that they were 50,000 or more years old.

124 **Historia precolonial de Nicaragua.** (Pre-Hispanic history of Nicaragua.)
Francisco Pérez Estrada. Managua: Editorial Nueva Nicaragua, Ministerio de Cultura, 1980. 41p.

A very brief outline of Nicaraguan prehistory, emphasizing the Nahuatl origins of the country. Gives a paragraph or two on each topic, including institutions, language, customs, government, social classes, etc.

125 **Las huellas de Acahualinca en el panorama arqueológico de Nicaragua.** (The footprints of Acahualinca in the archaeological panorama of Nicaragua.)
Joaquín Matillo Vilá. Managua: Editorial Unión, 1975. 45p. (Publicaciones del Museo Nacional, Serie Arqueología, no. 1).

A description of the early footprints found on the outskirts of Managua.

126 **Idolos de Nicaragua.** (Idols of Nicaragua.)
Frederick Thieck. León, Nicaragua: UNAN (Universidad Autónoma de Nicaragua), Departamento de Arqueología y Antropología, 1971. 218p. map. plates.

Illustrated album of stone statuary of Nicaragua. Includes the Squier-Zapatera collection (see *La colección Squier-Zapatera* above).

127 **Introducción al arte precolombino de Nicaragua.** (Introduction to the pre-Columbian art of Nicaragua.)
Jorge Eduardo Arellano. *Boletín Nicaragüense de Bibliografía y Documentación*, no. 40 (March-April 1981), p. 1-36. bibliog.

A well-documented and useful overview of preserved pre-Columbian art in Nicaragua, with an extensive bibliography, p. 32-36. This article serves as an introduction to the remainder of this issue of the *BNBD*, which contains several articles on pre-Columbian Nicaragua.

128 **The Maya and their neighbors.**
C. L. Hay (and others). New York: Appleton-Century,
1940. 606p.

This Festschrift in honour of A. M. Tozzer includes several important articles on
Nicaragua, notably those of F. B. Richardson, 'Non-Maya sculpture in Central
America', p. 395-416; Samuel K. Lothrop, 'South America as seen from Middle
America', p. 417-29; and A. V. Kidder, 'American penetrations in Middle
America', p. 441-55.

129 **Mesoamerican archaeology, a guide to the literature and
other information sources.**
Compiled by Susan F. Magee. Austin, Texas: Institute of
Latin American Studies, University of Texas, 1981. 71p.
bibliog.

A basic guide to archaeological sources for the region whose southern boundary
'extends from the mouth of the Ulúa River in Honduras to the Nicoya Peninsula
in Costa Rica'. This includes part of Nicaragua. Magee reviews the principal
general works on the region, guides to the literature, bibliographies, periodicals,
and indexes to abstracts, reviews, theses and dissertations, associations and societies, grants and research centres, international agencies, government agencies,
special library collections, Human Relations Area Files, museums, atlases and
maps, specialists, academic institutions and field schools, biographical dictionaries,
non-print materials and search techniques.

130 **Nicaraguan antiquities.**
Carl Bovallius. Stockholm: Kongl. Boktryckeriet, for the
Swedish Society of Anthropology and Geography, 1886.
Facsimile ed. with Spanish translation appended, Managua:
Banco de América, 1970. 50p.+41 plates. maps.

A beautifully illustrated description of Nicaraguan archaeological sites: specifically, statues in Punta del Sapote and Punta de las Figuras, rock carvings on the
island of Ceiba, and ceramic objects from Ometepec, Zapatera and Ceiba. Based
on a two-year residence in Nicaragua.

131 **Ometepe, isla de círculos y de espirales: estudio del arte
rupestre isleño.** (Ometepe, island of circles and spirals: a
study of the island's rupestrian art.)
Joaquín Matillo Vilá, Hildeberto María. Managua: Centro
de Investigaciones Rupestres, 1972. 213p. bibliog.

Heavily illustrated study of the rock pictographs on Ometepe Island in Lake
Nicaragua, with separate sections devoted to geography, ethnology, the pictographs and their locations, and an analysis of their significance.

132 **Pottery of Costa Rica and Nicaragua.**
Samuel K. Lothrop. New York: Museum of the American
Indian, Heye Foundation, 1926. 2 vols. (Contribution no. 8).

A magnificent collection and commentary on the region's prehistoric pottery.
Lothrop studied more than 30,000 items in museums and private collections in

Prehistory and Archaeology

Central America, the United States and Europe. These volumes are lavishly illustrated, often in full colour. The work represents the first modern, systematic study of Nicaraguan archaeology.

133 Pre-Columbian man finds Central America: the archaeological bridge.
Doris Zemurray Stone. Cambridge, Massachusetts: Harvard University, Peabody Museum Press, 1972. 231p. maps.

An excellent introduction to the archaeology of Nicaragua. Ms. Stone emphasizes Central America's important role as a cultural bridge between South America and Middle America, and her work is especially useful for understanding lower Central America (Nicaragua through Panama).

134 The prehistoric and modern subsistence patterns of the Atlantic coast of Nicaragua. A comparison.
Richard Werner Magnus. In: *Coastal adaptations: the economy and ecology of maritime Middle America.* Edited by Barbara L. Stark, Barbara Voorhies. New York: Academic Press, 1978, p. 61-80. maps. bibliog.

Compares archaeological and modern evidence of subsistence patterns along the Nicaraguan Caribbean coast, noting major differences between the two. For a more detailed study of the archaeology of this coast, see Magnus' 1974 Yale University PhD dissertation, *The prehistory of the Miskito coast of Nicaragua: a study in cultural relationships* (University Microfilms order no. 75-01381). A slightly different version of this excellent paper was also published in English by the Banco Central in Managua in 1976. See also his 'Prehistoric cultural relationships of the Miskito coast' in the 41st International Congress of Americanists *Actas* (Proceedings), Mexico City, 1974, vol. 3, p. 568-78.

135 Stone statues of Nicaragua.
Samuel K. Lothrop. *American Anthropologist*, vol. 23 (1921), p. 311-19.

A pioneering work in identifying principal Nicaraguan pre-Hispanic stone statuary.

Middle America: a culture history of the heartlands and frontiers.
See item no. 255.

Handbook of Middle American Indians.
See item no. 266.

Handbook of South American Indians.
See item no. 267.

The art and archaeology of pre-Columbian Middle America: annotated bibliography of works in English.
See item no. 694.

History

Central America general

136 América Central ante la historia. (A history of Central
America.)
Antonio Batres Jáuregui. Guatemala City: Marroquín
Hermanos, Casa Colorada, 1916-49. 3 vols.

A good general survey of Central American political history. Tends to favour the
Conservatives more than most of the histories written by Central Americans in
the late 19th or early 20th centuries. The first two volumes treat the colonial
period, the third volume covers the period 1821-1921.

137 The Cádiz experiment in Central America, 1808 to 1826.
Mario Rodríguez. Berkeley, California: University of
California Press, 1978. 316p. bibliog.

A detailed and persuasive account of the emergence of liberalism in Central
America as a result of the ideology that dominated the Cortes of Cádiz, which
directed Spanish resistance against Napoleon, 1804-14, and produced the notable
Constitution of 1812 with the collaboration of Spanish colonial representatives.
An impressive and highly significant scholarly work which is essential to understanding the philosophy, goals and methods of the Central American Liberals of
the 19th and 20th centuries.

138 Central America and the Caribbean.
New York: Arno Press, 1980. 412p. bibliog. (The Great
Contemporary Issues).

Facsimile reprints of articles from the *New York Times* tell the history of the
Caribbean region from 1868 to 1980. There is considerable coverage of Nicaragua, especially on the US interventions, Sandino and the Sandinistas.

139 **Central America, a nation divided.**
Ralph Lee Woodward, Jr.   New York: Oxford University
Press, 1976. 344p. maps. bibliog. (Latin American
Histories).

A general, socio-economic survey of Central American history from pre-Columbian times to 1975. Considers the five Central American states as a single unit, but substantial coverage is given to Nicaragua and its role within Central America. Includes an extensive bibliographical essay. A revised edition of this work, bringing it up to date, is scheduled to be published about 1985.

140 **The failure of union: Central America, 1824-1960.**
Thomas L. Karnes.   Chapel Hill, North Carolina:
University of North Carolina Press, 1961. 277p. bibliog. 2nd
ed., Tempe, Arizona: Center for Latin American Studies,
Arizona State University, 1976. 283p.

Karnes recounts the frequent attempts at Central American union from the establishment of the United Provinces in 1824 to the present. This is a scholarly and readable volume, a standard work in Central American history.

141 **The historiography of Central America since 1830.**
William J. Griffith.   *Hispanic American Historical Review*,
vol. 40 (Nov. 1960), p. 548-69.

A masterful description of the literature of 19th- and 20th-century Central American history, providing scholarly evaluation of the quality and quantity of historical writing on the region to 1960.

142 **History and Central America.**
Hubert Howe Bancroft.   San Francisco: History Co.,
1886-87. 3 vols.

Although heavily influenced by the Liberal historians of his time and certainly out of date in many respects, Bancroft's compendious work is still an important source for colonial and 19th-century Central American history.

143 **Middle American governors.**
Compiled by Glen W. Taplin.   Metuchen, New Jersey:
Scarecrow Press, 1972. 196p. bibliog.

A chronological listing of the chief executives of Nicaragua, 1522-1967, with the principal events of their administrations noted.

144 **The political influences of an interoceanic canal, 1826-1926.**
William W. Pierson.   *Hispanic American Historical Review*,
vol. 6 (1926), p. 205-31.

Overviews a century of efforts to build an isthmian canal and the role of Britain and the United States in those efforts.

145 **The romance and rise of the American tropics.**
Samuel Crowther. New York: Doubleday, Doran, 1929.
390p.

A rather strongly opinionated work glorifying American enterprise in Central America, with a great deal of attention paid to Nicaragua in the 19th and 20th centuries.

146 **Spanish Central America: a socioeconomic history, 1520-1720.**
Murdo J. MacLeod. Berkeley, California: University of California Press, 1973. 554p. maps. bibliog.

MacLeod's monumental study of Central America under Habsburg rule is essential to any study of the colonial period. He documents thoroughly the development of the population and economy during the first two centuries of Spanish rule in Central America, providing perceptive analysis and description. Although he is primarily concerned with social and economic development, he tells us a great deal about the political structure as well.

The Central American republics.
See item no. 5.

Middle America: a culture history of the heartlands and frontiers.
See item no. 255.

Handbook of Middle American Indians.
See item no. 266.

Vida militar de Centro América. (The military life of Central America.)
See item no. 374.

Research guide to Central America and the Caribbean.
See item no. 649.

Nicaragua general

147 **Artículos históricos.** (Historical articles.)
Alejandro Montiel Argüello. Managua: Banco Central de Nicaragua, 1978. 268p.

An interesting collection of articles on a broad range of topics in Nicaraguan economic, diplomatic, and political history.

148 **Bibliografía historiográfica de Nicaragua.** (Historiographical bibliography of Nicaragua.)
Carlos Molina Argüello. *Inter-American Review of Bibliography*, vol. 4 (1954), p. 9-22.

A basic guide to the principal historical literature of Nicaragua in Spanish. Despite its obvious shortcoming of not including works of the past thirty years, this is a useful guide to the principal works up to the mid-20th century.

149 **100 biografías centroamericanos.** (100 Central American biographies.)
Julián N. Guerrero C., Lola Soriano de Guerrero. Managua: Artes Gráficas, 1971-73. 2 vols.

The first two volumes of this projected series include biographies of a number of leading colonial figures, including in volume 1, Gil González Dávila, F. Hernández de Córdoba, Miguel Larreynaga, Rafael Landívar, Pedro de Alvarado, and Juan Vásquez de Coronado. Volume 2 includes Bartolomé de las Casas, Francisco de Montejo, Pedro de Betancourt, Rodolfo Argüello Escobar, and nineteen other brief biographies of modern figures, mostly Nicaraguan.

150 **Contribución a la historia de Centroamérica: monografías documentales.** (Contribution to the history of Central America: documentary monographs.)
Sofonías Salvatierra. Managua: Tipografía Progreso, 1939. 2 vols.

Of uneven quality, some of the sections are useful contributions and are based on research in Spanish archives. These volumes are principally concerned with the colonial period and the struggle for independence.

151 **Historia de Nicaragua desde los tiempos prehistóricos hasta 1860 en sus relaciones con España, México y Centroamérica.** (History of Nicaragua from prehistoric times to 1860 in its relations with Spain, Mexico and Central America.)
José Dolores Gámez. Managua: Banco de América, 1975. 3rd ed. 855p.

Less thorough than Tomas Ayón's *Historia de Nicaragua* (q.v.), but covers the period of independent Nicaragua through 1860. Useful for its detail, especially on diplomatic history. First published Managua 1889, 2nd ed. Madrid 1955. See also the author's *Historia moderna de Nicaragua* (q.v.).

152 **Historical dictionary of Nicaragua.**
Harvey K. Meyer. Metuchen, New Jersey: Scarecrow Press, 1972. 503p. (Latin American Historical Dictionaries, no. 6).

A very useful reference work, providing brief explanations of principal people, places and events in Nicaraguan history. Organized alphabetically.

153 **Obras de Don Pío Bolaños.** (Works of Pío Bolaños.)
Edited by Franco Cerutti. Managua: Fondo de Promoción Cultural, Banco de América, 1976-77. 2 vols. bibliog.

A collection of the writings of Pío Bolaños Alvarez (1873-1961), including of special value his *History of the city of Granada*, as well as shorter historical and biographical pieces of considerable utility to understanding 19th- and early 20th-century Nicaragua.

154 **Raíces indígenas de la lucha anticolonialista en Nicaragua.**
(Native roots of the Nicaraguan anticolonial struggle.)
Jaime Wheelock. New York: Bilingual Publications, 1979.
123p.

A succinct account of Indian opposition to Spanish domination from the Conquest through the late 19th century. Wheelock is one of Nicaragua's leading Marxist historians. Published in both English and Spanish. Originally published in Mexico in 1974.

155 **Revista de la Academia de Geografía e Historia de
Nicaragua.** (Nicaraguan Academy of Geography and History
review.)
Managua: AGHN, 1936-65. 30 vols. irregular.

Although published irregularly, this is important for historical articles and sources.

La Mosquitia en la revolución. (Mosquitia in the revolution.)
See item no. 38.

Central America early maps up to 1860.
See item no. 48.

Ensayos nicaragüenses. (Nicaraguan essays.)
See item no. 274.

Breve historia de la iglesia en Nicaragua, 1523-1979. (Brief history of the Church in Nicaragua, 1523-1979.)
See item no. 280.

Imperialismo y dictadura. Crisis de una formación social. (Imperialism and dictatorship. The crisis of a social structure.)
See item no. 300.

Gobernantes de Nicaragua, 1825-1947. (Governors of Nicaragua, 1825-1947.)
See item no. 325.

Desarrollo económico y político de Nicaragua, 1912-1947. (Economic and political development of Nicaragua, 1912-1947.)
See item no. 458.

Aspectos históricos de la moneda en Nicaragua. (Historical aspects of Nicaraguan currency.)
See item no. 484.

The coins and paper money of Nicaragua.
See item no. 488.

Technology versus tradition: the modernization of Nicaraguan agriculture, 1900-1940.
See item no. 542.

Cadiz to Cathay, the story of the long struggle for a waterway across the American isthmus.
See item no. 546.

The Nicaragua canal and the Monroe Doctrine, a political history of the isthmus transit, with special reference to the Nicaragua canal project and

the attitude of the United States government thereto.
See item no. 553.

Revista del Pensamiento Centroamericano. (Journal of Central American thought.)
See item no. 669.

Boletín de Referencias, Centro de Documentación. (Reference Bulletin, Documentation Centre.)
See item no. 697.

Local, urban, regional and departmental

156 **Corinto a través de la historia, 1514-1933.** (A history of Corinto, 1514-1933.)
Salvador D'Arbelles. Corinto, Nicaragua: Tipografía Saballos, 1933. 212p.

A history of Nicaragua's principal Pacific coast port.

157 **Historia de la Costa de Mosquitos, hasta 1894, en relación con la conquista española, los piratas y corsarios en las costas centroamericanas, los avances y protectorado del gobierno inglés en la misma costa y la famosa cuestión inglesa con Nicaragua, Honduras y El Salvador.** (History of the Mosquito Coast, to 1894, in relation to the Spanish conquest, the pirates and corsairs on the Central American coasts, the incursions and protectorate of the English government on the same coast and the famous English question with Nicaragua, Honduras and El Salvador.)
José Dolores Gámez. Managua: Talleres Nacionales, 1939. 346p.

The principal Nicaraguan history of the disputed Mosquito Coast region from the Spanish conquest through 1855. A brief final chapter by H. A. Castellón brings the story up to 1894, when the region was finally incorporated into Nicaragua. The work also deals with other Central American conflicts with the English in the 18th and 19th centuries.

158 **Historia de Diriamba, ciudad del Departamento de Carazo,**
   Nic. (History of Diriamba, city in the Department of
   Carazo, Nic.)
   Juan M. Mendoza.   Guatemala City: Imprenta Electra,
   1933. 532p.

An episodic and unanalytical narrative history of Diriamba, containing a great
deal of specific information, although unscientific in its methodology.

159 **Historia de Managua. Data desde el siglo xviii hasta hoy.**
   (History of Managua. Data from the 18th century to the
   present.)
   Gratus Halftermeyer.   Managua: Imprenta Nacional, 1971.
   5th ed. 383p.

A collection of anecdotes and historical data about people and places in
Managua. Not a professional history, but informative. Halftermeyer has published
several earlier books and articles similar to this on Managua.

An historical geography of western Nicaragua: the spheres of influence of
León, Granada and Managua, 1519-1965.
See item no. 36.

Historia de León Viejo. (History of Old León.)
See item no. 170.

Historia de el Realejo. (History of Realejo.)
See item no. 172.

Colonial Nicaragua (1524-1821)

160 **The Anglo-Spanish struggle for Mosquitia.**
   Troy S. Floyd.   Albuquerque, New Mexico: University of
   New Mexico Press, 1967. 235p. maps. bibliog.

A lively and scholarly account of the British and Spanish efforts to gain control
of the Mosquito Coast of Nicaragua to 1790. A major contribution to the history
of Nicaragua's Caribbean coast.

161 **Bourbon reforms in Central America: 1750-1786.**
   Miles Wortman.   *The Americas*, vol. 32 (Oct. 1975), p.
   222-38.

A useful overview of the Bourbon efforts to rejuvenate the Central American
economy in the late 18th century. Wortman pays considerable attention to Nicaragua in assessing the effects of the reforms in terms of economic development and
increasing provincial autonomy within the kingdom.

162 **Colección Somoza, documentos para la historia de Nicaragua.**
(Somoza Collection, documents for the history of
Nicaragua.)
Andrés Vega Bolaños. Madrid: Imprenta y Litografía Juan
Bravo, 1954-57. 17 vols.

A major collection of documents on the early history of Nicaragua, principally
from the first half of the 16th century, from Spanish archives. Since the national
archives of Nicaragua were destroyed by fire in 1931, this collection represents an
especially important source for Nicaragua's early history.

163 **Commercio terrestre de y entre las provincias de
Centroamérica.** (Trade from and among the provinces of
Central America.)
Manuel Rubio Sánchez. Guatemala City: Editorial del
Ejército, 1973. 366p.

Based on extensive study of colonial documents, Rubio traces trade and trade
policy from the Spanish conquest to the middle of the 18th century. As with most
of Rubio's works, there is little analysis, but an enormous amount of information,
quoting liberally from the documents. A projected future volume will continue
this story to 1821.

164 **Costa Rica, Nicaragua y Panama en el siglo XVI, su historia
y sus límites, según los documentos del Archivo de Indias de
Sevilla, del de Simancas, etc.** (Costa Rica, Nicaragua and
Panama in the 16th century, their history and boundaries,
according to documents from the Archives of the Indies in
Seville, the Simancas archives, etc.)
Manuel M. de Peralta. San José: M. Murillo, 1883. 832p.

Documents, with some notes and commentary. An important early collection.

165 **Forced native labor in sixteenth-century Central America.**
William L. Sherman. Lincoln, Nebraska: University of
Nebraska Press, 1979. 469p. bibliog.

One of the major works on 16th-century Central America, this thoroughly
researched history details much more than its title implies. Sherman's work
includes a very extensive bibliography. See also Sherman's 'Indian slavery and the
Cerato reforms', *Hispanic American Historical Review*, vol. 51 (1971), p. 25-50.

166 **El gobernador de Nicaragua en el siglo XVI, contribución al
estudio de la historia del derecho nicaragüense.** (The
governor of Nicaragua in the 16th century, contribution to
the study of Nicaraguan law.)
Carlos Molina Argüello. Seville, Spain: Escuela de
Estudios Hispano-Americanos, 1949. 251p.

A careful, well-documented study of executive institutions in 16th-century Nicaragua, providing a clear description of Spanish administration there under the
Habsburgs.

167 **Government and society in Central America, 1680-1840.**
Miles Wortman. New York: Columbia University Press, 1982. 373p.

Although the focus of this important study of colonial and early independent Central America is on Guatemala, it refers frequently to the province of Nicaragua. The work is a penetrating study of Central American society in its formative years, with considerable reliance on the author's research in the economic history of the period. See also his 'Government revenue and economic trends in Central America, 1787-1819', *Hispanic American Historical Review*, vol. 55 (May 1975), p. 251-86.

168 **The Guatemalan merchants, the government, and the 'provincianos', 1750-1800.**
Troy Floyd. *Hispanic American Historical Review*, vol. 41 (Jan. 1961), p. 90-110.

Floyd demonstrates the economic and political relationships between the several provinces of colonial Central America, and the obstacles that would contribute to the disruption of Central American union following independence.

169 **Hernández de Córdoba, capitán de conquista en Nicaragua.**
(Hernández de Córdoba, conquering captain in Nicaragua.)
Carlos Meléndez. Managua: Banco de América, 1976. 266p. bibliog. (Colección Cultural, Serie Histórica, no. 9).

A solid biography of the conquistador of Nicaragua, Francisco Hernández de Córdoba, with a documentary appendix. The author is a distinguished Costa Rican professor, and one of the leading historians of Central America.

170 **Historia de León Viejo.** (History of Old León.)
Alfonso Argüello Argüello. León, Nicaragua: Editorial Antorcha, 1969. 179p.

This is a history of the first city of León, established in 1524 and destroyed by earthquake and volcanic eruption in 1610.

171 **Historia de Nicaragua.** (History of Nicaragua.)
Tomas Ayón. Managua: Banco de América, 1977. 3rd ed. 3 vols. (Colección Cultural, Serie Histórica, nos. 10-12).

This is essentially a reprint of the second edition, published in Managua in 1956. The first edition was published in Managua in 1882-89 under the title *Historia de Nicaragua desde los tiempos más remotos hasta 1852* (History of Nicaragua from the earliest times to 1852). Despite the title, it covers only the colonial period (to 1821), a projected fourth volume having never been published. This is the most important 19th-century Nicaraguan history of the Spanish colonial period, and includes a great deal of information. It is worth noting that it was written before the Nicaraguan national archives were destroyed in 1931, so it is based on some materials which are no longer available to historians. Ayón (1821-87) was Nicaragua's most well known historian during the 19th century.

172 **Historia de el Realejo.** (History of Realejo.)
Manuel Rubio Sánchez, with notes by Eduardo
Pérez-Valle. Managua: Banco de América, 1975. 843p.
maps. bibliog. (Colección Cultural, Serie Fuentes Históricas,
no. 4).

A massive collection of documents and commentary on the history of the principal Pacific coast port of Nicaragua in the colonial period. The documents were
combed from the Archivo General de Centroamérica in Guatemala by the distinguished Guatemalan historian Manuel Rubio Sánchez. Explanatory footnotes have
been added by the Nicaraguan historian Eduardo Pérez-Valle.

173 **The Kemble papers.**
Stephen Kemble. New York: New York Historical Society,
1844-45. 2 vols. map. (New York Historical Society
Publications, vol. 16-17).

Stephen Kemble (1740-1829), a British officer in North America during the
American Revolution, was dispatched to Jamaica in 1780. From there he was
sent with reinforcements to the unsuccessful British campaign against Nicaragua,
1780-81. Brigadier-General Kemble's journals and correspondence of this campaign occupy most of volume 2 and are important sources for this invasion, also
offering an illuminating view of Nicaragua in the late 18th century.

174 **Memorial de mi vida.** (Memoir of my life.)
Blas Hurtado y Plaza, edited by Carlos Molina
Argüello. Managua: Banco de América, 1977. 322p.
bibliog. (Colección Cultural, Serie Ciencia Humana, no. 7).

Hurtado was a Nicaraguan Franciscan in the 18th century. This autobiographical
memoir reveals a great deal about life in Nicaragua and Costa Rica in that
century. Carlos Molina, the leading Nicaraguan colonial historian, has written a
very useful introduction and his notes greatly enhance the work.

175 **Misiones nicaragüenses en archivos europeos.** (Nicaraguan
missions in European archives.)
Carlos Molina Argüello. Mexico City: Instituto
Panamericano de Geografía e Historia, Comisión de
Historia, 1957. 163p. (Publicación no. 223).

An index to the documents on Nicaraguan history in Spanish archives consulted
and published by a series of Nicaraguan historians.

176 **Monumenta centroamericanae historica: colección de documentos y materiales para el estudio de la historia y vida de los pueblos de la América Central.** (Monument to the history of Central America: collection of documents and materials for the study of the history and life of the peoples of Central America.)
Edited by Federico Argüello Solórzano, Carlos Molina Argüello. Managua: Instituto Centroamericano de Historia, Universidad Centroamericana, 1965. 2 vols.
Publication of the colonial documents in the archive of the Colegio Centro América, later transferred to the Instituto Centroamericano de Historia of the Universidad Centroamericana in Managua.

177 **Nicaragua en los cronistas de Indias.** (Nicaragua in the chronicles of the Indies.)
Jorge Eduardo Arellano, Eduardo Pérez Valle. Managua: Fondo de Promoción Cultural, Banco de América, 1975-76. 3 vols. bibliog. (Colección Cultural, Serie Cronistas, nos. 1-3).
Extracts from the major chronicles of the 16th century. Includes selections from Pedro Martir, Pascual de Andagoya, Juan Sánchez Bortero, Bartolomé de las Casas, Toribio de Benavente Motolonía, Francisco López de Gómara, Girolano Benzoni, Antonio de Ciudad Real, Juan López de Velasco, Gonzalo Fernández de Oviedo, Antonio de Herrera y Tordesillas, Antonio de Remesal, and others.

178 **Realejo: forgotten colonial port and shipbuilding center in Nicaragua.**
David R. Radell, James J. Parsons. *Hispanic American Historical Review*, vol. 51 (May 1971), p. 295-312.
Scholarly article tracing the development of Nicaragua's principal Pacific coast port during the Hispanic period. See also *Historia de el Realejo* (q.v.).

179 **A statistical and commercial history of the Kingdom of Guatemala, in Spanish America. Containing important particulars relative to its productions, manufactures, customs, & c, an account of its conquest by the Spaniards, and a narrative of the principal events down to the present time: from original records in the archives; actual observation; and other authentic sources.**
Domingo Juarros, translated by John Baily. London: J. Hearne, 1823. Reprinted, New York: AMS Press, 1971. 520p.
Although much less informative about Nicaragua than Guatemala, this is still one of the basic source works for the end of the colonial period. Baily's translation is not complete, and the serious student will want to consult the original, *Compendio de la historia de la ciudad de Guatemala* (Guatemala City: Beteta, 1808-10).

2 vols.). This work includes a great deal of statistical data on population and economic affairs and is a useful source for understanding the changes that occurred in the kingdom near the close of the Hispanic era. It was, in fact, one of the principal sources for most histories of the late colonial period written in the 19th century.

180 **Les structures sociales du Nicaragua au XVIIIe siècle.** (The social structures of Nicaragua to the 18th century.) Germán Romero-Vargas. Lille, France: Atelier de Reproduction des Thèses, 1977. 802p.

A monumental work on colonial Nicaraguan society, written as the author's *doctorat d'état* thesis, University of Paris, 1976. Reprints of this limited publication are available from Slatkine, PO Box 765, Geneva 3, Switzerland.

181 **Vida del segoviano Rodrigo de Contreras, gobernador de Nicaragua, 1534-1544.** (Life of the Segovian Rodrigo de Contreras, governor of Nicaragua, 1534-1544.) Juan Contreras y López de Ayala (Marqués de Lozoya). Toledo, Spain: Editorial Católica Toledana, 1920. 366p. (Biblioteca de Historia Hispano-Americana).

A competent biography of an important early governor of Nicaragua, with a large documentary appendix (p. 195-366).

Some account of the Mosquito Territory: contained in a memoir written in 1757, while that country was in possession of the British. *See* item no. 67.

Spanish Central America: a socioeconomic history, 1520-1720. *See* item no. 146.

National origins in Central America. *See* item no. 256.

A bio-bibliography of Franciscan authors in colonial Central America. *See* item no. 696.

19th-century Nicaragua (1821-1912)

182 **Bosquejo político-estadístico de Nicaragua.** (Political and statistical sketch of Nicaragua.) Miguel González Saravía. Guatemala City: Beteta, 1824. 23p.

An important early description of Nicaragua immediately after independence. González Saravía, the son of a Spanish captain-general of colonial Central America, played an important role in the early political history of Nicaragua and wrote considerably on its development.

183 **The British role in Central America prior to the Clayton-Bulwer Treaty of 1850.**
Robert A. Naylor. *Hispanic American Historical Review*, vol. 40 (Aug. 1960), p. 361-82.

A thoroughly researched analysis of British activity in Central America during the first half of the 19th century, with particular emphasis on commercial activity. More extensive coverage may be found in Naylor's 1958 Tulane University PhD thesis, *British commercial relations with Central America, 1821-1851* (University Microfilms order no. 59-657).

184 **Central America, 1821-c.1870.**
Ralph Lee Woodward, Jr. In: *Cambridge History of Latin America*, vol. 3. Cambridge, England: Cambridge University Press, forthcoming.

A detailed discussion and interpretation of the first half-century of Central American independence, discussing the collapse of the Central American federation, the emergence of the independent Republic of Nicaragua, and social and economic problems of the new republic. This study provides greater depth on this period than the author's *Central America, a nation divided* (q.v.), and also contains a bibliographical essay which supplements that found in the earlier work.

185 **Central American commerce and maritime activity in the 19th century: sources for a quantitative approach.**
Thomas Schoonover. *Latin American Research Review*, vol. 13, no. 2 (1978), p. 157-69.

Schoonover identifies some sources of commercial activity in 19th-century Nicaragua and, although he overlooks others, this article definitely contributes to improved research in Nicaraguan economic history.

186 **Cuarenta años, 1838-1878, de historia de Nicaragua.** (Forty years, 1838-1878, of Nicaraguan history.)
Francisco Ortega Arancibia. Managua: Banco de América, 1974. 510p. (Colección Cultural, Serie Histórica, no. 6).

A fairly detailed, traditional narrative political history of the stormy mid-19th century in Nicaragua. It is in large part based on personal reminiscences of the author, who wrote it at an advanced age. First published in 1911, a second edition appeared in Madrid in 1957.

187 **De la historia de Nicaragua de 1889-1913: la dictadura del Presidente General José Santos Zelaya, y actuación del partido Conservador, hasta la restauración de la república.** (On the history of Nicaragua, 1889-1913: the dictatorship of President-General José Santos Zelaya, and the role of the Conservative Party, to the restoration of the republic.) José Joaquín Morales. Granada, Nicaragua: Editorial Magys, 1963. 389p.

A detailed political chronicle of the Zelaya period. Only part 1 was published, covering 1889-1909. It is strongly pro-Conservative Party and critical of Zelaya, seeking to redress the Liberal accounts of the Zelaya administration.

188 **Documentos para la historia de la guerra nacional contra los filibusteros en Nicaragua.** (Documents for the history of the National War against the filibusters in Nicaragua.) Angelita García Paz. San Salvador: Editorial Ahora, 1958. 233p.

An interesting collection of 113 documents relating to the Walker episode. From a wide range of published and archival sources, they include a number of documents regarding El Salvador's participation in the war against Walker.

189 **Estructuras socioeconómicas, poder y estado en Nicaragua, de 1821 a 1875.** (Socio-economic structures, power and the state in Nicaragua, 1821-1875.) Alberto Lanuza Matamoros. San José: Facultad de Ciencias Sociales de la Universidad de Costa Rica, 1976. 297p. bibliog. (Serie Tésis de Grado, no. 2).

An excellent thesis on social and economic development during the period indicated. The absence of archival sources has made this sort of research difficult for Nicaragua, but Lanuza has amassed considerable evidence from 19th-century published materials. This thesis was published in a very limited mimeographed edition, but three important chapters have been published in major Central American scholarly journals: 'Comercio exterior de Nicaragua (1821-1875)' (Foreign trade of Nicaragua, 1821-1875), *Estudios Sociales Centroamericanos*, vol. 5, no. 14 (May-Aug. 1976), p. 109-36; 'Nicaragua, territoria y población (1821-1875)' (Nicaragua, territory and population, 1821-1875), *Revista del Pensamiento Centroamericano*, vol. 31, no. 151 (April-June 1976), p. 1-22; 'La minería en Nicaragua (1821-1875)' (Mining in Nicaragua, 1821-1875), *Anuario de Estudios Centroamericanos*, vol. 3 (1977), p. 215-24.

190 **The filibuster; the career of William Walker.** Laurence Greene. Indianapolis, Indiana: Bobbs-Merrill, 1937. 350p. maps. bibliog.

A well-written, lively biography of William Walker.

191 **Filibusters and financiers, the story of William Walker and his associates.**
William O. Scroggs. New York: Macmillan, 1916. 408p.
This older work is still the best narrative history of the William Walker episode and the events surrounding it in Nicaragua.

192 **Freebooters must die! The life and death of William Walker, the most notorious filibuster of the nineteenth century.**
Frederick Rosengarten, Jr. Wayne, Pennsylvania: Haverford House, 1976. 226p. maps. bibliog.
This well-researched and lively history of the Walker episode adds little to what was previously known and reported in more scholarly works, but it is richly illustrated with maps, drawings and photographs of the period, making it an especially attractive, as well as informative, account.

193 **Fruto Chamorro.**
Pedro Joaquín Chamorro. Managua: Editorial Unión, 1960. 425p.
The principal biography of the founder of Nicaragua's Conservative Party, a major *caudillo* in mid-19th century Nicaraguan history.

194 **La guerra en Nicaragua: the war in Nicaragua as reported in *Frank Leslie's Illustrated Newspaper*, 1855-1857.**
Managua: Banco de América, 1976. 288p. (Colección Cultural, Serie Fuentes Históricas, no. 6A).
Facsimile reprint of the frequent articles on Nicaragua in this important US journal of the period. Richly illustrated.

195 **La guerra en Nicaragua: the war in Nicaragua as reported in *Harper's Weekly*, 1857-1860.**
Managua: Banco de América, 1976. 182p. (Colección Cultural, Serie Fuentes Históricas, no. 6B).
Facsimile reprint of coverage of events in Nicaragua in this major US journal of the period.

196 **Historia moderna de Nicaragua; complemento a mi historia de Nicaragua.** (Modern history of Nicaragua; supplement to my history of Nicaragua.)
José Dolores Gámez. Managua: Banco de América, 1975. 758p. (Colección Cultural, Serie Histórica, no. 7).
Although written in the 19th century, this work was not published until 1975. Like Gámez' numerous other works it is a pro-Liberal, narrative political history. Covering the period from 1810 to 1854, it is useful for its detailed information on political actors and events, despite its anachronistic organization and style.

197 **La invasión filibustera de Nicaragua y la guerra nacional.**
(The filibuster invasion of Nicaragua and the national war.)
J. Ricardo Dueñas Van Severen. San Salvador: Ministerio
de Educación, 1962. 2nd ed. 146p. (Colección Histórica, no.
8).
This well-documented history describes the political and social circumstances in
Nicaragua that preceded William Walker's invasion in 1855. Does a good job of
explaining the Nicaraguan reasons for Walker's presence. It was first published in
1959 (San Salvador: ODECA. 230p. [Biblioteca del Pensamiento Centroamericano, Colección de Estudios Históricos, no. 1]).

198 **José Santos Zelaya: a new look at Nicaragua's liberal
dictator.**
Charles L. Stansifer. *Revista Interamericana*, vol. 7 (fall
1977), p. 468-85.
Reviews the Zelaya régime, 1893-1909, pointing to the substantial impetus for
modernization which the Liberal dictator promoted. Stansifer challenges the harsh
treatment of Zelaya which some historians have given him. This is an English
translation of Stansifer's 'Una nueva interpretación de José Santos Zelaya, dic-
tador de Nicaragua, 1893-1909', *Anuario de Estudios Centroamericanos*, vol. 1
(1974), p. 47-60.

199 **The mahogany trade as a factor in the British return to the
Mosquito shore in the second quarter of the 19th century.**
Robert A. Naylor. *Jamaican Historical Review*, vol. 7
(1967), p. 40-67. map.
Explains how the diminishing mahogany reserves of Belize were a major factor in
British expansion along the Nicaraguan coast in the period 1823-50.

200 **Máximo Jerez, inmortal: comentario polémico.** (Máximo
Jerez, immortal: polemic commentary.)
Sofonías Salvatierra. Managua: Tipografía Progreso, 1950.
340p.
A sympathetic biography of one of the principal 19th-century Liberal Nicaraguan
commanders.

201 **Memorias para la historia de la revolución de Nicaragua y de
la guerra nacional contra los filibusteros, 1854 a 1857.**
(Memoirs for the history of the revolution in Nicaragua and
of the national war against the filibusters, 1854 to 1857.)
Jerónimo Pérez. Managua: Imprenta del Gobierno,
1865-73. 2 vols.
One of the first major historical works written by a Nicaraguan following
independence. It contains great detail on the tumultous events of the mid-1850s.
Reprinted in the author's *Obras históricas completas* (Managua, 1928. 2 vols.
2nd ed., Managua: Banco de América, 1977. 875p.).

202 **1840-1842: los atentados del superintendente de Belice.**
(1840-1842: the aggressions of the superintendent of Belize.)
Andrés Vega Bolaños.   Managua: Editorial Unión, 1971.
374p.
A collection of 121 documents in Spanish from the period 1840-42, relating to the efforts of the superintendent of Belize, Alexander Archibald MacDonald, to gain control of the eastern coast of Nicaragua. This is a useful compilation of historical records from a wide variety of published and manuscript Spanish and English sources on this major controversy between Great Britain and Central America. The volume contains a useful index, p. 335-74, a rarity in books published in Central America.

203 **Nicaragua en la independencia.** (Nicaragua in the
independence period.)
Chester Zelaya.   San José: Editorial Universitaria
Centroamericana (EDUCA), 1971. 349p. map. bibliog.
A well-documented, narrative study of Nicaragua from the late 18th century through the organization of the state government of Nicaragua in 1825. Important documents of the period are reprinted on p. 249-310. This work is a very useful contribution to understanding the political history of 19th-century Nicaragua.

204 **The Nicaragua route.**
David I. Folkman.   Salt Lake City, Utah: University of
Utah Press, 1972. 173p. map.
An attractively illustrated and fully documented account of the efforts to establish an interoceanic route across Nicaragua between 1848 and 1869. Includes appendixes showing dates and names of steamships connecting Nicaragua with the US east and west coasts and the numbers of passengers making the trip during these years.

205 **El Nicaragüense.** (The Nicaraguan.)
Granada, Nicaragua: El Nicaragüense, 1855-56.
approximately weekly.
This newspaper, published in English and Spanish, was the official organ of William Walker in Nicaragua once he took over the Nicaraguan government. As such, it is an interesting and important historical source for the Walker episode.

206 **A Palmerstonian diplomat in Central America: Frederick
Chatfield, Esq.**
Mario Rodríguez.   Tucson, Arizona: University of Arizona
Press, 1964. 385p. map. bibliog.
A major monograph based on extensive research in diplomatic correspondence, detailing the career of the British representative in Central America from 1833 to 1852. This volume is absolutely essential reading to any understanding of mid-19th-century Central America and the British role there.

207 **The political and economic foundations of modernization in Nicaragua: the administration of José Santos Zelaya, 1893-1909.**
Benjamin I. Teplitz. PhD dissertation, Howard University, 1973. 448p. (Available from University Microfilms, Ann Arbor, Michigan, order no. 75-2189).
A detailed study of the Zelaya period, in which the élitist Liberal Party directed the modernization of the country.

208 **Reflexiones sobre la historia de Nicaragua, de Gaínza a Somoza.** (Reflections on the history of Nicaragua from Gaínza to Somoza.)
José Coronel Urtecho. León, Nicaragua: Instituto Histórico Centroamericano, 1962. 2 vols.
The first two volumes of an ambitious project. Volume 1 deals with the independence movement in Nicaragua, while volume 2 treats the Civil War of 1824. These volumes contain some thought-provoking analysis, but are undocumented.

209 **Reseña histórica de Centro-América.** (Historical survey of Central America.)
Lorenzo Montúfar y Rivera Maestre. Guatemala City: El Progreso, 1878-87. 7 vols.
A detailed political history from the Liberal point of view. Deals with the period from 1821 to about 1875. Although it is primarily concerned with Guatemala, there is much on Nicaragua in these volumes. It has been a major source for subsequent historians of the isthmus, but its strong Liberal bias makes it unreliable in many instances. Montúfar was an important Liberal political leader in Central America in the mid- to late 19th century.

210 **Reseña histórica de Nicaragua desde el año 1887 hasta fines de 1895.** (Historical survey of Nicaragua from 1887 through the end of 1895.)
Manuel Castrillo Gámez. Managua: Talleres Nacionales, 1963. 580p.
Details Nicaraguan history from 1887 to 1895. Useful for political detail written by an eye-witness of the period.

211 **Sesquicentenario de la independencia de Centroamérica, 15 de septiembre, 1821-1971.** (Sesquicentennial of the independence of Central America, 15 September 1821-1971.)
León, Nicaragua: Universidad Nacional Autónoma de Nicaragua, 1971. 266p. (*Cuadernos Universitarios*, vol. 2, no. 6).
Commemorating the 150th anniversary of Central American independence, this special issue of *Cuadernos Universitarios* reprints several older articles, plus four excellent new pieces on the late 18th and early 19th centuries.

212 **The war in Nicaragua.**
William Walker. Mobile, Alabama: Goetzel, 1860. 431p.
Reprinted, Detroit, Michigan: Blaine-Ethridge, 1971.
Walker's own account of his adventure in Nicaragua. Various Spanish editions have also been published.

213 **William Walker.**
Enrique Guier. San José: Lehmann, 1971. 353p.
One of the more objective of the Spanish biographies of Walker. Guier is a popular writer of historical works in Costa Rica.

214 **William Walker: ideales y propósitos.** (William Walker: ideals and intentions.)
Alejandro Hurtado Chamorro. Granada, Nicaragua: Editorial Unión, 1965. 300p.
A scholarly, well-disciplined study of Walker's activities in Central America.

215 **With Walker in Nicaragua.**
James Carlson Jamison. Columbia, Missouri: E. W. Stephens, 1909. 181p.
A memoir written by a captain in Walker's army. It is passionately pro-Walker, and glorifies the Americans' activities in Central America. It relates Walker's later attempts to invade Central America, including an eye-witness description of Walker's execution in Honduras in 1860. An attractive Spanish translation, *Con Walker en Nicaragua*, was produced and published in 1977 in Masaya, Nicaragua, by Alejandro Bolaños Geyer.

216 **The world and William Walker.**
Albert Z. Carr. New York: Harper & Row, 1963. 289p. map. bibliog.
A very readable and well-researched biography of Walker. Carr's work is less detailed than Scroggs', but is especially good for its effort to analyse the personality and psychological characteristics of Walker.

The state of Nicaragua of the Greater Republic of Central America.
See item no. 34.

West Indies directory, part VI. The north coast of South America from Trinidad westward, and the coast to the Bay of Honduras.
See item no. 64.

Travels in Central America, 1821-1840.
See item no. 68.

Incidents of travel in Central America, Chiapas and Yucatan.
See item no. 72.

Diario de John Hill Wheeler, ministro de los Estados Unidos en Nicaragua, 1854-1857. (Diary of John Hill Wheeler, United States minister in Nicaragua, 1854-1857.)
See item no. 78.

History. 19th-century Nicaragua (1821-1912)

Reminiscences of the 'Filibuster' War in Nicaragua.
See item no. 82.

The states of Central America: their geography, topography, climate, population, resources, production, commerce, political organization, aborigines, etc., etc., comprising chapters on Honduras, San Salvador, Nicaragua, Costa Rica, Guatemala, Belize, the Bay Islands, the Mosquito Shore, and the Honduras Inter-Oceanic Railway.
See item no. 83.

Nicaragua: past, present and future; a description of its inhabitants, customs, mines, minerals, early history, modern filibusterism, proposed inter-oceanic canal and manifest destiny.
See item no. 84.

The Cádiz experiment in Central America, 1808 to 1826.
See item no. 137.

Historia de la Federación de la América Central, 1823-1840. (History of the Central American Federation, 1823-1840.)
See item no. 319.

Estudios de historia militar de Centroamérica. (Studies in Central American military history.)
See item no. 370.

La unión de Centroamérica. (The Central American union.)
See item no. 392.

Manifest destiny denied.
See item no. 408.

Orígines de la reincorporación nicaragüense de la costa miskita. (Origins of the Nicaraguan reincorporation of the Miskito Coast.)
See item no. 430.

La revolución liberal en la historia económica de Nicaragua. (The liberal revolution in Nicaraguan economic history.)
See item no. 477.

The mahogany tree: its botanical characters, qualities and uses, with practical suggestions for selecting and cutting it in the region of its growth, in the West Indies and Central America, with notices of the projected interoceanic communications of Panama, Nicaragua, and Tehuantepec, in relation to their productions, and the supply of fine timber for shipbuilding and all other purposes.
See item no. 516.

Archivo histórico de la República de Nicaragua, tomo I: 1821-1826. (Historical archives of the Republic of Nicaragua, volume I: 1821-1826.)
See item no. 646.

Los 'incunables' de Nicaragua: 1829-1859. (The 'incunabulas' of Nicaragua: 1829-1859.)
See item no. 650.

Editoriales de *La Prensa*. (Editorials from *La Prensa*.)
See item no. 654.

United States occupation (1912-34)

217 **Con Sandino en Nicaragua. La hora de la paz.** (With
Sandino in Nicaragua. The hour of peace.)
Ramón Belausteguigoitia. Madrid: Espasa Calpe, 1934.
244p. Facsimile ed., Managua: Editorial Nueva Nicaragua,
1981.
One of the best early accounts of the Sandino revolt, written by a Basque journalist, following extensive interviews with the guerrilla chieftain.

218 **The dawn of nationalism and its consequences in Nicaragua.**
Charles Edward Frazier, Jr. PhD dissertation, University of
Texas, 1958. 616p. (Available from University Microfilms,
Ann Arbor, Michigan, order no. 58-1651).
An informative study of the period of United States intervention in Nicaragua.
See also the author's 'Colonel Henry L. Stimson's Peace Mission to Nicaragua,
April-May, 1927', *Journal of the West*, vol. 2 (Jan. 1963), p. 66-84; and 'August
Cesar Sandino: good devil or perverse god?', *Journal of the West*, vol. 3 (Oct.
1964), p. 517-36.

219 **Dollars for bullets: the story of American intervention in
Nicaragua.**
Harold N. Denny. New York: Dial Press, 1929. 411p.
Account by a *New York Times* reporter who spent six months in Nicaragua
during the US intervention. Although this pro-US account is not especially objective, it is interesting for its description of events and colourful reporting. Since it
is not always reliable for factual information, however, it must be used with care.

220 **The five republics of Central America, their political and
economic development and their relations with the United
States.**
Dana G. Munro, edited by David Kinley. New York:
Russell & Russell, 1967. 332p.
Munro's descriptive survey of Central America is especially useful for its analysis
and description of the region during the first two decades of the 20th century.
Munro was an official of the State Department present in Central America
during much of the period, and his astute observations provide excellent insight
into the period. His historical surveys of earlier eras have less value today. Originally published by the Carnegie Endowment for International Peace, 1918. See
also Dana Munro's *A student in Central America, 1914-1916* (New Orleans:
Tulane University, Middle American Research Institute, 1983 [Publication no.
51]).

221 **The last night of General August C. Sandino.**
Domingo Ibarra Grijalva, translated by Gloria Bonitz. New
York: Vantage, 1973. 256p.
Includes a number of documents, previously unpublished, that the author used to
prepare *El verdadero Sandino* (q.v.).

222 **El pensamiento vivo de Sandino.** (The living ideas of
Sandino.)
Selected and edited by Sergio Ramírez. Managua:
Editorial Nueva Nicaragua, Ministerio de Cultura, 1981.
rev. ed. 560p. bibliog.
A chronical compilation of the letters, manifestos and other writings of Augusto
C. Sandino by a leading Nicaraguan intellectual who subsequently became a
member of the Sandinista ruling junta following the overthrow of the Somoza
dynasty in 1979. The 192 selections from Sandino's writings are preceded by a
perceptive explanatory note by Ramírez. The first edition (San José: EDUCA,
1974) and several subsequent editions, including German (1975), Italian (1976),
and Swedish (1977), contain only 160 documents.

223 **Sandino.**
Gregorio Selser, translated by Cedric Belfrage. New York:
Monthly Review Press, 1981. 250p. bibliog.
First published in Spanish in Buenos Aires in 1955, Selser's work is competent
and detailed. It is strongly sympathetic to Sandino's war against the US Marines,
1927-33, and includes many of his writings. There have been many Spanish
editions of this work under the title *Sandino, general de hombres libres*, and it
has had very wide circulation in Latin America.

224 **The Sandino Affair.**
Neill Macaulay. Chicago: Quadrangle Books, 1967. 319p.
bibliog.
Solidly researched and vigorously written, Macaulay's work remains the best single volume on Sandino. Macaulay emphasizes Sandino's guerrilla warfare tactics
and is critical of the United States role in Nicaragua.

225 **Sandino, bibliografía fundamental.** (Sandino, basic
bibliography.)
Instituto de Estudio del Sandinismo, Centro de
Documentación. *Boletín de Referencias*, vol. 1 (Jan.-March
1982), p. 1-70.
An annotated list of 115 books, articles and other publications regarding Augusto
César Sandino. Organized topically, with an author index. Includes reprints of
some important Sandino documents.

226 **Sandino! Estudio completo del heroe de las Segovias.**
(Sandino! A complete study of the hero of the Segovias.)
G. Alemán Bolaños. Mexico City, Buenos Aires: Imprenta
de la República, 1932. 82p.

The first major study of Sandino, containing many documents which have subsequently been published in other works. It is heavily documented, but hardly the 'complete study' claimed by the title. Twenty years laters Alemán Bolaños published a substantially expanded biography on Sandino, *Sandino el libertador* (Sandino the liberator), Mexico City: Ediciones del Caribe, 1952. 244p. (2nd ed., San José: EDUCA, 1980. 244p.).

227 **Sandino o la tragedia de un pueblo.** (Sandino, or the tragedy
of a people.)
Sofonías Salvatierra. Madrid, 1934. 291p.

An important early eye-witness account of Sandino by one of those involved in arranging the peace treaty with him. It is favourable toward Sandino.

228 **Sandino: patriot or bandit?**
Joseph O. Baylen. *Hispanic American Historical Review*,
vol. 31 (Aug. 1951), p. 394-419.

A scholarly, pro-Somoza account of the life and career of Augusto C. Sandino, based principally on US sources.

229 **The United States Marines in Nicaragua.**
R. W. Cushman, Jr., Bernard C. Nalty. Washington, DC:
Historical Branch, G-3 Division Headquarters, United States
Marine Corps, 1962. mimeographed. 39p. map. bibliog.
(Marine Corps Historical Reference Series, no. 21).

Although brief, this is a fairly detailed description of US Marine Corps operations in Nicaragua.

230 **El verdadero Sandino o el Calvario de las Segovias.** (The true
Sandino, or the Calvary of the Segovias.)
Anastasio Somoza. Managua: Editorial y Litografía San
José, 1976. 566p.

Somoza's account of Sandino, justifying his repression and trying to discredit Sandino and 'Sandinismo'. Originally published in 1936, it was actually put together by National Guard lieutenants Domingo Ibarra and Guillermo Cuadra, and was based on documents in the possession of the National Guard. Despite its anti-Sandino bias, the work contains data that his defenders have used to laud him.

Our neighbor Nicaragua.
See item no. 97.

Influencia de la crisis del 29 en Nicaragua. (Influence of the 1929
depression on Nicaragua.)
See item no. 301.

History. United States occupation (1912-34)

A. C. Sandino y el FSLN. (A. C. Sandino and the FSLN.)
See item no. 335.

Augusto César Sandino.
See item no. 337.

The constabulary in the Dominican Republic and Nicaragua: progeny and legacy of United States intervention.
See item no. 368.

American intervention in Nicaragua, 1909-33; an appraisal of objectives and results.
See item no. 394.

Dollar diplomacy in Nicaragua, 1909-1913.
See item no. 402.

Intervention and dollar diplomacy, 1900-1921.
See item no. 404.

The Mexican crisis and intervention in Nicaragua.
See item no. 409.

Nicaragua and the United States, 1909-1927.
See item no. 411.

Nicaraguan elections of 1928.
See item no. 412.

Quijote on a burro: Sandino and the Marines, a study in the formation of foreign policy.
See item no. 414.

A search for stability, United States diplomacy toward Nicaragua, 1925-1933.
See item no. 417.

The shark and the sardines.
See item no. 418.

The United States and the Caribbean in the twentieth century.
See item no. 420.

The United States and the Caribbean republics, 1921-1933.
See item no. 421.

The United States and Nicaragua, 1927-1932: decisions for de-escalation and withdrawal.
See item no. 423.

United States in Nicaraguan politics: supervised elections, 1927-1932.
See item no. 427.

The banana empire: a case study of economic imperialism.
See item no. 453.

Tropical enterprise: the Standard Fruit and Steamship Company in Latin America.
See item no. 506.

Sandino en la plástica de América. (Sandino in the art of America.)
See item no. 642.

Somoza dynasty (1935-79)

231 **Anastasio Somoza García: a brief history of Nicaragua's 'enduring' dictator.**
Richard Millett. *Revista Interamericana*, vol. 7, no. 3 (1977), p. 486-508.
A biographical article on the dictator of Nicaragua (1936-56), with considerable attention to his political methods and relations with the United States.

232 **Dictators never die: a portrait of Nicaragua and the Somozas.**
Eduardo Crawley. New York: St. Martin's Press, 1979. 180p. maps.
A journalistic history of the Somoza era with serious limitations in that it includes errors of fact and judgment and is undocumented.

233 **Guardians of the dynasty.**
Richard Millett. Maryknoll, New York: Orbis Books, 1977. 284p. map. bibliog. illus.
A thoroughly researched history of the US-created Guardia Nacional de Nicaragua and the Somoza family. A major contribution to 20th-century Nicaraguan historiography. It is both hard-hitting and objective, as it details in dispassionate but vigorous prose the US involvement in the formation and continuance of the Somoza régimes. See also *Death of the dynasty* (q.v.), the author's follow-up to this volume.

234 **Mi rebelión: la dictadura de los Somoza.** (My rebellion: the dictatorship of the Somozas.)
Luís G. Cardenal. Managua: El Pez y la Serpiente, 1979. 2nd. ed. 379p.
First published in Mexico (Costa-Amic) in 1979. Engineer Cardenal claims to be a friend of Tachito Somoza and to know the Somoza family well. He was related both to the Somozas and to the opposition newspaper editor, Pedro Joaquín Chamorro Cardenal, leader of the unsuccessful 1959 attempt to oust the Somozas by a parachute drop from Costa Rica into the Department of Chontales. This book tells Cardenal's own personal story and gives an account of that invasion.

235 **Sandino: death and aftermath.**
Joseph O. Baylen. *Mid-America: an Historical Review*, vol. 36 (April 1954), p. 116-39.
A perceptive account by a US diplomatic historian of the events surrounding Sandino's assassination and the rise of Anastasio Somoza. Argues that Sandino's assassination should be understood in the context of internal Nicaraguan politics, denying any US complicity in the act.

236 **Somoza and the legacy of U.S. involvement in Central America.**
Bernard Diederich. New York: E. P. Dutton, 1981. 352p.
A biography of the Somoza dynasty by a *Time Magazine* reporter, based largely on news reports and personal recollections. It is also an important first-hand description of the Sandinista revolution that ended the Somoza régime.

Area handbook for Nicaragua.
See item no. 2.

Development and dictatorship in Nicaragua, 1950-1960.
See item no. 323.

Nicaragua.
See item no. 326.

Nicaragua betrayed.
See item no. 327.

Presidential leadership in Nicaragua.
See item no. 328.

The Christian Democratic movement in Nicaragua.
See item no. 332.

The Nicaraguan political system: the flow of demands and the reactions of the regime.
See item no. 334.

Nicaragua, an ally under siege.
See item no. 349.

Nicaragua, año cero, la caída de la dinastía Somoza. (Nicaragua, year zero, the fall of the Somoza dynasty.)
See item no. 350.

Te dió miedo la sangre? (Did the blood frighten you?)
See item no. 627.

Sandinista revolution (1979-present)

237 **50 años de lucha sandinista.** (50 years of Sandinista struggle.)
Humberto Ortega Saavedra. Managua: Ministerio del Interior, 1979. 125p. (Colección Las Segovias).
What might be considered the official history of the Sandinista movement in Nicaragua, written by a leading member of the FSLN (Frente Sandinista de Liberación Nacional) directorate. Several other editions have appeared.

238 **Death of the dynasty: the end of the Somoza rule in Nicaragua.**
Richard Millett.   Maryknoll, New York: Orbis Books, forthcoming [1983?].

Millett follows up his study of the Nicaraguan National Guard (*Guardians of the dynasty*, q.v.) with a scholarly and careful analysis of the collapse of the Somoza dynasty.

239 **Gaspar vive.** (Gaspar lives.)
Manuel Rodríguez García.   San José: Artes Gráficas, 1981. 397p.

A sympathetic biography of a Spanish priest, Gaspar García Laviana, who came to Nicaragua in 1970 and later became a *comandante* in the Sandinista movement, dying in combat in 1978. His career as a revolutionary soldier-priest stands as a symbol for the Christian revolutionary movement in Nicaragua.

Dr. Pedro Joaquín Chamorro (1924-1978), the Conservative Party, and the struggle for democratic government in Nicaragua.
See item no. 341.

Nicaragua in revolution.
See item no. 352.

Nicaragua, the land of Sandino.
See item no. 354.

Nicaragua, a people's revolution.
See item no. 355.

Nicaragua: the Sandinist revolution.
See item no. 356.

Power and consolidation in the Nicaraguan revolution.
See item no. 359.

Nicaragua in revolution: the poets speak/Nicaragua en revolución: los poetas hablan.
See item no. 596.

Population

240 **Aspectos del desarrollo demográfico.** (Aspects of demographic development.)
F. C. A. Maglione. Managua: Oficina Ejecutiva de Encuestas y Censos, 1978. 57p. (Boletín Demográfico no. 2).
A discussion of world population trends and projections of the Nicaraguan population through the year 2000.

241 **Censo general de población de la República de Nicaragua, 1950.** (General census of the population of the Republic of Nicaragua, 1950.)
Dirección General de Estadística. Managua: Dirección General de Estadística, 1951. 6 vols.
Official publication of the 1950 census. Previous censuses were taken in 1778, 1800, 1813, 1834, 1845-46, 1867, 1890, 1906, 1920 and 1940, but all those before 1920 have very serious limitations.

242 **Censos nacionales 1963: población, vivienda, agropecuario.** (1963 national census: population, housing, agriculture and grazing.)
Dirección General de Estadística. Managua: Departamento de Publicaciones, 1964-67. 5 vols.
Official reports on the 1963 census. Available in microfilm from Research Publications Inc., Westbridge, Connecticut (International Population Census Publications, 1945-67: Nicaragua [1963.5] [1963.9]).

243 **Censos nacionales 1971.** (1971 national census.)
Oficina Ejecutiva de Encuestas y Censos. Managua: Oficina Ejecutiva de Encuestas y Censos, 1974-75. 4 vols.
Official report for the 1971 census.

244 **Corología de la población de Nicaragua.** (Chorology of the
population of Nicaragua.)
Román Perpiña. Madrid: Consejo Superior de
Investigaciones Científicas, Instituto 'Balmes' de Sociología,
1959. 121p. map.
A careful study of the Nicaraguan population based on the census of 1950.
Especially concerned with location and movement of the population. Detailed
statistical tables are appended.

245 **Demographic Yearbook.**
Department of Economic and Social Affairs, United Nations
Statistical Office. New York: United Nations, 1948-
annual.
Detailed statistics on population, including birth and mortality rates, migration,
marriages, annulment, divorce, marital status and household composition.
Information for Nicaragua is not complete for all categories, but this yearbook
will provide a great deal of information on Nicaragua's population. In English
and French.

246 **Human resources of Central America, Panama, and Mexico,
1950-1980, in relation to some aspects of economic
development.**
L. A. Ducoff. New York: United Nations, 1960. 155p.
A thorough statistical study of population trends, the labour force and their
relation to the economic development of the region.

247 **La población de Centroamérica y sus perspectivas.** (The
population of Central America and its perspectives.)
Jorge Arías de Blois. Guatemala City: Universidad de San
Carlos de Guatemala, Facultad de Ingeniería, 1966. 59p.
Surveys population and related statistics, including distribution characteristics,
growth and its implications.

248 **Población de Nicaragua: análisis de los resultados de la
encuesta de hogares de 1980.** (Population of Nicaragua:
analysis of the results of the home survey of 1980.)
Edited by Jaime Ocón Abaunza. Managua: Instituto
Nacional de Estadísticas y Censos, 1981. 88p. (Boletín
Demográfico, no. 7).
Statistics and demographic analysis based on a summary of homes (family units)
in Nicaragua during August and September of 1980.

Population

249 **Población de Nicaragua: compendio de las cifras censales y proyecciones por departamentos y municipios, años 1971-1980.** (Population of Nicaragua: a compendium of census figures and projections for departments and municipalities, 1971-1980.)
Managua: Instituto Nacional de Estadística y Censos, 1980. 2nd ed. 53p. (Boletín Demográfico, no. 1).

An overview and statistical summary of the Nicaraguan population, 1971-80. Other issues of the *Boletín Demográfico* deal with special aspects of the Nicaraguan population.

250 **Population densities using a new approach: a preliminary report.**
Robert E. Nunley. *Revista Geográfica* (Instituto Panamericano de Geografía e Historia, Brazil), no. 66 (June 1967), p. 55-93. maps.

Preliminary findings of a research project designed to develop more effective approaches to studying the distribution of human populations. Deals with Nicaragua, Guatemala, Honduras, El Salvador, Costa Rica and Belize. The article is useful for its information on and comparisons of population densities in Central America.

251 **Population growth and the quality of life in Nicaragua.**
David C. Korten. Managua: INCAE (Instituto Centroamericano de Administración de Empresas), 1973. 11p.

A brief but very competent essay on demographic challenges facing Nicaragua.

252 **The population of Central America, including Mexico, 1950-1980: future population estimates by sex and age, report 1.**
United Nations Statistical Office. Millwood, New York: Kraus Reprint, 1974. 84p. (UN Population Studies, no. 16).

First published in 1954, this is a projection of population through 1980. Its usefulness has now largely expired, however.

A sociological study of the relations of man to the land in Nicaragua.
See item no. 298.

Salud pública y crecimiento demográfico en Centro América. (Public health and population growth in Central America.)
See item no. 307.

Anuario Estadístico. (Statistical annual.)
See item no. 447.

Nationalities and Minorities

General

253 Cultural surveys of Panama - Nicaragua - Guatemala - El Salvador - Honduras.
Richard N. Adams. Washington, DC: Pan American Union, 1957. 669p. maps. bibliog.

A very comprehensive survey of the peoples of each of the Central American states. Although now dated, it remains an important introduction to the anthropology of the Central American states. See also Adams' 'Cultural components of Central America', *American Anthropologist*, vol. 58 (1956), p. 881-907, in which the various modifications of Indian and Spanish culture in Central America are classified.

254 Frontier adaptations in lower Central America.
Edited by Mary W. Helms, Franklin O. Loveland. Philadelphia: Institute for the Study of Human Issues, 1976. 178p. bibliog. refs.

Nine carefully researched essays deal with a relatively unknown region of Central America, stressing the continuity and alterations that have occurred with culture contact by several 'frontier' Indian groups. Those essays dealing with Nicaragua include: Franklin Loveland, 'Tapirs and manatees: cosmological categories and social process among Rama Indians of eastern Nicaragua' (p. 67-82), and 'Afterword: anthropological research in lower Central America' (p. 165-70); William V. Davidson, 'Black Carib (Garifuna) habitats in Central America' (p. 85-94); and Dorothy J. Cattle, 'Dietary diversity and nutritional security in a coastal Miskito Indian village, eastern Nicaragua' (p. 117-30).

255 **Middle America: a culture history of the heartlands and frontiers.**
Mary W. Helms. Englewood Cliffs, New Jersey: Prentice Hall, 1975. 367p. maps. bibliog. Reprinted, Washington, DC: University Press of America, 1982.

A history of Mexico and Central America from an anthropological point of view, examining the culture of the region from pre-Columbian times to the present and contrasting developments in northern Mexico and lower Central America (the frontiers) with Mesoamerica (the heartland). Nicaragua is in the frontier region. Helms emphasizes the effects of previous cultures and institutions on nation-building developments today.

256 **National origins in Central America.**
Francis Merriman Stanger. *Hispanic American Historical Review*, vol. 12 (Feb. 1932), p. 18-45.

A thoughtful article attributing the separate development of the Central American states to their isolation and closer contact with outside powers than with one another. They also differ racially in their relationship to the native peoples.

Area handbook for Nicaragua.
See item no. 2.

La costa atlántica de Nicaragua. (The Nicaraguan Atlantic coast.)
See item no. 35.

Ensayos nicaragüenses. (Nicaraguan essays.)
See item no. 274.

Nicaragua in revolution.
See item no. 352.

El habla nicaragüense, estudio morfológico y semántico. (Spoken Nicaraguan, a morphologic and semantic study.)
See item no. 635.

Selección de la obra *La costa atlántica de Nicaragua*. (Selection from the work *The Atlantic coast of Nicaragua*.)
See item no. 702.

Indians

257 **Anthropological bibliography of aboriginal Nicaragua.**
Jorge A. Lines, Edwin M. Shook, Michael D. Olien. San José: Tropical Science Center, 1965. 98p. (Tropical Science Center Occasional Paper no. 3).

An extensive list of basic works on Nicaragua, broader than the title would imply.

258 **Asang, adaptations to culture contact in a Miskito community.**
Mary W. Helms. Gainesville, Florida: University of Florida Press, 1971. 268p. bibliog.

A well-researched and clearly written ethnographic study of a Miskito community on Nicaragua's Caribbean coastal region. There is an extensive bibliography of works dealing with the Miskito region, including many items on the Moravian missions there, p. 251-60.

259 **Between land and water: the subsistence economy of the Miskito Indians, eastern Nicaragua.**
Bernard Q. Nietschmann. New York: Seminar Press, 1973. 279p.

A soundly researched and interesting study of the Miskito Indian turtle-fishing village of Tasbapauni on the Caribbean coast. Originally the author's doctoral dissertation at the University of Wisconsin (1970).

260 **Caribbean edge, the coming of modern times to isolated people and wildlife.**
Bernard Nietschmann. Indianapolis: Bobbs-Merrill, 1979. 280p. maps.

An account of events, places, people and animals encountered during research on the Miskito coast of Nicaragua. Concerned with both the Miskito Indians and the turtles and other animals found there. Nietschmann's other works deal with the scientific results of his research among the Miskitos. This is a more personal account. See also Nietschmann's 'Nicaraguan skin connection', *Natural History*, vol. 86 (Jan. 1977), p. 28-30, an anecdotal account of a crocodile-skin dealer in Bluefields.

261 **Class, ethnicity and state among the Miskitu Amerindians of northeastern Nicaragua.**
Philippe Bourgois. *Latin American Perspectives*, vol. 8, no. 2 (spring 1981), p. 22-39.

Traces the economic and political history of the Miskito people and their participation in the Sandinista revolution during its first year. Bourgois recognizes the Miskitos' desire for cultural identity, and points to serious problems in the administration of the region, noting the need for some autonomy so that the Miskitos' fear of ladino domination may be alleviated. Argues that socialism will be to the advantage of the Miskitos and other Amerindian groups, and that every effort should be made to integrate them peacefully. A different version of this article appeared in *Nicaragua in revolution* (q.v.).

262 **Dialectical aspects of natural symbols: order and disorder in Rama cosmology.**
Franklin O. Loveland. PhD dissertation, Duke University, 1975. 513p. (Available from University Microfilms, Ann Arbor, Michigan, order no. 76-8761).
Analyses the oral history, literature and cosmology of the Rama Indians of eastern Nicaragua from several perspectives.

263 **El estado actual de la etnología en la América Central.** (The present state of ethnology in Central America.)
Doris Stone. In: *XXXVI Congreso Internacional de Americanistas, España 1964. Actas y Memorias.* Seville, Spain, 1966, p. 11-18. bibliog.
A useful, if brief, overview of Indian ethnology in Central America.

264 **Ethnographical survey of the Miskito and Sumu Indians of Honduras and Nicaragua.**
Edward Conzemius. Washington, DC: Bureau of American Ethnology, 1932. 191p. bibliog. (Bulletin no. 106). Facsimile ed., New Haven, Connecticut: Human Relations Area Files, 1958.
The principal traditional ethnographic study of the region, with a great deal of data on the life and activities of the people.

265 **Garifuna of Pearl Lagoon: ethnology of an Afro-American enclave in Nicaragua.**
William V. Davidson. *Ethnohistory*, vol. 27 (winter 1980), p. 31-47. map. bibliog.
Describes the six small Garifuna-speaking communities around Pearl Lagoon, Nicaragua, isolated for about a century from the larger Black Carib population around the Bay of Honduras. Davidson traces the history of these people and their migration from northeastern Honduras. The two modern villages, Orinoco and La Fé, are mapped in detail, showing the progressions and patterns of settlement. In recent years this Carib enclave has been in decline owing to pressures from other Nicaraguans. Based heavily on oral accounts, but also utilizing a wide range of published sources. See also Davidson's more extensive bibliography on the Pearl Lagoon settlements in his 'The Caribs of Central America: a map of their realm and a bibliography of research', *National Studies* (Belize), vol. 2 (Nov. 1974), p. 15-25.

266 **Handbook of Middle American Indians.**
Edited by Robert Wauchope (and others). Austin, Texas: University of Texas Press, 1964- . 16 vols. plus supplement.
Edited at the Middle American Research Institute of Tulane University, this is a massive collaborative collection of information, interpretation and bibliography. The work is broad in scope and contains not only materials specifically relating to Indians, but also a great deal on the region's geography, archaeology, history, population, linguistics, flora and fauna, economic development and culture.

Volume titles, listed here with their editors, only begin to indicate the breadth and utility of this remarkable collection: 1. *Natural environment and early cultures*, Robert C. West; 2, 3. *Archaeology of southern Mesoamerica*, Gordon R. Willey; 4. *Archaeological frontiers and external connections*, Gordon Ekholm, Gordon R. Willey; 5. *Linguistics*, Norman A. McQuown; 6. *Social anthropology*, Manning Nash; 7, 8. *Ethnology*, Evon Z. Vogt; 9. *Physical anthropology*, T. Dale Stewart; 10, 11. *Archaeology of northern Mesoamerica*, Gordon Ekholm, Ignacio Bernal; 12-15. *Guide to ethno-historical sources*, Howard Cline; 16. *Sources cited and artifacts illustrated*, Margaret A. L. Harrison; *Supplement*, Victoria Bricker: vol. 1, *Archaeology*, Jeremy A. Sabloff; vol. 2, *Language and literature*, Munro S. Edmundson.

267 **Handbook of South American Indians.**
Edited by Julian H. Steward. Washington, DC: Smithsonian Institution, Bureau of American Ethnology, 1946-59. 7 vols. (Bulletin no. 143).

Although primarily concerned with South American Indians, this major collection includes several articles that deal with Nicaraguan Indians and archaeology, and the serious student should not overlook it. W. D. Strong's 'The archaeology of Costa Rica and Nicaragua', vol. 4, p. 121-42, is an excellent guide to the literature on Nicaraguan archaeology through about 1945.

268 **Negro or Indian? the changing identity of a frontier population.**
Mary W. Helms. In: *Old roots in new lands, historical and anthropological perspectives on black experiences in the Americas.* Edited by Ann Pescatello. Westport, Connecticut; London: Greenwood Press, 1977, p. 157-72.

A major contribution to understanding the Miskito peoples of the Nicaraguan Caribbean coast. Helms reviews the ethnohistorical evidence regarding these peoples from the 17th century to the present, with particular reference to the mixing of Negros and Indians there.

269 **Nicaragua Indígena.** (Indigenous Nicaragua.)
Managua: Instituto Indigenista Nacional, 1946-47, 1954-69. irregular.

This organ of the Nicaraguan Indian Institute published both important articles on Nicaragua's indigenous population and government decrees and other edicts affecting that population.

270 **Los nicarao y los chorotega según las fuentes históricas.**
(The Nicarao and Chorotega Indians according to historical sources.)
Anne MacKaye Chapman. San José: Universidad de Costa Rica, 1960. 115p. bibliog. (Serie Historia y Geografía, no. 4).

A very competent study of the Indian tribes of western Nicaragua. See also the author's PhD dissertation, Columbia University, 1958, *An historical analysis of the tropical forest tribes on the southern border of Mesoamerica* (University Microfilms order no. 58-2528).

271 **Rural-urban dynamics: the Miskito coast of Nicaragua.**
Christine Loveland. *Urban Anthropology*, vol. 2 (fall 1973), p. 182-93. bibliog.

Loveland concentrates on the Rama Indians in rural areas surrounding Bluefields, on the Nicaraguan Caribbean coast.

272 **The Sandinistas and the Indians, the 'problem' of the Indians in Nicaragua.**
Richard N. Adams. *Caribbean Review*, vol. 10 (winter 1981), p. 23-25, 55-56.

An informative and perceptive essay on the situation regarding the Miskito and other Indians of Nicaragua's Caribbean coast with respect to the Sandinista revolution.

Raíces indígenas de la lucha anticolonialista en Nicaragua. (Native roots of the Nicaraguan anticolonial struggle.)
See item no. 154.

Nuevo estudio sobre la religión de los Nicaraos. (New study on the religion of the Nicaraos.)
See item no. 288.

Religión de los Nicaraos: análisis y comparación de tradiciones culturales Nahuas. (Religion of the Nicaraos: analysis and comparison of Nahua cultural traditions.)
See item no. 290.

The health and the customs of the Miskito Indians of northern Nicaragua: interrelationships in a medical program.
See item no. 311.

The Costeños and the revolution in Nicaragua.
See item no. 339.

The creole English of Nicaragua's Miskito Coast; its socio-linguistic history and a comparative history of its lexicon and syntax.
See item no. 632.

Diccionario trilingüe Miskito-Español-Inglés. (Trilingual Miskito-Spanish-English dictionary.)
See item no. 634.

Foreign immigrants

273 **German colonial projects on the Mosquito Coast, 1844-1848.**
   G. B. Henderson.   *English Historical Review,* vol. 59
   (1944), p. 257-71.
Reviews development of the Mosquito Coast and discusses the unsuccessful German colonization schemes there in the mid-19th century. Correspondence regarding the projects, 1844-49, from documents in the Public Records Office in London, is appended, p. 261-71.

Folklore

274 Ensayos nicaragüenses. (Nicaraguan essays.)
Francisco Pérez Estrada. Managua: Fondo de Promoción
Cultural, Banco de América, 1976. 191p. bibliog. (Colección
Cultural, Serie Ciencias Humanas, no. 1).
Anthropological studies, including articles on the Nahuas in Nicaragua, Nicarag-
uan folk customs, the Nicaraguan folk hero Guegüense, and a socio-economic
history of land tenure in Nicaragua. Several of these articles previously appeared
in *Nicaragua Indígena* (q.v.).

275 Folklore de Nicaragua. (Nicaraguan folklore.)
Enrique Peña Hernández. Masaya, Nicaragua: Editorial
Unión, 1968. 410p. bibliog.
A major illustrated compendium of Nicaraguan folklore. It includes description of
national and regional folkloric characteristics and folkloric theatre, dress, dance,
music, food and drink, games, stories, sayings and other colloquial expressions, a
glossary of folklore in Nicaragua, a calendar of festivals, a chapter on the teaching of folklore in Nicaragua, and other information related to the subject.

276 El folklore en la literatura de Centro América. (Folklore in
Central American literature.)
Rafael Heliodoro Valle. *Journal of American Folklore*, vol.
36 (April-June 1923), p. 105-34. bibliog.
A brief overview of Central American folklore in literature, including discussion
of Nicaragua on p. 109-10, followed by an extensive bibliography, p. 110-34.

277 **Folklore nicaragüense y mestisaje.** (Nicaraguan folklore and race mixture.)
Eduardo Zepeda-Henríquez. *Boletín Nicaragüense de Bibliografía y Documentación*, no. 18 (July-Aug. 1977), p. 173-84.
Surveys Nicaraguan folk traditions from the earliest times, focusing especially on the Mestizo Nicaraguan folk hero, Guegüense.

278 **The Guegüence: a comedy ballet in the Nahuatl-Spanish dialect of Nicaragua.**
D. G. Brinton. Philadelphia: Library of Aboriginal American Literature, 1883. 94p.
An important early contribution to describing this major Nicaraguan folk hero dance. The Nahuatl-Spanish dialect text of this work, obtained in Nicaragua by Dr. C. H. Behrendt, is published here, along with an English translation, introduction and notes. The music is also given.

Frontier adaptations in lower Central America.
See item no. 254.

Romances y corridos nicaragüenses. (Nicaraguan ballads and songs.)
See item no. 644.

Religion

279 **Apuntes para una teología nicaragüense.** (Notes for a
Nicaraguan theology.)
Centro Antonio Valdivieso, with the Instituto Histórico
Centroamericano, Universidad Centroamericana. San José:
Departamento Ecuménico de Investigación, 1981. 198p.
The proceedings of a conference on this subject held in Managua, 8-14 September 1980. It presents the theology of liberation viewpoint and its relation to
the Sandinista revolution. Topics include the relation of Christian social faith to
revolutionary Nicaragua, the Catholic Church in the revolution, the Protestant
Evangelical Church, problems created by the division of the Church in the revolutionary process, and questions of theology with respect to the revolution.

280 **Breve historia de la iglesia en Nicaragua, 1523-1979.** (Brief
history of the Church in Nicaragua, 1523-1979.)
Jorge Eduardo Arellano. Managua, 1980. 147p. bibliog.
Reprinted from the *Boletín del Archivo General de la Nación*, no. 2-3 (Managua,
Jan.-June 1980), updated with a section on the Church in the 1970s and a
documentary appendix. It is an excellent survey of the Catholic Church's development in Nicaragua since the Spanish conquest, but its emphasis is on the Church
in the 20th century. Well documented and with a substantial bibliographic essay.

281 **The Catholic Church in Central America.**
Frederick D. Pike. *Review of Politics*, vol. 21 (Jan. 1959),
p. 83-113.
A good historical overview of the Catholic Church's role in Central America
through the 1960s, with considerable attention paid to Nicaragua.

282 **Evangelism-in-depth; experimenting with a new type of evangelism; as told by team members of the Latin American Mission.**
Moody Bible Institute.   Chicago: Moody Press, 1961. 126p.
An account of Baptist evangelical effort in Nicaragua.

283 **Fé cristiano y revolución sandinista en Nicaragua.** (Christian faith and Sandinista revolution in Nicaragua.)
Edited by Alvaro Argüello, SJ.   Managua: Instituto Histórico Centroamericano, 1979 [1980]. 375p. bibliog.
(Apuntes Para el Estudio de la Realidad Nacional, no. 3).
The proceedings of a seminar on this topic held in Managua, 24-28 September 1979. An important collection of essays for understanding the highly significant role of Christianity in the Sandinista revolution. Articles by Roberto Rivera Mendizábal, Jaime Wheelock, Juan Hernández Picó, Alvaro Argüello, Ronald Mendoza, José Miguel Torres, Sergio Arce, Raúl Gómez Treto, Pablo Richard and Napoleón Alvarado.

284 **Historia de la Compañía de Jesús en Nicaragua: 1873-1880.**
(History of the Society of Jesus in Nicaragua: 1873-1880.)
Franco Cerutti.   *Revista del Pensamiento Centroamericano,* vol. 32, no. 156 (July-Sept. 1977), p. 120-43; no. 157 (Oct.-Dec. 1977), p. 101-10.
One of several scattered articles by Cerutti on the Jesuits in Nicaragua. This Italian-born historian of Nicaragua promises that a book on the subject is forthcoming.

285 **La iglesia en América Central y el Caribe.** (The Church in Central America and the Caribbean.)
Isidoro Alonso, Ginés Garrido.   Bogotá: Oficina Internacional de Investigaciones Sociales de FERES (Federación Internacional de los Institutos Católicos de Investigaciones Sociales y Socio-religiosas), 1962. 282p. maps. (Estudios Socio-religiosos Latinoamericanos, no. 4).
A useful overview of the Church in the 1950s. Not a history of the Church in the region.

286 **Love in practice - the Gospel in Solentiname.**
Ernesto Cardenal, translated by Donald D. Walsh.   Maryknoll, New York: Orbis Books; London: Search Press, 1976-79. 3 vols.
A sometimes awkward, but understandable translation of an important work by one of the leaders of liberation theology in Nicaragua. Cardenal's ideas of bringing the gospel to the masses comes through clearly in these dialogues on the Gospels between the author and community members of Solentiname, Nicaragua. Cardenal is minister of culture in the Sandinista government.

Religion

287 **Nicaraguan bishops on socialism.**
M. Obando y Bravo. *Christianity and Crisis*, vol. 40 (12
May 1980), p. 147.

A revealing statement by Nicaragua's archbishop on the attitudes of the ecclesias-
tical hierarchy of the country on socialism and revolution. This issue also includes
articles by Nicaragua's foreign minister, Father Miguel d'Escoto, and an article
by W. H. Cohen, 'Nicaragua: the revolution takes hold', p. 137-40.

288 **Nuevo estudio sobre la religión de los Nicaraos.** (New study
on the religion of the Nicaraos.)
Antonio Esqueva. *Boletín Nicaragüense de Bibliografía y
Documentación*, no. 25 (Sept.-Oct. 1978), p. 1-9.

A brief description of the religion of the Nicaraguan Indians based on the
account of 16th-century chronicler, Gonzalo Fernández de Oviedo. This article
was reprinted in the *BNBD*, vol. 40 (March-April 1981), p. 37-45.

289 **Protestantism in Nicaragua: its historical roots and influences
affecting its growth.**
George Irwin Ferris, Jr. PhD dissertation, Temple
University, 1981. 287p. bibliog. (Available from University
Microfilms, Ann Arbor, Michigan, order no. 81-15870).

Emphasizes the origins and influence of Protestantism in Nicaragua and notes the
significant difference between western Nicaragua and the Caribbean coast in
missionary activities. Protestant efforts in the more heavily populated western
region have been much less successful than those among the Indians of the
eastern coast. Ferris pays considerable attention to Church-state relations in
Nicaragua.

290 **Religión de los Nicaraos: análisis y comparación de
tradiciones culturales Nahuas.** (Religion of the Nicaraos:
analysis and comparison of Nahua cultural traditions.)
Miguel León-Portilla. Mexico City: UNAM (Universidad
Autónoma de México), 1972. 116p. maps. bibliog.

A very thoroughly researched and revealing study of the Nahuat-speaking
Nicarao Indians, based largely on the chronicles of Oviedo. Notes similarities to
Mexican religious practices. A major scholarly study by a noted Mexican
ethno-historian.

291 **Religión, iglesia, cristianismo y revolución en el diario
Barricada.** (Religion, Church, Christianity and revolution in
the daily *Barricada*.)
René Rodríguez Masís. *Boletín Nicaragüense de
Bibliografía y Documentación*, no. 40 (March-April 1981),
p. 86-90.

Lists sixty-four articles on this topic published in the Sandinista daily *Barricada*
during the period 1979-81.

292 **Religion in Central America.**
Kenneth Grubb. London: World Dominion Press, 1937.
147p. maps.
Describes Protestant missions in Central America.

293 **Reseña histórica de la Diócesis de Nicaragua.** (Historical
survey of the Diocese of Nicaragua.)
Arturo Aguilar S. León, Nicaragua: Tipografía Hospicio,
1929. 308p.
A useful, if not very professional, history of the Nicaraguan Church. It has more
detail on the early period, however, than Arellano's *Breve historia...* (q.v.).

Area handbook for Nicaragua.
See item no. 2.

Memorial de mi vida. (Memoir of my life.)
See item no. 174.

Gaspar vive. (Gaspar lives.)
See item no. 239.

Asang, adaptations to culture contact in a Miskito community.
See item no. 258.

Social Conditions

General

294 **Las contradicciones de la transición: clases, nación y estado en Nicaragua.** (Contradictions in the transition: classes, nation and state in Nicaragua.)
Carlos M. Vilas. *Estudios Sociales Centroamericanos*, vol. 11, no. 31 (Jan.-April 1982), p. 95-114.
A Nicaraguan sociologist describes the complexities of the transition from imperialism to socialism in revolutionary Nicaragua.

295 **Dynamics of societal diversity: notes from Nicaragua for a sociology of survival.**
Richard N. Adams. *American Ethnologist*, vol. 8 (Feb. 1981), p. 1-20. bibliog.
A leading anthropologist who has specialized in Central America comments perceptively on the Nicaraguan revolution and its consequences for society in the country.

296 **Family recovery following a natural disaster: the case of Managua, Nicaragua.**
Patricia Bolton. PhD dissertation, University of Colorado, 1979. 165p. bibliog. (Available from University Microfilms, Ann Arbor, Michigan, order no. 79-23213).
Case study of a family recovery following the Managua earthquake of December 1972.

297 **La nueva Nicaragua: antimperialismo y lucha de clases.** (The new Nicaragua: anti-imperialism and the class struggle.)
Adolfo Gilly. Mexico City: Nueva Imágen, 1980. 2nd ed. 141p.
First-hand description of social conditions in Nicaragua.

298 **A sociological study of the relations of man to the land in Nicaragua.**
Edgar G. Nesman. PhD dissertation, University of Florida, 1969. 233p. map. bibliog. (Not available from University Microfilms).
This useful dissertation examines land tenure, the size of farms, land division, surveys and titles, settlement patterns and systems of agriculture in Nicaragua. The study is unique and is principally based on direct observation and personal interviews with hundreds of Nicaraguans in thirty rural communities, as well as on the 1963 census. The study offers a great deal of data on rural Nicaragua not found elsewhere in English. Unfortunately, this dissertation is not available from University Microfilms, but a photocopy may be purchased directly from the University of Florida.

299 **World handbook of political and social indicators.**
Bruce Russett (and others). New Haven, Connecticut: Yale University Press, 1972. 2nd ed. 443p.
Of considerable use to social scientists in comparing Nicaragua to other countries statistically, in terms of human resources, government and politics, communications, wealth, health, education, marriage, immigration and religion.

Area handbook for Nicaragua.
See item no. 2.

Terremoto '72: elites y pueblo. (Earthquake '72: élites and the people.)
See item no. 45.

The prehistoric and modern subsistence patterns of the Atlantic coast of Nicaragua. A comparison.
See item no. 134.

Raíces indígenas de la lucha anticolonialista en Nicaragua. (Native roots of the Nicaraguan anticolonial struggle.)
See item no. 154.

Ensayos nicaragüenses. (Nicaraguan essays.)
See item no. 274.

Estadísticas del desarrollo social de Nicaragua, 1960-1967 y proyecciones, 1968-1972. (Statistics on the social development of Nicaragua, 1960-1967, and projections for 1968-1972.)
See item no. 305.

Principales leyes económicas y sociales: leyes bancarias y financieras. (Principal economic and social laws: banking and financial laws.)
See item no. 442.

Anuario Estadístico. (Statistical annual.)
See item no. 447.

A case study of an international development project: the Instituto Nacional de Comercio Exterior y Interior in Ciudad Sandino, Nicaragua. *See* item no. 495.

Breve historia de la tenencia de tierra en Nicaragua. (Brief history of land tenure in Nicaragua.) *See* item no. 524.

Social structure

300 **Imperialismo y dictadura. Crisis de una formación social.** (Imperialism and dictatorship. The crisis of a social structure.)
Jaime Wheelock Román. Mexico City: Siglo XXI, 1975. 2nd ed., 1979. 206p. 3rd ed., *Nicaragua: imperialismo y dictadura*, Havana: Editorial de Ciencias Sociales, 1980. 213p. bibliog.

A major interpretation of Nicaraguan social development since the late 19th century within the dependency framework. Wheelock blames Nicaragua's social and economic problems on the capitalist-dependent development of coffee and other agro-exports and describes the failure of the national bourgeoisie to meet the crisis.

301 **Influencia de la crisis del 29 en Nicaragua.** (Influence of the 1929 depression on Nicaragua.)
Edelberto Torres Rivas. In: *América Latina en los años treinta* (Latin America in the thirties). Edited by Pablo González Casanova. Mexico City: UNAM (Universidad Autónoma de México), Instituto de Investigaciones Sociales, 1977, p. 89-112.

A very important article by one of Central America's leading social scientists. Torres analyses the effects of declining prices on the Nicaraguan economy, but also points out that the US intervention was a more devastating factor. This is a well-documented study of the economy and class structure within Nicaragua during this period.

302 **Interpretación del desarrollo social centroamericano, procesos y estructuras de una sociedad dependiente.** (Interpretation of Central American social development, processes and structures of a dependent society.)
Edelberto Torres Rivas. Ciudad Universitaria Rodrigo Facio, Costa Rica: EDUCA (Editorial Universitaria Centroamericana), 1971. 317p. bibliog.

A major contribution toward understanding the socio-economic dynamics of the Central American countries, this has been a very influential work among Central

American social scientists. It analyses the economy of Central America within a dependency framework. See also his 'El estado contra la sociedad: las raíces de la revolución nicaragüense', *Estudios Sociales Centroamericanos*, vol. 9, no. 27 (Sept.-Dec. 1980), p. 79-96.

303 **Nicaragua: the transition to a new society.**
James Petras. *Latin American Perspectives*, vol. 8, no. 2 (spring 1981), p. 74-94.
A US sociologist describes the transition from capitalism to socialism in Nicaragua. Petras argues that a mixed economy or social democratic solution is both unlikely and undesirable in Nicaragua. Rather, Nicaragua must move quickly toward a committed socialist state. See also Petras' 'Whither the Nicaraguan revolution?', *Monthly Review*, vol. 31 (Oct. 1979), p. 1-22.

Les structures sociales du Nicaragua au XVIIIe siècle. (The social structures of Nicaragua to the 18th century.)
See item no. 180.

Estructuras socioeconómicas, poder y estado en Nicaragua, de 1821 a 1875. (Socio-economic structures, power and the state in Nicaragua, 1821-1875.)
See item no. 189.

Las contradicciones de la transición: clases, nación y estado en Nicaragua. (Contradictions in the transition: classes, nation and state in Nicaragua.)
See item no. 294.

Migraciones rurales y estructura agraria en Nicaragua. (Rural migrations and agrarian structure in Nicaragua.)
See item no. 535.

Social problems

304 **Progressive drug involvement: marihuana use careers among Nicaraguan private secondary school students.**
Harvey R. Williams, III. PhD dissertation, Vanderbilt University, 1977. 193p. bibliog. (Available from University Microfilms, Ann Arbor, Michigan, order no. 78-12439).
Examining marihuana use among nearly 10,000 Nicaraguan adolescents, this study identifies definite career patterns of drug involvement from tobacco to alcohol to marihuana, and describes characteristics of their use. Findings are consistent with theoretical premises and are also generally consistent with related investigations of North American youth.

Social Services, Health and Welfare

General

305 **Estadísticas del desarrollo social de Nicaragua, 1960-1967 y proyecciones, 1968-1972.** (Statistics on the social development of Nicaragua, 1960-1967, and projections for 1968-1972.)
Sector Social, Oficina de Planificación, Consejo Nacional de Economía. Managua: Comisión Nacional de Economía, 1968. unpaginated.
Statistics on social programmes and conditions.

306 **Health policy making in a revolutionary context: Nicaragua, 1979-1981.**
T. J. Bossert. *Social Science and Medicine (Medical Economics),* vol. 15C (Dec. 1981), p. 225-31.
Acknowledges that the Sandinista régime has made great strides toward the achievement of equality of access to health services. The emphasis has been on preventive rather than curative services and encouragement of community participation. Bossert notes that equity of access increased much more for urban than rural areas, but he suggests that as militant Sandinistas gain more important roles in the Ministry of Health, greater rural progress may be expected. Based principally on six weeks in Nicaragua in 1980.

307 **Salud pública y crecimiento demográfico en Centro América.**
(Public health and population growth in Central America.)
Instituto Centroamericano de Población y Familia, Carlos
Gehlert Mata, Carlos Orellana. Guatemala City:
ICAPF-IDESAC (Instituto Centroamericano de Población y
Familia-Instituto Para el Desarrollo Económico Social de
América Central), 1968. 81p. bibliog. (Colección
Monografías Diagnósticas, no. 1).
A concise report, principally statistical, of population and health care in each
Central American country. Successive sections analyse the population, present
indicators of the health situation, and discuss public health resources in Central
America.

Nicaragua in revolution.
See item no. 352.
Anuario Estadístico. (Statistical annual.)
See item no. 447.

Health

308 **Breve historia hospitalaria de Nicaragua.** (Brief hospital
history of Nicaragua.)
Rafael Alvarado Sarria. León, Nicaragua: Editorial
Hospicio, 1969. 148p.
Surveys hospital development throughout Nicaragua from the establishment of the
country's first hospital, in León in 1624, through about 1965. A brief sketch on
each hospital in the country makes up the bulk of this work.

309 **The ecology of malnutrition in Mexico and Central America:
Mexico, Guatemala, British Honduras, Honduras, El
Salvador, Nicaragua, Costa Rica and Panama.**
Jacques Meyer May, Donna L. MacLellan. New York:
Hafner, 1972. 395p. maps. bibliog. (Studies in Medical
Geography, no. 11).
Demographic, economic and dietary information related to nutrition in each coun-
try. Nicaragua is dealt with on p. 239-81.

310 **The ecology of malnutrition in Sandy Bay, Nicaragua.**
Mary Ruth Horner. PhD thesis, University of Wisconsin,
1978. 372p. bibliog. (Available from University Microfilms,
Ann Arbor, Michigan, order no. 79-15111).
Studies causes and effects of widespread malnutrition in a Miskito Indian com-
munity. Effects of physical environment on the nutrition of the community was a

major factor in the problem. Recommendations for improvement on the basis of feasibility are included.

311 The health and the customs of the Miskito Indians of northern Nicaragua: interrelationships in a medical program.
Michel Pijoan. *América Indígena*, vol. 6 (1946), p. 41-66, 157-83.

Detailed description of a plan for a co-operative medical and sanitary programme. It reveals many of the customs of the Miskito Indians with respect to health care, and comments on the problems of developing modern health care in more primitive societies.

312 Health and revolution in Nicaragua.
Medical Aid Committee.   London: Nicaragua Solidarity Committee, 1980. 40p.

Briefly describes health service efforts of the Sandinista government.

Human Rights

313 **Cuarto informe oficial, julio 79-dic. 81.** (Fourth official
report, July 79-Dec. 81.)
Comision Permanente de Derechos Humanos de
Nicaragua. Managua: CPDHN, 1982. varied pagination.
A voluminous report on existing laws and guarantees of human rights in Nicaragua and of violations of human rights which the commission is investigating. The Nicaraguan Permanent Commission of Human Rights (CPDHN) was formed in 1977 to help document and expose violations of human rights in the Somoza régime. Its continuation has been a source of embarrassment for the Sandinista régime, as it has exposed new violations by Sandinista officials. This report also documents hostile activities against the Human Rights Commission. With the three previous reports (*Informe oficial, abril 1977-febrero 1978*; *Segundo informe, hasta el 10 de junio 1978*; and *Tercer informe, hasta junio 1979*), the CPDHN has documented in great detail the human rights situation in Nicaragua. See also the *Informe de la Comisión Permanente de Derechos Humanos de Nicaragua a la Comisión Interamericana de Derechos Humanos* (Managua: CPDHN, Oct. 1980. 16p.).

314 **Human rights and basic needs in the Americas.**
Edited by Margaret Crahan. Washington, DC: Georgetown
University Press, 1982. 343p. (Studies in Ethics).
Argues that achievement of security and the promotion of human rights are not antithetical but complementary, and criticizes US support of authoritarian régimes in Latin America. Coverage of Nicaragua is limited, but important, especially in the selection on 'Economic performance and basic needs' by Elizabeth Dore and John Weeks. For a more theoretical and philosophical approach to the subject, see, in the same series, *Human rights in the Americas: the struggle for consensus*, edited by Alfred Hennelly, SJ, and John Langan, SJ (1982).

315 **Human rights and United States policy toward Latin America.**
Lars Schoultz. Princeton, New Jersey: Princeton University Press, 1981. 421p. bibliog.

A scholarly study of US policy on human rights with respect to Latin America. There is frequent reference to human rights in Nicaragua in this work, especially during the Carter administration. Schoultz is an associate professor of political science at the University of North Carolina.

316 **Report on the situation of human rights in Nicaragua.**
Organization of American States, Inter-American Commission on Human Rights. Washington, DC: Secretariat-General of the Organization of American States, 1978. 78p.

Detailed and grisly report on violations of human rights in Nicaragua during the last years of the Somoza régime.

317 **The Republic of Nicaragua: an Amnesty International report including the findings of a mission to Nicaragua, 10-15 May 1976.**
Amnesty International. London: Amnesty International Publications, 1977. 75p.

Detailed report on human rights violation by the Somoza régime in the 1970s. A Spanish edition was published in the *Revista del Pensamiento Centroamericano*, vol. 32, no. 157 (1977), p. 111-51. See also the *Annual Reports* and *Monthly Newsletters* of Amnesty International for ongoing reporting on human rights in Nicaragua.

Politics

Central and Latin American political characteristics

318 **Ciencias políticas y temas afines.** (Political science and related topics.)
Managua: Biblioteca y Servicios de Información, Banco Central de Nicaragua, 1979. 12p. (Mini-bibliografía no. 12).
Lists 170 items, including periodical articles, dealing with politics, held by the Banco Central library. The section on Nicaragua contains thirty-four entries. Other sections deal topically with works on other regions or in general, including but not exclusively limited to Latin America. The Nicaraguan section lists many articles by principals in the Sandinista revolution.

319 **Historia de la Federación de la América Central, 1823-1840.**
(History of the Central American Federation, 1823-1840.)
Pedro Joaquín Chamorro y Zelaya. Madrid: Ediciones Cultura Hispánica, 1951. 644p.
This is the most extensive history of the Central American Federation, written by a leading Nicaraguan historian.

320 **Obras.** (Works.)
Carlos Cuadra Pasos. Managua: Fondo de Promoción Cultural, Banco de América, 1976-77. 2 vols.
Extensive political essays and personal reminiscences by a well-known Nicaraguan journalist.

321 **Sinners and heretics: the politics of military intervention in Latin America.**
Mauricio Solaún, Michael A. Quinn. Urbana, Illinois: University of Illinois Press, 1972. 228p. bibliog. (Illinois Studies in the Social Sciences, no. 58).

A study of thirty military *coups* in Latin America, including the 1947 Nicaraguan *coup*. But there are many other references to the Nicaraguan political system in this important interpretive study of Latin American politics. Solaún, a sociologist at the University of Illinois, later served as US ambassador to Nicaragua under President Jimmy Carter.

The Central American republics.
See item no. 5.

Nicaragua, patria libre. (Nicaragua, free country.)
See item no. 12.

La Mosquitia en la revolución. (Mosquitia in the revolution.)
See item no. 38.

The Cádiz experiment in Central America, 1808 to 1826.
See item no. 137.

Middle American governors.
See item no. 143.

World handbook of political and social indicators.
See item no. 299.

Nicaraguan political characteristics

322 **The bureaucratic function and system support: a comparison of Guatemala and Nicaragua.**
Germán D. Luján. *Comparative Politics*, vol. 7 (July 1975), p. 559-76.

An analytical study of the bureaucracies of these two Central American states, presenting models and flow charts to show their functions and relationships to societal groups. Notes significant differences between the two systems, while showing that both systems confirm several behaviouralist theories of bureaucracy.

323 **Development and dictatorship in Nicaragua, 1950-1960.**
Peter H. Smith. *American Economist*, vol. 7 (June 1963), p. 24-32.

An informative review of the economic policy of the Somoza dynasty in the 1950s, with particular reference to the application of the Alliance for Progress in Nicaraguan development in the early 1960s. Smith notes the remarkable economic growth that Nicaragua achieved in this decade under Somoza's strongarmed guidance.

324 **Estirpe sangriente: los Somozas.** (Bloody stock: the
Somozas.)
Pedro Joaquín Chamorro Cardenal. Mexico City: Diógenes,
1979. 283p.
Originally published in Buenos Aires (Editorial Triángulo) in 1959, this is one of
the most articulate and bitter denunciations of the Somoza dynasty. The editor
was the editor of the opposition daily, *La Prensa*, and a long-time leader in the
Conservative Party.

325 **Gobernantes de Nicaragua, 1825-1947.** (Governors of
Nicaragua, 1825-1947.)
Sara Luisa Barquero. Managua: Ministerio de Instrucción
Pública, 1945. 2nd ed. 248p.
Biographical sketches of the rulers of Nicaragua from the first chief of state in
1825 through 1945.

326 **Nicaragua.**
Susanne Jonas. *NACLA's Latin America and Empire
Report*, vol. 10, no. 2 (Feb. 1976). 40p.
Highly critical of the Somoza régime, this report contains much information on
the period and on the US role in Nicaragua, including details of US investment
in Nicaragua. This report comprises the entire issue.

327 **Nicaragua betrayed.**
Anastasio Somoza Debayle, Jack Cox. Boston,
Massachusetts; Los Angeles: Western Islands Publishers,
1980. 431p.
Somoza's own account of his régime and his overthrow, as told by Jack Cox. It is
useful not only as a representation of Somoza's viewpoint and a defence of his
régime, but because of the very candid and revealing personal relationships which
Somoza (through Cox) explains in the volume. Although it must be used with
care, owing to its strong biases, this volume provides an inside veiw of one of the
region's most hated dictatorships.

328 **Presidential leadership in Nicaragua.**
Chester Yeager Williams. PhD dissertation, Indiana
University, 1977. 347p. bibliog. (Available from University
Microfilms, Ann Arbor, Michigan, order no. 77-30332).
Suggests that rather than being an absolute dictator, Anastasio Somoza Debayle
was limited in his actions by the strengths of competing élites. Studies the
bureaucratic politics of Nicaragua with special emphasis on the presidency under
Somoza. Challenges common notions about Somoza's authoritarian practices.

329 **Un pueblo y su conductor, terremoto de Managua 1972.** (A
people and their leader, the Managua earthquake of 1972.)
Silvio Campos Meléndez. Managua: San José, 1973.
151p.+photos.

A description of the earthquake with many photographs, and praise of Somoza's
leadership in overcoming the disaster.

Area handbook for Nicaragua.
See item no. 2.

Nicaragua: dictatorship and revolution.
See item no. 11.

Central America and the Caribbean.
See item no. 138.

The dawn of nationalism and its consequences in Nicaragua.
See item no. 218.

Te dió miedo la sangre? (Did the blood frighten you?)
See item no. 627.

Editoriales de *La Prensa*. (Editorials from *La Prensa*.)
See item no. 654.

Political parties

330 **Alrededor del problema unionista de Centro América.**
(Regarding the unionist problem of Central America.)
Salvador de Mendieta. Barcelona, Spain: Maucci, 1934. 2
vols.

Mendieta considered this work to be a part of his *La enfermedad de Centro
América* (see below). Volume 1 is a somewhat autobiographical account of Men-
dieta and his struggles for unionism on the isthmus, while volume 2 contains
historical data on unionist efforts. See also the biography of Mendieta by Warren
H. Mery, mentioned below in the annotation to *La enfermedad de Centro
América*.

331 **Central American political parties: a functional approach.**
Charles W. Anderson. *Western Political Quarterly*, vol. 15
(March 1962), p. 125-39.

A useful overview of Central American political parties, placed in the context of
western political systems and the role of parties in the Central American political
process. Specific attention to Nicaragua, while not extensive, is perceptive. See
also Anderson's 1960 University of Wisconsin PhD dissertation, *Political ideology
and the revolution of rising expectations in Central America, 1944-1948* (425p.
University Microfilms order no. 60-3161).

332 **The Christian Democratic movement in Nicaragua.**
Thomas W. Walker. Tucson, Arizona: University of
Arizona Press, 1970. 71p. bibliog. (Comparative Government
Studies no. 3, Institute of Government Research, University
of Arizona).
A very competent study of the Christian Democratic Party, a moderate opposition
group to the Somoza régime, 1948-69. The study is also useful for its revelations
regarding the nature of political activity under the Somozas.

333 **La enfermedad de Centro América.** (The Central American
illness.)
Salvador de Mendieta. Barcelona, Spain: Maucci, 1934. 3
vols.
Salvador de Mendieta was Nicaragua's great advocate for Central American
unity in the early 20th century and the founder of the Unionist Party. This work
is a stinging condemnation of much that was wrong with Central America as
Mendieta saw it. Volume 1 contains a very detailed description of Central
America as of about 1906-07. Volume 2 is a sort of history, not particularly
useful. Volume 3 contains Mendieta's recommendations as to what should be
done. Mendieta continued this work in *Alrededor del problema unionista de
Centro América* (see above). See also the biography of Mendieta by Warren H.
Mery, *Salvador de Mendieta: escritor y apostol de la unión centroamericana*
(Salvador de Mendieta: writer and apostle of Central American union), Birmingham, Alabama: Birmingham Southern College, 1971, a publication based on the
author's PhD dissertation at the University of Alabama, 1968 (University Microfilms order no. 68-15500).

334 **The Nicaraguan political system: the flow of demands and
the reactions of the regime.**
Mariano Fiallos Oyanguren. PhD dissertation, University
of Kansas, 1968. 204p. (Available from University
Microfilms, Ann Arbor, Michigan, order no. 68-17381).
A careful study of the political structure of the Somoza régime.

Por el Rescate de la Revolución Democrática Nicaragüense. (For the
rescue of the Nicaraguan democratic revolution.)
See item no. 28.

Sandinista revolution, 1979

335 **A. C. Sandino y el FSLN.** (A. C. Sandino and the FSLN.)
Managua: Biblioteca y Servicios de Información, Banco
Central de Nicaragua, June-July 1979. 5p. (Bibliografía
Corta no. 14).

Lists forty-six books and articles dealing with Sandino and the struggle of the
Frente Sandinista de Liberación Nacional (Sandinista Front for National Liberation) to overthrow the Somoza dynasty. Some are primary sources. Ninety-seven
additional items, from *Imprenta Semanal, Extra Semanal* and *Semana,* 1959-72,
comprise a *Selección bibliográfica sobre Sandino y el Sandinismo* (Bibliografía
Corta no. 16. 7p.).

336 **The agony of a dictatorship: Nicaraguan chronicle.**
O. Ignatiev, G. Borovik. Moscow: Progress Books, 1980.
159p.

A panoramic picture of events culminating in the downfall of the Somoza
dynasty. A moving, pro-Marxist account by two Soviet writers who visited Central America in the months prior to the Sandinista victory.

337 **Augusto César Sandino.**
Edited by Sergio Ramírez. Managua: Ministerio de
Cultura, Juventud y Deportes, 1978. 408p. (Pensamiento de
América, no. 11).

An excellent collection of the scattered writings, interviews, letters, and other
documents of Sandino, effectively introduced and edited by Ramírez.

338 **La caída del somocismo y la lucha sandinista en Nicaragua.**
(The fall of Somozism and the Sandinista struggle in
Nicaragua.)
Julio López C., Orlando Núñez S., Carlos Fernando
Chamorro Barrios, Pascual Serres. San José: EDUCA
(Editorial Universitaria Centroamericana), 1979. 2nd ed.
385p. (Colección Seis).

Essentially a history the Sandinista movement, 1977-79. This series of essays was
previously published in *Pensamiento Crítico.*

339 **The Costeños and the revolution in Nicaragua.**
Phillip A. Dennis. *Journal of Interamerican Studies and
World Affairs,* vol. 23 (Aug. 1981), p. 271-96.

Based on field-work in Nicaragua in 1978-79, Dennis surveys the history of the
Miskitos and their involvement in the Sandinista revolution. He describes the
development of MISURASATA (Miskito, Sumu, Rama, Sandinista Aslatakanka
united together) as a peoples' organization representing the several Nicaraguan
coastal Indian tribes.

340 **Crisis in Nicaragua.**
Alejandro Bedaña. *NACLA Report on the Americas*, vol.
12, no. 6 (Nov.-Dec. 1978), p. 1-42.
An intelligent review of the situation in Nicaragua during the war against
Somoza, from the point of view of a pro-Sandinista Nicaraguan.

341 **Dr. Pedro Joaquín Chamorro (1924-1978), the Conservative
Party, and the struggle for democratic government in
Nicaragua.**
Ralph Lee Woodward, Jr. *Annals of the Southeastern
Council on Latin American Studies*, vol. 10 (March 1979),
p. 38-46.
Surveys the life of the courageous editor of *La Prensa* (Managua) and the
peculiar role of the Nicaraguan Conservative Party as the only important legal
opposition party to the Somoza dynasty.

342 **Doris Tijerino: inside the Nicaraguan revolution, as told to
Margaret Randall.**
Margaret Randall. Vancouver, British Columbia: New Star
Books, 1978. 176p.
A personal account of life under the Somoza dynasty in Nicaragua and the
growing struggle against that régime. Emphasizes the repressiveness of Somoza
and the National Guard.

343 **The end and the beginning: the Nicaraguan revolution.**
John A. Booth. Boulder, Colorado: Westview Press, 1982.
279p.
Explaining and analysing the political and social changes that occurred in the
first years of the Sandinista government, Booth also explores the antecedents to
the revolution and focuses on the impact of the revolution, ideology, power align-
ments and policies. He emphasizes the distinctive nature of the Nicaraguan
revolution and examines its implications for understanding revolutionary move-
ments in general in Latin America. This is the best general study of the revolution and its backgrounds yet to appear in English.

344 **Entre Sandino y Fonseca Amador.** (Between Sandino and
Fonseca Amador.)
Jesús Miguel Blandón. Managua: Tipografía Villalta, 1954.
224p.
A chronicle of the antecedents to the Sandinista Front for National Liberation
formed by Carlos Fonseca Amador.

345 **Escritos.** (Writings.)
Carlos Fonseca Amador. Managua: FSLN, Secretaría
Nacional de Propaganda y Educación Popular, 1979. 78p.
The principal writings of the founder of the Sandinista movement.

346 **Ideology of the Nicaraguan revolution.**
H. E. Vanden. *Monthly Review*, vol. 34 (June 1982), p.
25-41.
An historical survey of the Sandinista movement by a US political scientist.
Describes as the 'genius of FSLN ideology' its practical application of Sandino's
nationalist thought and Marxist concepts and methodology to Nicaraguan reality.

347 **La insurección nicaragüense, 1978-1979: la lucha armada del
FSLN y el pueblo contra la dictadura somocista, en la prensa
nacional y extranjera.** (The Nicaraguan insurrection,
1978-1979: the armed struggle of the FSLN and the people
against the Somoza dictatorship, in the national and foreign
press.)
Compiled by René Rodríguez Masís, Antonio Acevedo
Espinosa. Managua: Biblioteca y Servicios de Información,
Banco Central de Nicaragua, Oct. 1979. 173p.
A selection of 125 newspaper articles on the Sandinista insurrection.

348 **Micro-political explanation of the 1979 Nicaraguan
revolution.**
A. G. Cuzan, R. J. Heggen. *Latin American Research
Review*, vol. 17, no. 2 (1982), p. 156-70.
Presents a theory of Latin American government and suggests a model of coercive
versus persuasive tendencies to determine how a government achieves its ends.
Sees increasing use of coercion as likely in Nicaragua.

349 **Nicaragua, an ally under siege.**
Edited by Belden Bell. Washington, DC: Council on
American Affairs, 1978. 148p.
A group of essays generally defensive of the Somoza régime and critical of US
policy, which the contributors perceived as seeking the overthrow of the Somoza
dynasty. Contributors include Carl Curtis, Jeffrey Gayner, Jeffrey St. John, William Schneider, Jr., Otto Scott, John J. Tierney, Jr., and William Yarborough.

350 **Nicaragua, año cero, la caída de la dinastía Somoza.**
(Nicaragua, year zero, the fall of the Somoza dynasty.)
Mayo Antonio Sánchez. Mexico City: Editorial Diana,
1979. 166p. map. bibliog.
One of the first published works describing the overthrow of Somoza and the
history of the Sandinista movement. This pro-Sandinista account includes a
number of interesting photographs.

351 **Nicaragua, the course of revolution.**
R. Burbach. *Monthly Review*, vol. 31 (Feb. 1980), p. 28-39.

An informative and sympathetic description of the first six months of the Sandinista revolution, the structure of government, mass organizations, difficulties of establishing a socialist state while the bourgeoisie remains powerful and active, and economic progress and obstacles in the new Nicaragua. Argues in favour of more rapid socialization of the country.

352 **Nicaragua in revolution.**
Edited by Thomas W. Walker. New York: Praeger, 1982. 410p.

A collaborative effort by more than twenty scholars to explain the Nicaraguan revolution and its programmes. Walker and his twenty-three fellow contributors not only examine the insurrection itself, but pay painstaking attention to the important programmes and policies of the Sandinista government: economic and agrarian reform, literacy, public health, treatment of indigenous minorities, foreign policy, etc. This is one of the most important books published on the Nicaraguan revolution.

353 **Nicaragua, June 1978-July 1979.**
Susan Meiselas, edited by Claire Rosenberg. New York: Pantheon Books, 1981. 120p.

A first-hand description of the war against Somoza.

354 **Nicaragua, the land of Sandino.**
Thomas W. Walker. Boulder, Colorado: Westview Press, 1981. 137p.

A sympathetic and at times over-simplified history of the Nicaraguan revolution. Walker relates the revolution to Nicaragua's history, but the book's principal value is its description of the revolution and the first year of rule by the Sandinistas. Walker is a political scientist who has specialized in Nicaragua.

355 **Nicaragua, a people's revolution.**
EPICA Task Force. Washington, DC: EPICA (Ecumenical Program for Inter-American Communication and Action), 1980. 103p. bibliog.

A heavily illustrated description of the Sandinista overthrow of the Somoza régime.

356 **Nicaragua: the Sandinist revolution.**
Henri Weber, translated by Patrick Camiller. London: Verso, 1981. 154p. bibliog.

Briefly surveys Nicaraguan history as a background to discussing the fall of the Somoza dynasty and the Sandinista revolution. Analyses the conditions that fostered the revolutionary crisis, the increasing isolation of the Somozas from the Nicaraguan élite, from neighbouring governments and from the United States, and the concomitant growth of the FSLN. Explains the growth of socialism in

Politics. Sandinista revolution, 1979

Nicaragua, discusses the personnel and institutions of the new state and assesses their progress and the relation of the revolution to the general crisis in Central America in a climate of renewed Cold War. The work is based on somewhat limited sources, but is a well-written Marxist account of Nicaraguan history and the revolution. Weber is a Soviet-born professor of philosophy at the University of Paris VIII.

357 The Nicaraguan revolution.
Edited by Pedro Camejo, Fred Murphy. New York: Pathfinder Press, 1979. 79p.

A brief volume published shortly after the fall of Somoza. Its principal value is that it reprints the speeches by leading Sandinistas, an interview with Jaime Wheelock and the translation of the new Statute of Rights in Nicaragua.

358 Nicaragua's revolution.
Roger Burbach, Tim Draimin. *NACLA Report on the Americas*, vol. 14, no. 3 (May-June 1980), p. 1-35.

A valuable, sympathetic assessment of the Sandinista revolution during its first year following the overthrow of Somoza. Includes discussion both of the war and of the philosophy and system being established in revolutionary Nicaragua.

359 Power and consolidation in the Nicaraguan revolution.
Stephen M. Gorman. *Journal of Latin American Studies*, vol. 13, no. 1 (May 1981), p. 133-49.

An excellent account of the Sandinista success in consolidating power following the revolution. Gorman shows the structure of the government and the means by which power was consolidated. See also Gorman's brief but informative 'Sandinista chess, how the left took control', *Caribbean Review*, no. 10 (winter 1981), p. 15-17.

360 Revolution and peace: the Nicaraguan road.
Ernesto Cardenal. *Journal of Peace Research*, vol. 18, no. 2 (1981), p. 201-07.

A speech by the Nicaraguan minister of cultural affairs upon receiving the Peace Prize of the German Book Trade Association in Frankfurt-am-Main in October 1980. He defends the Nicaraguan revolution as creating not only the economic conditions for the economic development of its people, but also a major cultural revolution that preaches brotherhood and peace for its former enemies. Cardenal says that the Nicaraguan revolution incorporates Christian principles and is part of a world-wide historical process of evolution, of reconciliation between men as well as between man and nature. For a report on this speech see Rudolf J. Siebert, 'Ernesto Cardenal and the Nicaraguan revolution from theological theory to revolutionary praxis', *Cross Currents*, vol. 30 (fall 1980), p. 241-51.

361 Revolution in Nicaragua: another Cuba?
W. M. LeoGrande. *Foreign Affairs*, vol. 58 (fall 1979), p. 28-50.

Reviews the history of the Sandinista revolution, with particular reference to US policy. The author, a political scientist at the American University, argues that the US 'consistently tried to fit a square peg of policy into the round hole of reality', and failed to understand the dynamics of Somoza's decline. Also describes the various ideological tendencies within the revolution and the likelihood of radicalization. A thoughtful consideration of the US response to the transformation of the social structure of Nicaragua. An important article arguing for US understanding and sympathy toward Nicaragua as the best means of avoiding 'another Cuba'.

362 Sandinistas speak.

Tomás Borge (and others). New York: Pathfinder Press, 1982. 250p.

Speeches, writings and interviews with the leaders of Nicaragua's revolution. Included are the Sandinista manifestos: 'The historic program of the FSLN' and 'The role of religion in the new Nicaragua'; Carlos Fonseca Amador, 'Nicaragua: zero hour'; Daniel Ortega, 'Nothing will hold back our struggle for liberation' and 'An appeal for justice and peace'; an interview with Humberto Ortega; Tomás Borge, 'On human rights in Nicaragua' and 'The second anniversary of the Sandinista revolution'; and Jaime Wheelock, 'Nicaragua's economy and the fight against imperialism'.

363 Sandino's daughters.

Margaret Randall. Trumansburg, New York: Crossing Press, 1982. 220p.

The author, who has written a series of works on women in Latin American countries, describes the role of women in revolutionary Nicaragua.

364 Somocistas on trial.

J. K. Skinner. *Monthly Review*, vol. 33 (March 1982), p. 49-59.

Vivid description of trials of 4,550 civilian and military collaborators of the Somoza régime between December 1979 and February 1981. Provides statistical details on outcome of the trials and sentences and case histories of a number of the more celebrated cases.

365 Target Nicaragua.

George Black, Judy Butler. *NACLA Report on the Americas*, vol. 16, no. 1 (Jan.-Feb. 1982), p. 1-45.

Focuses on threats to the Nicaraguan revolution, especially from the United States. Also reviews the progress of the revolution.

366 Triumph of the people, the Sandinista revolution in Nicaragua.

George Black. London: Zed Press, 1981. 368p. bibliog.

A detailed account of the fall of Somoza and of Sandinismo. Black deals sympathetically with the Sandinistas and is critical of those who question the revolution. This is one of the most informative works on the revolution to date.

367 **The wider war: Honduras, Nicaragua, Guatemala.**
Judy Butler. *NACLA Report on the Americas*, vol. 15, no.
3 (May-June 1981), p. 20-37.
A report on the growing US involvement against the Nicaraguan revolution and
other peoples' revolutions in Central America. This article reflects the escalation
of the civil war in the Central American countries.

El pensamiento vivo de Sandino. (The living ideas of Sandino.)
See item no. 222.

Sandino, bibliografía fundamental. (Sandino, basic bibliography.)
See item no. 225.

Dictators never die: a portrait of Nicaragua and the Somozas.
See item no. 232.

Somoza and the legacy of U.S. involvement in Central America.
See item no. 236.

50 años de lucha sandinista. (50 years of Sandinista struggle.)
See item no. 237.

Death of the dynasty: the end of the Somoza rule in Nicaragua.
See item no. 238.

Apuntes para una teología nicaragüense. (Notes for a Nicaraguan
theology.)
See item no. 279.

Fé cristiano y revolución sandinista en Nicaragua. (Christian faith and
Sandinista revolution in Nicaragua.)
See item no. 283.

Nicaraguan bishops on socialism.
See item no. 287.

Counterrevolution in Nicaragua: the U.S. connection.
See item no. 399.

Situación económica y alianzas políticas. (The economic situation and
political alliances.)
See item no. 479.

**Nicaragua in revolution: the poets speak/Nicaragua en revolución: los
poetas hablan.**
See item no. 596.

Apocalypse and other poems.
See item no. 620.

Zero hour and other documentary poems.
See item no. 624.

Sandino en la plástica de América. (Sandino in the art of America.)
See item no. 642.

Boletín de Referencias, Centro de Documentación. (Reference Bulletin,
Documentation Centre.)
See item no. 697.

**Celebrating the demise of Somocismo, fifty recent Spanish sources on the
Nicaraguan revolution.**
See item no. 699.

Armed forces

368 **The constabulary in the Dominican Republic and Nicaragua: progeny and legacy of United States intervention.**
Marvin Goldwert. Gainesville, Florida: University of Florida Press, 1962. 55p. bibliog. (Latin American Monographs, no. 17).

A scholarly monograph comparing the problems of the United States in its efforts to train national police forces in these two Caribbean countries. In both cases, Goldwert points out, dictatorial rule was the result. Goldwert's treatment of the Nicaraguan National Guard is much less thorough than Millett's *Guardians of the dynasty* (q.v.).

369 **Defending the revolution.**
A. Sukhostat. *World Marxist Review*, vol. 24 (Aug. 1981), p. 60-67.

A perceptive article, from a strongly pro-Marxist point of view, describing the economic difficulties and progress and various police and military organizations formed to defend the Sandinista revolution against counter-revolutionaries and US imperialism.

370 **Estudios de historia militar de Centroamérica.** (Studies in Central American military history.)
José N. Rodríguez. Guatemala City: Tipografía Nacional, 1930. 385p. bibliog.

A useful survey of Central American military history through the 19th century.

371 **In search of the new soldier: junior officers and the prospect of social reform in Panama, Honduras and Nicaragua.**
Stephen C. Ropp. PhD dissertation, University of California, Riverside, 1971. 213p. bibliog. (Available from University Microfilms, Ann Arbor, Michigan, order no. 72-17063).

A penetrating study of the structure of the military in three Central American countries, noting the rapid evolution of the junior officer corps in recent years.

372 **Militarism and social revolution in the third world.**
Miles D. Wolpin. Totowa, New Jersey: Allanheld, 1981. 260p.

Although only occasionally referring specifically to Nicaragua, this work has much relevance to the Nicaraguan experience, both for the Somoza years and under Sandinista rule. This thoroughly documented study deals with both rightist and leftist military régimes.

373 **The United States and militarism in Central America.**
Don L. Etchison. New York: Praeger, 1975. 150p. bibliog.
A scholarly account of the role of armed forces in contemporary politics in each
Central American state. Analyses the policies of John Kennedy, Lyndon Johnson
and Richard Nixon with respect to the Central American military, with considerable attention to Nicaragua. Statistical appendixes enhance this work.

374 **Vida militar de Centro América.** (The military life of Central
America.)
Pedro Zamora Castellanos. Guatemala City: Tipografía
Nacional, 1924. 562p.
A standard military history of Central America, principally dealing with the 19th
century, although there is a brief colonial section.

**Sinners and heretics: the politics of military intervention in Latin
America.**
See item no. 321.

Foreign Relations

General

375 **Anglo-American isthmian diplomacy, 1815-1915.**
Mary Wilhelmine Williams. Washington, DC: American
Historical Association, 1916. 356p.

A survey of US-British relations with respect to Central America, with much
attention to Nicaragua, canal projects and the Mosquito Coast. Although more
recent historiography has revised, refined and expanded upon Williams' classic
study, this work remains a useful narrative of the topic.

376 **Boundaries, possessions, and conflicts in Central and North
America and the Caribbean.**
Gordon Ireland. Cambridge, Massachusetts: Harvard
University Press, 1941. 432p. maps.

The standard reference work on border disputes in the region to 1940. Nicaraguan disputes are dealt with on p. 2-24 and 129-210, the dispute with Honduras
being especially drawn out.

377 **Los cancilleres de Nicaragua, influencias y reminiscencias,
1838-1936.** (The foreign ministers of Nicaragua, influences
and reminiscences, 1838-1936.)
Máximo Navas Zepeda. Managua: La Nación, 1976. 279p.
bibliog.

Although this work is not very professional in style or content, it does provide a
great deal of information and documentation on Nicaragua's foreign ministers
during the indicated period.

101

378 **Central America, international dimensions of the crisis.**
Edited by Richard E. Feinberg. New York: Holmes &
Meier, 1982. 280p. bibliog.

A collection of essays on the international aspects of the crisis in Central
America, brought on in large measure by the Nicaraguan revolution. Considers
alternatives for US policy, Cold War implications, and the role of Mexico and
Venezuela in the region. Contributors include Robert Bond, Margaret Crahan,
Wolf Grabendorff, Margaret Daly Hayes, René Herrera Zúñiga, Mario Ojeda,
John Purcell, James Rosenau, Jiri Valenta, and Francisco Villagran Kramer.

379 **Inside Central America.**
María Elena Hurtado. *South, the Third World Magazine*,
no. 21 (July 1921), p. 16-22.

Three separate articles deal with the present crisis in Central America, with
special reference to Nicaragua: 'The man in the eye of the storm' deals with
Mexico's role in the crisis and President José López Portillo's peace initiative (p.
16-17); 'Fall of a valuable pawn' reviews recent development in Central America
with respect to US strategy (p. 19-21); and 'Pressure on a "dangerous" experiment' examines Nicaragua's search for social justice and the progress of its
revolution (p. 21-22).

380 **José de Marcoleta: padre de la diplomacia nicaragüense.**
(José de Marcoleta: father of Nicaraguan diplomacy.)
José Ramírez M. Managua: Imprenta Nacional, 1975. 2
vols. bibliog.

A biography of a Nicaraguan diplomat, José de Marcoleta, whose services
extended over some of the most important events of the mid-19th century. Of
related interest is the interesting collection of Marcoleta's papers, mostly concerned with the great fire in San Juan del Norte in 1855 and the Kinney expedition to Nicaragua, published under the title *Documentos diplomáticos de Don
José de Marcoleta, ministro de Nicaragua en los Estados Unidos, 1854* (Diplomatic papers of José de Marcoleta, Nicaraguan minister to the United States in
1854), Managua: Banco de América, Fondo de Promoción Cultural, 1976. 2nd
ed. 84p.

Nicaragua in revolution.
See item no. 352.

Nicaragua: el impacto de la mutación política. (Nicaragua: the impact of
the political mutation.)
See item no. 469.

With other Central American states

381 **Autonomy or dependence as regional integration outcomes: Central America.**
Philippe C. Schmitter. Berkeley, California: University of California, Institute of International Studies, 1972. 87p. bibliog.

A well-documented but rather narrowly conceived monograph on the common market experience, from a dependency point of view. Blames foreign, especially United States, interests for the failure of the integration movement in Central America.

382 **Central American regional integration.**
Joseph P. Nye. New York: Carnegie Endowment for International Peace, 1967. 66p. (*International Conciliation,* no. 562).

A good account of the political-bureaucratic aspect of the integration movement, Nye describes the new class of technocrats in all five Central American states who led the way in the movement.

383 **Enclave colonialista en Nicaragua.** (Colonialist enclave in Nicaragua.)
Luís Pasos Argüello. Managua: Unión, 1978. 283p. bibliog.

Challenges Colombian control of San Andrés Island, off Nicaragua's Caribbean coast.

384 **Historia de las relaciones interestatuales de Centro América.** (History of Central American interstate relations.)
Laudelino Moreno. Madrid: Compañía Iberoamericana de Publicaciones, 1928. 507p. map. bibliog.

A thorough examination of Central American interstate relations through 1923, with detailed examination of the pertinent documents, treaties, etc. An important contribution to the history of Central American union and disunion.

385 **The Honduras-Nicaragua boundary dispute, 1957-1963: the peaceful settlement of an international conflict.**
Wayne Earl Johnson. PhD dissertation, University of Denver, 1964. 181p. maps. bibliog. (Available from University Microfilms, Ann Arbor, Michigan, order no. 65-285).

A scholarly description of the settlement of a long-standing dispute, on which there was voluminous publication by both Honduras and Nicaragua.

386 **Nuestros límites con Nicaragua: estudio histórico.** (Our
boundaries with Nicaragua: historical study.)
Luís Fernando Sibaja Chacón. San José: Comisión
Nacional de Conmemoración Histórica, 1974. 279p. maps.
bibliog.
Costa Rican side of boundary disputes between that country and Nicaragua.

387 **La ODECA: sus antecedentes históricos y su aporte al
derecho internacional americano.** (The ODECA: its historical
antecedents and its contribution to American international
law.)
Marco Tulio Zeledón. San José: Colegio de Abogados de
Costa Rica, 1966. 192p. bibliog.
A history of the Organization of Central American States, written by one of its
former secretary-generals. Also deals with efforts at Central American unification
before the formation of ODECA in 1951.

388 **Regional integration in Central America.**
Isaac Cohen Orantes. Lexington, Massachusetts: D. C.
Heath, 1972. 126p. bibliog.
A survey of the Central American integration effort to 1972. See also Browning's
The rise and fall of the Central American Common Market below.

389 **The Republic of El Salvador against the Republic of
Nicaragua; complaint of the Republic of El Salvador, with
appendices.**
El Salvador, translated by Harry Van Dyke. Washington,
DC: Gibson Brothers, 1917. 85p.
The Salvadoran case against Nicaragua's lease of a naval base in the Gulf of
Fonseca to the United States, as argued before the Central American Court of
Justice. See also Salvador Rodríguez González, *El Golfo de Fonseca y el tratado
Bryan-Chamorro celebrado entre los Estados Unidos de Norte América y Nicar-
agua: doctrina Meléndez* (The Gulf of Fonseca and the Bryan-Chamorro treaty
between the United States of America and Nicaragua: the Meléndez doctrine)
(San Salvador: Imprenta Nacional, 1917. 458p. map), which is the official statement and protest of the Salvadoran government against the Bryan-Chamorro
treaty published together with substantial documentary support. President Carlos
Meléndez of El Salvador strongly opposed establishment of a US naval base in
the Gulf of Fonseca, arguing that the waters of that gulf were held jointly by El
Salvador, Honduras and Nicaragua, and that Nicaragua could not unilaterally
grant rights to the United States for the use of these waters.

390 **The rise and fall of the Central American Common Market.**
David Browning. *Journal of Latin American Studies*, vol.
6, no. 1 (May 1974), p. 161-68.
A review essay of Isaac Orantes, *Regional integration in Central America* (see
above), D. H. McClelland, *The Central American Common Market* (q.v.), and

Gary W. Wynia, *Politics and planners* (q.v.) by an historical geographer. Provides critical analysis of recent literature on the subject.

391 **The thirty years war between Figueres and the Somozas: international intrigue in Costa Rica and Nicaragua.**
Charles D. Ameringer. *Caribbean Review*, vol. 8, no. 4 (1979), p. 4-7, 40-41.

José Figueres and Anastasio Somoza regarded each other as a threat to their respective survivals. Each tried fervently to overthrow the other. This led to strained relations and occasional outbreaks of violence between Costa Rica and Nicaragua. The rivalry was continued by his sons following Somoza's assassination, until the final overthrow of Tachito Somoza in 1979. Ameringer summarizes this rivalry and the United States role in it.

392 **La unión de Centroamérica.** (The Central American union.)
Alberto Herrarte. Guatemala City: Centro Editorial José Pineda Ibarra, Ministerio de Educación Pública, 1964. 2nd ed. 428p.

First published in 1955, Herrarte's work remains one of the more important standard works on the efforts of Central Americans to reunify the isthmus politically.

The failure of union: Central America, 1824-1960.
See item no. 140.

With the United States

393 **The acquisition of the Nicaragua canal route: the Bryan-Chamorro treaty.**
Peter E. Brownback. Unpublished PhD dissertation, University of Pennsylvania, 1952. (Not available from University Microfilms; copies can be obtained from the University).

394 **American intervention in Nicaragua, 1909-33; an appraisal of objectives and results.**
Joseph O. Baylen. *Southwestern Social Science Quarterly*, vol. 35 (Sept. 1954), p. 128-54.

A leading US diplomatic historian reviews the intervention, concluding that it was carried out because of a combination of self-interest and idealism. The intervention failed to achieve the desired results and instead created much anti-Americanism. A multi-lateral intervention would have been preferable.

Foreign Relations. With the United States

395 American policy in Nicaragua.
Henry L. Stimson. New York: C. Scribner, 1927. 129p.

Strong defence of US policy in Nicaragua by one of the participants. Stimson claims the United States was primarily interested in establishing democracies in Central America. Se also *The dawn of nationalism and its consequences in Nicaragua* (q.v.).

396 Anglo-American diplomatic relations with regard to Nicaragua and Venezuela: February 1894-January 1896.
Gary Meredith Ross. PhD dissertation, Washington State University, 1966. 367p. (Available from University Microfilms, Ann Arbor, Michigan, order no. 67-1576).

Deals with the highly significant diplomatic manoeuvres as the United States challenged British hegemony in the Caribbean region, specifically in Nicaragua and Venezuela. In the case of Nicaragua, the United States helped to resolve Britain's long-standing disputes with Nicaragua in a manner favourable to Nicaragua.

397 A bibliography of United States-Latin American relations since 1810; a selected list of eleven thousand published references.
Compiled and edited by David F. Trask, Michael C. Meyer, Roger R. Trask. Lincoln, Nebraska: University of Nebraska Press, 1968. 441p.

An extensive bibliography, containing more than just relations with the US narrowly defined. A large section deals with Nicaraguan relations. See also the *Supplement to a bibliography of United States-Latin American relations since 1810*, compiled and edited by Michael C. Meyer (Lincoln, Nebraska: University of Nebraska Press, 1979. 193p.), with 3,568 additional entries, partially annotated.

398 Charles Evans Hughs and Nicaragua, 1921-1925.
Virginia Leonard Greer. PhD dissertation, University of New Mexico, 1954. 197p. (Available from University Microfilms, Ann Arbor, Michigan, order no. 00-09726).

A very competent analysis of the Nicaraguan policy of United States secretary of state Charles Evans Hughs, 1921-25. Greer describes much of the internal history of Nicaragua and the Americanization process that occurred under US occupation. Although successful in several aspects, according to Greer, in the final analysis Hughs' Nicaragua policy was a failure. See also Greer's 'State Department policy in regard to the Nicaraguan election of 1924', *Hispanic American Historical Review*, vol. 34 (Nov. 1954), p. 445-567.

399 Counterrevolution in Nicaragua: the U.S. connection.
Jeff McConnell. *Counter Spy*, vol. 6 (May-June 1982), p. 11-23.

Details US support of counter-revolution and destabilization efforts during the Carter and Reagan administrations, and argues, with considerable documentation, that such efforts are substantial and ongoing.

400 **La diplomacia norteamericana y la reincorporación de la Mosquitia.** (United States diplomacy and the reincorporation of Mosquitia.)
John Fielding. *Boletín Nicaragüense de Bibliografía y Documentación*, no. 26 (Nov.-Dec. 1978), p. 15-24. map.

Based on both published and manuscript sources, this is a competent historical narrative of the US role in the restoration of the Miskito Coast to Nicaragua. Fielding argues that control of the canal route, rather than protection of local American interests, was the principal motive for US action here at the close of the 19th century. This entire issue of the *BNBD* is devoted to the Miskito Coast.

401 **Diplomatic correspondence of the United States, inter-American affairs, 1831-1860. Vol. 3 - Central America, 1831-1850, documents 723-995; Vol. 4 - Central America 1851-1860, documents 996-1578.**
Selected and arranged by William R. Manning. Washington, DC: Carnegie Endowment for International Peace, 1933-34. 2 vols.

These two volumes of diplomatic correspondence contain a large volume of material relevant to Nicaragua during 1831-60, during which period the United States began to challenge British hegemony in the Central American region. For the period 1821-31, a small group of documents (nos. 430-38) are found in *Diplomatic correspondence of the United States concerning the independence of the Latin American nations*, compiled by W. R. Manning (New York: Oxford University Press, 1925. 3 vols.). Additional US diplomatic correspondence with Central America for this period and subsequently until the last twenty-five years may be obtained on microfilm from the National Archives of the United States. A catalogue of such materials already filmed is available from the National Archives in Washington.

402 **Dollar diplomacy in Nicaragua, 1909-1913.**
Dana G. Munro. *Hispanic American Historical Review*, vol. 38 (May 1958), p. 208-34.

A leading US authority on the period and region concludes that US policy was concerned more with political than financial considerations. Munro, however, is critical of the US intervention.

403 **Fiscal intervention in Nicaragua.**
Roscoe R. Hill. New York: Paul Maisel, 1933. 117p. maps. bibliog.

An important early study on the financial aspects of the US intervention in Nicaragua. Hill argues that establishing financial order could not guarantee political order in Nicaragua. Hill argues also that a major American motive for the intervention in Nicaragua was protection of the Panama Canal.

Foreign Relations. With the United States

404 Intervention and dollar diplomacy, 1900-1921.
Dana G. Munro. Princeton, New Jersey: Princeton
University Press, 1964. 553p.

This careful and scholarly history of US relations with the Caribbean region during the period of aggressive US involvement gives considerable attention to events in Nicaragua. Munro was actively involved in Nicaragua during the period as a US Foreign Service officer in Central America.

405 The looting of Nicaragua.
Rafael Nogales y Méndez. New York: R. M. McBride, 1928. 304p.

A detailed work by a Venezuelan reporter on the US intervention in Nicaragua. Nogales supports arguments that dollar diplomacy was the principal US motive in the intervention. This was an influential work in both the United States and Latin America.

406 Machine-gun diplomacy.
John A. H. Hopkins, Melinda Alexander. New York:
Lewis Copeland, 1928. 216p.

Highly critical of the role of Wall Street bankers in the US intervention in Nicaragua.

407 The making of the good neighbor policy.
Bryce Wood. New York: W. W. Norton, 1961. 438p.

This standard history of Franklin Roosevelt's Good Neighbor Policy contains a chapter on the US intervention in Nicaragua. Wood gives much importance to the Mexican revolution in prompting US intervention in Nicaragua, and suggests that the United States government learned some important, if expensive, lessons in Nicaragua.

408 Manifest destiny denied.
James Thomas Wall. Washington, DC: University Press of
America, 1982. 339p. bibliog.

Emphasizing the diplomatic problems of the United States, Wall surveys the story of Cornelius Vanderbilt, William Walker, Henry L. Kinney and other Americans in Nicaragua in the mid-19th century. His account of Kinney is especially useful, since it is less well known. Based principally on New York newspapers and US diplomatic correspondence, the works stems from the author's 1975 dissertation at the University of Tennessee, *American intervention in Nicaragua, 1848-1861* (University Microfilms order no. 75-3651).

409 The Mexican crisis and intervention in Nicaragua.
Charles W. Hackett. *Current History*, vol. 25 (March
1927), p. 870-77.

The relationship between the Mexican revolution and the events in Nicaragua in the 1920s is noted by a historian specializing in Latin America. See also his 'US intervention in Nicaragua', *Current History*, vol. 26 (April 1927), p. 104-07, and his 'Review of our policy in Nicaragua', *Current History*, vol. 29 (Nov. 1928), p. 285-88.

410 **The new empire, an interpretation of American expansion, 1860-1898.**
Walter LaFeber. Ithaca, New York: Cornell University Press, for the American Historical Association, 1963. 444p. bibliog.

Useful for understanding the background to US expansionism in Central America in the early 20th century. Attention specifically to Nicaragua is limited, but perceptive in its explanation of the US displacement of the British there.

411 **Nicaragua and the United States, 1909-1927.**
Isaac J. Cox. In: *World Peace Foundation Pamphlets*, vol. 10, no. 7. Boston, Massachusetts: World Peace Foundation, 1927, p. 703-887.

An important contemporary study defending the US intervention in Nicaragua. Includes a number of charts and documents in appendixes.

412 **Nicaraguan elections of 1928.**
Vinson A. McNeil. *Marine Corps Gazette*, vol. 50, no 9 (Sept. 1966), p. 32-33, 36-39.

A review of the Marine Corps-supervised 1928 election in Nicaragua. The author was a Marine officer in Nicaragua during this period and his observations and personal recollections are useful, although some of his assumptions regarding Nicaraguan history are dubious. This article is drawn from his MA thesis, University of North Carolina at Chapel Hill, 1963.

413 **Our jungle diplomacy.**
William Franklin Sands, Joseph M. Lalley. Chapel Hill, North Carolina: University of North Carolina Press, 1944. 250p.

A critical appraisal of US policy in the Caribbean region, with emphasis on Panama and Nicaragua. There is considerable converage of Nicaragua, however, where the authors believe the US Marine Corps was reduced to a collection agency. This is to a considerable extent a personal memoir.

414 **Quijote on a burro: Sandino and the Marines, a study in the formation of foreign policy.**
Lejeune Cummins. Mexico City: La Impresora, 1958. 206p.

Originally an MA thesis at the University of California (1951) directed by the Chilean scholar Arturo Ríoseco, this is a biting criticism of US diplomacy in the Sandino affair. It is sympathetic to Sandino. A Spanish translation was published in Managua by the Instituto de Estudio del Sandinismo in 1981.

415 **Relations between the United States and Nicaragua, 1896-1916.**
Anne I. Powell. *Hispanic American Historical Review*, vol. 8 (Feb. 1928), p. 43-64.

A scholarly review of US-Nicaraguan relations during the period indicated. Defends US intervention and emphasizes the beneficial results that accrued to Nicaragua: financial stability, economic and social progress, and orderly political development. But Powell also recognized the existence of considerable anti-American sentiment in Nicaragua and said that it must be eradicated if pan-Americanism was to succeed. See also Powell's 1929 University of Texas PhD dissertation, *Relations between the United States and Nicaragua, 1898-1925.*

416 **Rompiendo cadenas: las del imperialismo en Centro América y en otras repúblicas del continente.** (Breaking chains: those of the imperialism in Central America and in other republics of the continent.)
Vicente Saenz. Mexico City: Departamento Editorial, Unión Demócrata Centroamericano, 1951. 2nd ed. 289p.

A classic condemnation of the United States, first published in 1933. This second edition is updated, and blames the United States for the permanency of the Somoza régime. A third edition appeared in Buenos Aires (Palestra, 1961. 354p.).

417 **A search for stability, United States diplomacy toward Nicaragua, 1925-1933.**
William Kamman. Notre Dame, Indiana: University of Notre Dame Press, 1968. 263p. bibliog.

In this serious and heavily documented study of the period, the author argues that financial matters were not the principal reason for the US intervention in Nicaragua, but they did become an important part of US involvement in the country. This work has an extensive bibliography, but with some notable omissions.

418 **The shark and the sardines.**
Juan José Arévalo, translated by Jane Cobb, Raul Osegueda. New York: Lyle Stuart, 1961. 256p.

Strongly anti-American attack by the former president of Guatemala (1945-50). Arévalo describes several cases of US exploitation of Latin America, but especially uses Nicaragua as an example of the shark (US) gobbling up the sardine (Nicaragua).

419 **The southern dream of a Caribbean empire, 1854-1861.**
Robert E. May. Baton Rouge, Louisiana: Louisiana State University Press, 1973. 286p. bibliog.

A scholarly study, focusing on the US southern attitude and action toward Central America in the 1850s, with two chapters on Nicaragua. Although this work has an extensive bibliography, the author does not appear to have used Spanish-language or Central American sources.

420 **The United States and the Caribbean in the twentieth century.**
Lester D. Langley. Athens, Georgia: University of Georgia Press, 1980. 334p. bibliog.
A synthesis of US policy in the Caribbean Basin in the 20th century. Places the US intervention in Nicaragua in the proper perspective of broader US Caribbean policy.

421 **The United States and the Caribbean republics, 1921-1933.**
Dana G. Munro. Princeton, New Jersey: Princeton University Press, 1974. 571p. bibliog.
Munro's own experience in the State Department during this period make this careful study especially valuable. Includes two chapters on Nicaragua.

422 **The United States and Central America: the policy of Clay and Knox.**
George Weitzel. *Annals of the American Academy of Political and Social Scientists*, vol. 132 (July 1927), p. 115-29.
The former United States minister to Nicaragua defends US policy from charges of imperialism and dollar diplomacy. He compares the Central American policy of Philander C. Knox favourably with that of Henry Clay in the early 19th century. Both secretaries of state were attempting to improve trade and diplomatic relations between the Americas. This issue of the *Annals* also contains several other articles regarding US policy in Nicaragua, notably H. W. Dodds, 'The United States and Nicaragua' (p. 134-41), and Whiting Williams, 'Geographic determinism in Nicaragua' (p. 141-45).

423 **The United States and Nicaragua, 1927-1932: decisions for de-escalation and withdrawal.**
John J. Tierney, Jr. PhD dissertation, University of Pennsylvania, 1969. 380p. bibliog. (Available from University Microfilms, Ann Arbor, Michigan, order no 70-16225).
Investigates decisions made during the administration of Herbert Hoover, principally by secretary of state Henry L. Stimson, regarding the withdrawal of the US Marines from Nicaragua. Views the confrontation between Sandino and the US as a precedent for the revolutionary developments of the post-World War II era. Critical of US intervention in Nicaragua and the manner in which US decisions were made, but steps taken to de-escalate and withdraw the troops served US national interests better than continuation of the conflict.

424 **The United States and Nicaragua, a survey of the relations from 1909 to 1932.**
US Department of State. Washington, DC: US Government Printing Office, 1932. 134p.
The official point of view, prepared by Henry L. Stimson.

425 **United States commercial pressure for a Nicaraguan canal in the 1890's.**
P. H. Schieps. *The Americas*, vol. 20 (1964), p. 333-58.
An excellent, heavily documented synthesis of the voluminous literature supporting the Nicaraguan canal idea, following the bankruptcy of the Nicaraguan Canal Construction Commission in 1893.

426 **United States efforts to foster peace and stability in Central America: 1923-1954.**
Anne Warrick Lommel. PhD dissertation, University of Minnesota, 1967. 336p. (Available from University Microfilms, Ann Arbor, Michigan, order no. 68-1628).
Traces the failure of US policy to achieve peace and stability in Central America during the indicated period.

427 **United States in Nicaraguan politics: supervised elections, 1927-1932.**
Thomas J. Dodd, Jr. PhD dissertation, George Washington University, 1967. 347p. (Available from University Microfilms, Ann Arbor, Michigan, order no. 66-11523).
A careful study of US political supervision in Nicaragua, with particular emphasis on the role of Henry L. Stimson. A Spanish version appeared in the *Revista del Pensamiento Centroamericano*, vol. 30, no. 148 (July-Sept. 1975), p. 5-102.

Dollars and dictators, a guide to Central America.
See item no. 9.

Sandino's dream was Somoza's nightmare and our hope.
See item no. 16.

Nicaragua: past, present and future; a description of its inhabitants, customs, mines, minerals, early history, modern filibusterism, proposed inter-oceanic canal and manifest destiny.
See item no. 84.

Las impresiones de un general de las fuerzas confederadas sobre Centroamérica en los años finales del siglo XIX. (The impressions of a Confederate general in Central America in the last years of the 19th century.)
See item no. 90.

Our neighbor Nicaragua.
See item no. 97.

The romance and rise of the American tropics.
See item no. 145.

Documentos para la historia de la guerra nacional contra los filibusteros en Nicaragua. (Documents for the history of the National War against the filibusters in Nicaragua.)
See item no. 188.

Filibusters and financiers, the story of William Walker and his associates.
See item no. 191.

Freebooters must die! The life and death of William Walker, the most notorious filibuster of the nineteenth century.
See item no. 192.

La invasión filibustera de Nicaragua y la guerra nacional. (The filibuster invasion of Nicaragua and the national war.)
See item no. 197.

The war in Nicaragua.
See item no. 212.

William Walker.
See item no. 213.

William Walker: ideales y propósitos. (William Walker: ideals and intentions.)
See item no. 214.

With Walker in Nicaragua.
See item no. 215.

The dawn of nationalism and its consequences in Nicaragua.
See item no. 218.

The five republics of Central America, their political and economic development and their relations with the United States.
See item no. 220.

Sandino.
See item no. 223.

The United States Marines in Nicaragua.
See item no. 229.

Somoza and the legacy of U.S. involvement in Central America.
See item no. 236.

Influencia de la crisis del 29 en Nicaragua. (Influence of the 1929 depression on Nicaragua.)
See item no. 301.

Human rights and United States policy toward Latin America.
See item no. 315.

Nicaragua.
See item no. 326.

Nicaragua, an ally under siege.
See item no. 349.

Revolution in Nicaragua: another Cuba?
See item no. 361.

Target Nicaragua.
See item no. 365.

The constabulary in the Dominican Republic and Nicaragua: progeny and legacy of United States intervention.
See item no. 368.

The Republic of El Salvador against the Republic of Nicaragua; complaint of the Republic of El Salvador, with appendices.
See item no. 389.

Development assistance in Central America.
See item no. 459.

Masterminding the mini-market: U.S. aid to the Central American Common Market.
See item no. 467.

Interest in a Nicaraguan canal, 1903-1931.
See item no. 549.

The Nicaragua canal and the Monroe Doctrine, a political history of the isthmus transit, with special reference to the Nicaragua canal project and the attitude of the United States government thereto.
See item no. 553.

The adaption of technology in Nicaragua.
See item no. 589.

Soberanía. (Sovereignty.)
See item no. 664.

With Europe

428 **Los alemanes en Nicaragua.** (The Germans in Nicaragua.)
Goetz von Houwald. Managua: Banco de América, 1975.
479p. (Colección Cultural, Serie Histórica, no. 2).
Provides a detailed narrative of Germans who came to Nicaragua from the Conquest (1524) to the present. Discusses their activities, organizations, and influence in the country.

429 **France in Central America: Félix Belly and the Nicaraguan canal.**
Cyril Allen. New York: Pageant Press, 1966. 163p. bibliog.
A useful work on the French agent who sought to get a French canal contract with Nicaragua in the 19th century. Based on the author's PhD dissertation at the University of Minnesota, 1950. See also Allen's article on Belly in the *Hispanic American Historical Review*, vol. 37 (1957), p. 46-59. For Belly's important memoir on Central America, see *A travers l'Amérique Centrale...* (q.v.).

430 **Orígines de la reincorporación nicaragüense de la costa miskita.** (Origins of the Nicaraguan reincorporation of the Miskito Coast.)
Larry K. Laird. *Revista Conservadora del Pensamiento Centroamericano*, vol. 28, no. 140 (May 1972). 57p. map. bibliog.

A translation of the author's University of Kansas 1970 MA thesis, this is a heavily documented account of Nicaragua's recovery of the Miskito Coast at the close of the 19th century. Appendixes include lists of the Miskito kings, British and other foreign businesses on that coast in 1892 and 1900, a table of population, taxes and schools in 1894, and the treaty between Nicaragua and Great Britain of 1905, in which the British finally recognized Nicaraguan sovereignty over the Miskito Coast. Laird documents the influential role of the United States in this episode.

431 **Otnosheniia Rossii so stranami Tsentral'noi Ameriki vo vtoroi polovine XIX veka.** (Relations between Russia and the Central American states in the second half of the 19th century.)
Novaia i Noveishaia Istoriia, vol. 4 (1972), p. 106-19.

A brief group of documents revealing Russian involvement in Central America, 1850-1900. This unsigned article contains information about a little-studied topic not found elsewhere.

432 **La política inglesa en Centro América durante el siglo XIX.** (English policy in Central America during the 19th century.)
Virgilio Rodríguez Beteta. Guatemala City: Editorial del Ministro de Educación Pública 'José de Pineda Ibarra', 1963. 243p.

Anti-British, journalistic tirade, adding little new.

Historia de la Costa de Mosquitos, hasta 1894, en relación con la conquista española, los piratas y corsarios en las costas centroamericanas, los avances y protectorado del gobierno inglés en la misma costa y la famosa cuestión inglesa con Nicaragua, Honduras y El Salvador. (History of the Mosquito Coast, to 1894, in relation to the Spanish conquest, the pirates and corsairs on the Central American coasts, the incursions and protectorate of the English government on the same coast and the famous English question with Nicaragua, Honduras and El Salvador.)
See item no. 157.

The Anglo-Spanish struggle for Mosquitia.
See item no. 160.

The Kemble papers.
See item no. 173.

The British role in Central America prior to the Clayton-Bulwer Treaty of 1850.
See item no. 183.

The mahogany trade as a factor in the British return to the Mosquito shore in the second quarter of the 19th century.
See item no. 199.

1840-1842: los atentados del superintendente de Belice. (1840-1842: the aggressions of the superintendent of Belize.)
See item no. 202.

A Palmerstonian diplomat in Central America: Frederick Chatfield, Esq.
See item no. 206.

Anglo-American diplomatic relations with regard to Nicaragua and Venezuela: February 1894-January 1896.
See item no. 396.

With the United Nations

433 **Las Naciones Unidas en el ámbito centroamericano; guía de estudio.** (The United Nations in the Central American environment; a study guide.)
José Vicente Moreno. San Salvador: Dirección de Cultura, Ministerio de Educación, 1970. 206p. (Colección Estudios y Documentos, no. 31).
Guide to UN activities in Central America.

434 **Yearbook of the United Nations.**
United Nations Office of Public Information. New York: United Nations, 1947- . annual.
Provides an indexed, concise and accurate record of the activities of the UN with reference to its documents. Useful for checking on UN activities related to Nicaragua, such as development assistance, social and health conditions, etc.

Nicaragua: el impacto de la mutación política. (Nicaragua: the impact of the political mutation.)
See item no. 469.

Constitution, Laws and Judicial System

435 **Boletín Estadístico de la Corte Suprema de Justicia.**
(Statistical bulletin of the Supreme Court of Justice.)
Corte Suprema de Justicia, Sección de Estadística y
Publicaciones. Managua: Corte Suprema de Justicia,
1969-72. 10 issues. irregular.
Provides detailed statistics on judicial proceedings in the Nicaraguan Supreme
Court and appellate courts.

436 **Boletín Judicial.** (Judicial bulletin.)
Managua: Departamento de Justicia, 1912-41(?). irregular
(title varies).
Includes sentences and decisions of the Supreme Court and appellate courts of
Nicaragua.

437 **Constitución y leyes de reforma de la República de
Nicaragua, 1893-1894-1895.** (Constitution and reform laws
of the Republic of Nicaragua, 1893-1894-1895.)
Managua: Tipografía Nacional, 1896. 400p.
An important collection of the laws embodying the Liberal Reform inaugurated
by José Santos Zelaya in 1893.

438 **Las constituciones de Nicaragua.** (The constitutions of
Nicaragua.)
Emilio Alvarez Lejarza. Madrid: Ediciones Cultura
Hispánica, 1958. 1,004p. bibliog. notes.
Detailed commentary with texts of Nicaragua's several constitutions.

Constitution, Laws and Judicial System

439 **Constitution of the Republic of Nicaragua, 1974.**
Washington, DC: General Secretariat of the Organization of
American States, 1974. 61p.

An English translation of the last Nicaraguan constitution under the Somozas,
published originally in *La Gaceta* (Managua), no. 89, 24 April 1974. Action by
the Sandinista government has modified much of this constitution. See also *Constitución política: ley de ámparo y ley marcial de la República de Nicaragua*
(Managua, 1975. 160p.).

440 **Jurisprudencia civil nicaragüense.** (Nicaraguan civil
jurisprudence.)
Alejandro Montiel Argüello. Managua: Imprenta Nacional,
1972. 3 vols.

Arranged alphabetically by subject, and chronologically within subjects, these
volumes provide an index to 20th-century court cases with brief synopses of the
content and decisions.

441 **Nuevo diccionario de jurisprudencia nicaragüense.** (New
dictionary of Nicaraguan jurisprudence.)
Juan Huembes y Huembes. Masaya, Nicaragua: Imprenta
Nacional, 1972. 644p.

A substantially enlarged edition of Huembes' *Diccionario de jurisprudencia nicaragüense* (Managua: Editorial Alemana, 1964. 291p.).

442 **Principales leyes económicas y sociales: leyes bancarias y
financieras.** (Principal economic and social laws: banking
and financial laws.)
Banco Central de Nicaragua. Managua: Banco Central de
Nicaragua, 1976-77. 3rd ed. 5 vols.

First published in 1963, this is a very useful guide to the principal economic and
social legislation through 1976.

443 **Recopilación de las leyes, decretos y acuerdos ejecutivos de la
República de Nicaragua, en Centro América.** (Compilation of
the laws, decrees and executive agreements of the Republic
of Nicaragua, in Central America.)
Jesús de la Rocha. Managua: Imprenta del Gobierno,
1867. 6 vols.

Collection of Nicaraguan laws from period 1825-61. See also de la Rocha's
Código de la legislación de la República de Nicaragua, en Centro América
(Code of legislation of the Republic of Nicaragua, in Central America),
Managua: Imprenta El Centro Americano, 1873-74. 2 vols.

444 A statement of the laws of Nicaragua in matters affecting business.

José Antonio Tijerino, Mario Palma Ibarra. Washington, DC: Organization of American States, 1978. 4th ed. 323p.

A very handy survey of Nicaraguan law, with successive chapters on the constitution and form of government, nationality and immigration, rights and duties of foreigners, foreign investments, industrial development, commercial companies, registers, notarial law, bankruptcy and insolvency, contracts and obligations, agency, suretyship, transportation, taxation, labour and social legislation, exploitation of natural resources, agrarian legislation, forestry legislation, water legislation, mining legislation, petroleum legislation, monopolies and exclusive privileges, patents and trademarks, copyright, negotiable instruments, banking, exchange control, insurance, property rights, mortgages and other liens, bailments, succession, marriage and divorce, the family domicile, administration of justice, drug legislation, territorial waters, continental shelf, fishing rights, commercial treaties, and codes in force. While some of this will have been rendered obsolete by the Sandinista revolutionary legislation, the work remains a useful guide to much Nicaraguan law. Hopefully, a 5th edition will soon be forthcoming.

Código de comercio de Nicaragua, concordado y anotado. (Commercial code of Nicaragua, with concordat and annotations.)
See item no. 497.

Administration and Local Government

445 **Gobierno municipal de Nicaragua.** (Municipal government of
Nicaragua.)
Ministerio de Gobernación. Managua: Talleres Nacionales,
1959. 103p.
Publication of basic laws governing municipalities in Nicaragua.

446 **Tax reform in Nicaragua.**
Carlos A. Aguirre, Raymond L. Richman. International
Monetary Fund, Fiscal Affairs Department, 1972. 77p.
This typewritten report indicates 'Restricted circulation, not for public use', but a
copy is available to the public in the Library of the Banco Central de Nicaragua.
Although now dated, especially since the Sandinista revolution, it is most useful
for its discussion of the Nicaraguan tax system. There is also a Spanish edition.

Anuario Estadístico. (Statistical annual.)
See item no. 447.

Statistics

447 **Anuario Estadístico.** (Statistical annual.)
Banco Central de Nicaragua, Ministerio de Economía y
Comercio, Oficina Ejecutiva de Encuestas y
Censos. Managua: Ministerio de Economía y Comercio,
1938- . annual (title varies).
Statistics on population, housing, education, health and social services, employment and salaries, public services, construction, agriculture, industry, banking and
finance. The Banco Central has also issued a biannual *Boletín Estadístico*, and
since October 1977 a monthly *Estadísticas Económicas Mensuales*. Between 1907
and 1938 the Dirección General de Estadística issued a *Boletín de Estadística*
somewhat irregularly.

448 **Anuario Estadístico Centroamericano de Comercio Exterior.**
(Central American statistical annual of external trade.)
Guatemala City: Secretaría Permanente del Tratado General
de Integración (SIECA), 1967- . annual.
Presents detailed statistical data on the trade of the five Central American states.
Publication of this work has been increasingly in arrears. The most recent volume,
published in 1978, covered the period 1972-73.

449 **Compendio Estadístico Centroamericano.** (Central American
statistical compendium.)
Mexico City: United Nations, 1957; New York: United
Nations, 1962; Guatemala City: Secretaría Permanente del
Tratado General de Integración (SIECA), 1963-67. 5 vols.
Compilation of statistics on the Central American Common Market states.
Emphasis is on trade statistics, although other topics are included in the five
volumes published between 1957 and 1963. This series was continued by the
preceding item.

Statistics

450 **Statistical Abstract of Latin America, volume 21.**
Edited by James W. Wilkie. Los Angeles: University of
California, Los Angeles, Latin American Center, 1981.
671p. maps.
Issued more or less annually, this statistical compendium has become a major
reference work for Latin American studies. This latest edition contains 666 statistical tables, showing social, economic and political trends and data. In addition to
the *Statistical Abstract*, the UCLA Latin American Center periodically issues
various topical supplements.

451 **Statistical Yearbook.**
United Nations Department of Economic and Social Affairs,
Statistical Office. New York: United Nations, 1948- .
annual.
This annual contains an enormous variety of statistical information on population,
manpower, agricultural and industrial production, mining, manufacturing, construction, energy, trade, transport, communications, consumption, national
accounts, finance, development assistance, housing, health, education, science and
technology, and culture. Published in English and French. The UN *Statistical
Yearbook* succeeds the *Statistical Yearbook of the League of Nations* (Geneva:
League of Nations, Economic and Financial Section, 1927-44. annual. title
varies), but the amount of information on Central America in the League of
Nations volumes is disappointing in most categories.

452 **Statistical Yearbook for Latin America, 1979.**
United Nations Economic Commission for Latin
America. London: HM Stationery Office; New York:
Unipub. 1981. 457p. New York: International Publishers
Service, 1982. 471p.
Official UN statistics on Latin America on a broad range of topics.

The Caribbean Year Book.
See item no. 3.

Centro América 1982, Análisis Económicos y Políticos Sobre la Región.
(Central America 1982, economic and political analyses of the region.)
See item no. 6.

Centro América, subdesarrollo y dependencia. (Central America,
underdevelopment and dependency.)
See item no. 7.

Datos básicos sobre Nicaragua. (Basic data on Nicaragua.)
See item no. 8.

**A statistical and commercial history of the Kingdom of Guatemala, in
Spanish America. Containing important particulars relative to its
productions, manufactures, customs, & c, an account of its conquest by
the Spaniards, and a narrative of the principal events down to the present
time: from original records in the archives; actual observation; and other
authentic sources.**
See item no. 179.

Central American commerce and maritime activity in the 19th century: sources for a quantitative approach.
See item no. 185.

Censo general de población de la República de Nicaragua, 1950. (General census of the population of the Republic of Nicaragua, 1950.)
See item no. 241.

Censos nacionales 1971. (1971 national census.)
See item no. 243.

Demographic Yearbook.
See item no. 245.

La población de Centroamérica y sus perspectivas. (The population of Central America and its perspectives.)
See item no. 247.

Población de Nicaragua: compendio de las cifras censales y proyecciones por departamentos y municipios, años 1971-1980. (Population of Nicaragua: a compendium of census figures and projections for departments and municipalities, 1971-1980.)
See item no. 249.

World handbook of political and social indicators.
See item no. 299.

Estadísticas del desarrollo social de Nicaragua, 1960-1967 y proyecciones, 1968-1972. (Statistics on the social development of Nicaragua, 1960-1967, and projections for 1968-1972.)
See item no. 305.

Development assistance in Central America.
See item no. 459.

Economic integration in Central America.
See item no. 461.

Indicadores Económicas de Nicaragua. (Nicaraguan economic indicators.)
See item no. 465.

Plan nacional de reconstrucción y desarrollo, 1975-1979. (National plan for reconstruction and development, 1975-1979.)
See item no. 471.

Yearbook of National Account Statistics.
See item no. 483.

Boletín Anual. (Annual bulletin.)
See item no. 485.

Informe Anual. (Annual report.)
See item no. 492.

Comercio Exterior de Nicaragua. (Foreign trade of Nicaragua.)
See item no. 498.

FAO Trade Yearbook.
See item no. 501.

Yearbook of International Trade Statistics.
See item no. 507.

Yearbook of Forest Products Statistics.
See item no. 518.

Statistics

Diagnóstica socio-económico del sector agropecuario. (Socio-economic diagnosis of the agricultural and grazing sector.)
See item no. 526.

FAO Production Yearbook.
See item no. 528.

Tenencia de la tierra y desarrollo rural en Centroamérica. (Land tenure and rural development in Central America.)
See item no. 543.

Road user charges in Central America.
See item no. 558.

Labor law and practice in Nicaragua.
See item no. 564.

Statistics for the analysis of the education sector: Nicaragua.
See item no. 587.

Economics

453 The banana empire: a case study of economic imperialism.
Charles David Kepner, Jr., Jay Henry Soothill. New York:
Vanguard Press, 1935. 392p. bibliog. Reprinted, New York:
Russell & Russell, 1967.
Classic attack on the banana companies as examples of economic imperialism.
Highly critical of the United Fruit Company, this study provides a basic frame-
work of what the harmful effects of the banana industry were on early 20th-
century Central America.

454 Bibliografía económica selectiva de Nicaragua. (Selective
economic bibliography of Nicaragua.)
Managua: Biblioteca y Servicios de Información, Banco
Central de Nicaragua, Oct.-Dec. 1980. 30p. (Bibliografía
Corta no. 23).
Based on books in the library of the Banco Central, this list of about 400 items
interprets 'economy' broadly and includes many historical works, travel accounts
and other works that comment on the Nicaraguan economy. Most of the works
are in Spanish and much of the list is taken up with the voluminous publications
of the Banco Central and other government offices.

455 Caribbean Basin Economic Survey.
Edited by Donald Baer. Atlanta, Georgia: Federal Reserve
Bank of Atlanta, 1975-81. quarterly. 7 vols.
This useful quarterly newsletter focused on the economic development of Central
America and the Caribbean. Specific coverage of Nicaragua was uncommon, but
Nicaragua was included in the frequent topical articles on the whole region.
Ceased publication in 1981.

456 Central America: regional integration and economic development.

Roger D. Hansen. Washington, DC: National Planning Association, 1967. 106p. (Studies in Development Progress, no. 1).

A non-technical description of the Central American Common Market with emphasis on the problems facing the integration movement.

457 Central American economic integration, the politics of unequal benefits.

Stuart Fagan. Berkeley, California: Institute of International Studies, University of California, 1970. 79p. bibliog. (Research Series no. 15).

Reviews the history of the CACM in the 1960s and then analyses the resulting unequal benefits in the balances of payments of member countries. Specifically, he examines the cases of Honduras' demand for preferential treatment and the balance of payments difficulties and fiscal shortages of Costa Rica and Nicaragua. This study provides the material for seriously evaluating the possibilities of adaptation, reformulation of attitudes and expectations, and redefining regional tasks in response to continuing crises.

458 Desarrollo económico y político de Nicaragua, 1912-1947.

(Economic and political development of Nicaragua, 1912-1947.)

Marco Antonio Valle Martínez. San José: CSUCA (Consejo Superior Universitario Centroamericano), 1976. 208p. (Serie Tesis de Grado, no. 1).

This licenciatura thesis at the University of Costa Rica provides an excellent analysis and description of the political and economic development of Nicaragua during the first half of the 20th century.

459 Development assistance in Central America.

John F. McCamant. New York: Praeger, 1968. 351p.

An excellent description of the multiplicity of foreign and international agencies involved in Central America and the nature of their activities. The work includes a considerable amount of statistical information and is useful for understanding the degree of involvement of the United States in internal Central American development.

460 The economic development of Nicaragua.

International Bank for Reconstruction and Development. Baltimore, Maryland: Johns Hopkins University Press, for the IBRD, 1953. 424p.

Prepared by the IBRD at the request of the Nicaraguan government, this is the most thorough study of the Nicaraguan economy in the mid-20th century. It examines and evaluates the economic potential of the country, development programmes, investments, agriculture, industry, energy, transportation and communication, and the fiscal system, and recommends substantial reforms. Much of the policy of the Somoza régime since the 1950s was based on this report.

461 Economic integration in Central America.
Edited by William R. Cline, Enrique Delgado. Washington, DC: Brookings Institution, 1978. 712p.

Jointly sponsored by the Brookings Institution and by the Secretariat for Economic Integration in Central America (SIECA), this mammoth study contains a great deal of information and analysis on the integration movement in the last decade. A basic source for any study of the Central American Common Market and the integration movement.

462 The economy of Nicaragua.
Richard W. O. Lethander. PhD dissertation, Duke University, 1968. 414p. bibliog. (Available from University Microfilms, Ann Arbor, Michigan, order no. 69-9462).

A thorough examination of the Nicaraguan economic system in the 1950s and 1960s. Includes chapters on natural resources, the transportation system, population and labour force, economic structure, agriculture, industry, trade, the tax system, and the financial system.

463 External financing of the Nicaraguan development experiment.
Robert P. Vichas. PhD dissertation, University of Florida, 1967. 206p. bibliog. (Available from University Microfilms, Ann Arbor, Michigan, order no. 68-9572).

An important study of foreign investment in Nicaragua during the Somoza years.

464 Family and other business groups in economic development: the case of Nicaragua.
Harry W. Strachan. New York: Praeger, 1976. 129p.

A useful and careful study of the principal business groups operating in the Nicaraguan economy in the 1960s and early '70s and their implications for business administration.

465 Indicadores Económicas de Nicaragua. (Nicaraguan economic indicators.)
Departamento de Estudios Económicos. Managua: Departamento de Estudios Económicos, 1975-78. irregular (title varies slightly).

Detailed statistical tables on Nicaraguan population, agricultural and industrial production, currency and banking, finance, trade, construction and services.

Economics

466 **La integración de Centroamérica.** (Central American
integration.)
Félix Guillermo Fernández-Shaw y Baldasano. Madrid:
Ediciones Cultura Hispánica, 1965. 1,086p.

Valuable for early years of the integration movement, this work contains commentary on and reprints of many documents of the period. It is heavily documented.

467 **Masterminding the mini-market: U.S. aid to the Central
American Common Market.**
Suzanne Jonas. *Latin America and Empire Report*, vol. 7,
no. 5 (May-June 1973), p. 3-21. bibliog.

Leftist view of extensive US involvement in the common market, arguing that development of a market for US goods is more important to US policy than real regional development. See also in the same issue 'The U.S. investment bubble in Central America', p. 23-29, which documents the expanding US investment in agro-exports.

468 **Nicaragua.**
American Embassy, Managua. *Foreign Economic Trends
and Their Implications for the United States*, no. 81-122
(Nov. 1981). 12p. (US Department of Commerce,
Marketing Information Series).

Surveys the Nicaraguan economic situation, production of specific commodities and minerals, and commerce. Notes commercial and investment opportunities. These reports, prepared by the US embassy in Managua, are published about once a year.

469 **Nicaragua: el impacto de la mutación política.** (Nicaragua:
the impact of the political mutation.)
Comisión Económica para América Latina. Santiago de
Chile: United Nations, 1981. 126p.

Surveys the enormous damage to the Nicaraguan economy caused by the civil war of 1978-79 and describes the plans for reconstruction and rehabilitation, both in terms of Nicaraguan programmes and international assistance. Appendixes, p. 105-26, contain the Nicaraguan junta's plan for reconstruction and the resolutions by the Economic Commission for Latin America and the United Nations General Assembly. See also, published in both English and Spanish, *International cooperation: the complement of our effort to rebuild Nicaragua* (Managua: Fondo Internacional Para la Reconstrucción, 1982. 30p.).

470 **Plan de reactivación económica en beneficio del pueblo.** (Plan
for economic reactivation for the public benefit.)
Ministerio de Planificación. Managua: Centro de
Publicaciones de la Secretaría Nacional de Propaganda y
Educación Política del FSLN, 1980. 142p.

This is the basic Sandinista plan for development of the country following the overthrow of Somoza. See also *Programa económica de austeridad*, listed below.

471 **Plan nacional de reconstrucción y desarrollo, 1975-1979.**
(National plan for reconstruction and development,
1975-1979.)
Dirección de Planificación Nacional.   Managua: Consejo de
Planificación Nacional, 1975. 2 vols.
Plan of the Somoza government for continued reconstruction and development of
Nicaragua after the devastating earthquake of 1972.

472 **Politics and planners; economic development in Central
America.**
Gary Wynia.   Madison, Wisconsin: University of Wisconsin
Press, 1972. 227p. bibliog.
A study of public policy making in Central America, with considerable attention
to Nicaragua. Emphasizes the contrast between Nicaragua and Costa Rica.

473 **Las primeras bases de infraestructura en Nicaragua,
1875-1936.** (The first foundations of infrastructure in
Nicaragua, 1875-1936.)
Cristina Chamorro B.   Managua: Universidad
Centroamericana, Facultad de Humanidades, 1976. 93p.
Although not entirely exhaustive of available sources, this scholarly examination
of the foundations of infrastructure in Nicaragua is a useful contribution to the
economic history of the country.

474 **Programa económica de austeridad y eficiencia, 1981.**
(Economic programme of austerity and efficiency, 1981.)
Managua: Ministerio de Planificación, 1981. 180p.
The Planning Ministry's report on economic measures necessary to get Nicar-
agua's economy on its feet again. A similar report was published in 1980 under
the title *Plan de reactivación económica en beneficio del pueblo* (see above).

475 **Quarterly Economic Review of Nicaragua, Costa Rica,
Panama.**
London: Economist Intelligence Unit, 1974- . quarterly.
Concise and informative review of the economy of these countries. An excellent
source for up-to-date trends on Nicaragua's economy. Supersedes the *Quarterly
Economic Report of Central America.*

476 **Report on the Central American national development plans
and the process of economic integration.**
Inter-American Economic and Social Council, Committee of
Nine.   Washington, DC: Pan American Union, 1966. 170p.
Pessimistic evaluation of the integration effort, noting the failure of the pro-
gramme to significantly improve prosperity in the region.

Economics

477 **La revolución liberal en la historia económica de Nicaragua.**
(The liberal revolution in Nicaraguan economic history.)
José S. Quant Varela. Licenciatura thesis, Universidad
Autónoma de Nicaragua, Managua, 1975. 109p. bibliog.

Although limited in scope, this thesis is useful in its documentation of the very
substantial economic change that occurred in Nicaragua under the Zelaya régime
(1893-1909), especially in terms of increased exports and increased foreign debt.

478 **Seguros.** (Insurance.)
Managua: Biblioteca y Servicios de Información, Banco
Central de Nicaragua, April-May 1979. 19p. (Bibliografía
Corta no. 13).

The series of disasters that has befallen Nicaragua in the past decade (the earthquake of 1972, the 1978-79 civil war, and the 1982 flood) has made insurance
especially important to the Nicaraguan economy and society. Many of the items
listed in this bibliography deal with insurance in general or in other countries, but
a considerable number focus on Nicaragua. The bibliography, including both
books and articles but limited to items in the library of the Banco Central, is
organized topically, except for a section (p. 15-19) listing chronologically articles
from the Nicaraguan daily press dealing with damages and insurance claims
during the civil war.

479 **Situación económica y alianzas políticas.** (The economic
situation and political alliances.)
Donald Castillo. *Revista Mexicana de Sociología*, vol. 42
(1980), p. 501-21.

Reviews Nicaragua's economic situation, its economic ties to the United States,
and the trend from private sector to public sector development since the Sandinista take-over. A well-documented and informative treatment.

480 **Supply and demand for Nicaraguan milk and dairy products:
1958-1977 period. An econometric analysis.**
Manuel Antonio Vanegas-Fonseca. PhD dissertation,
University of Minnesota, 1982. (Available from University
Microfilms, Ann Arbor, Michigan, order no 82-21344).

Quantifies economic, social, demographic and institutional factors that have
affected the supply of and consumer demand for milk and dairy products during
the period stated. Concludes that consumption and retail prices of dairy products
are related to farm prices, energy costs, and hourly earnings of farm workers,
although the responses of retail prices to the last two variables are small.

481 **Taxes and tax harmonization in Central America.**
Virginia G. Watkins. Cambridge, Massachusetts: Law
School of Harvard University, 1967. 519p. bibliog.

A major work on tax programmes within the Central American integration movement. Separate chapters also deal with each country, and although the Sandinista
revolution has reduced the value of the chapter on Nicaragua (p. 373-433), it
may still have some utility. It is based on tax law in effect in Nicaragua on 31
December 1965.

482 The United Fruit Company in Latin America.
Stacy May, Galo Plaza. Washington, DC: National
Planning Association, 1958, reprinted 1976. 263p. (American
Business Abroad Series).
A defence of the United Fruit Company against widespread criticism of its opera-
tions. Published as a case study of American business performance overseas, this
is a sympathetic description of one of the most important of all US business
enterprises ever to operate in Central America.

483 Yearbook of National Account Statistics.
United Nations Department of Economic and Social Affairs,
Statistical Office. New York: United Nations, 1957- .
annual.
Detailed national accounts estimates, total and per capita gross national products,
national incomes, and other economic data on income and expenditures. These
annual volumes provide much information on the condition and growth of the
Nicaraguan economy, but the information is not complete in all categories.

Area handbook for Nicaragua.
See item no. 2.

The Caribbean Year Book.
See item no. 3.

The Central American republics.
See item no. 5.

Centro América 1982, Análisis Económicos y Políticos Sobre la Región.
(Central America 1982, economic and political analyses of the region.)
See item no. 6.

Dollars and dictators, a guide to Central America.
See item no. 9.

**Exposición sumaria de viajes y trabajos geográficos sobre Nicaragua
durante el siglo XIX.** (Summary description of travels and geographic
works on Nicaragua during the 19th century.)
See item no. 69.

**The prehistoric and modern subsistence patterns of the Atlantic coast of
Nicaragua. A comparison.**
See item no. 134.

**The five republics of Central America, their political and economic
development and their relations with the United States.**
See item no. 220.

Ensayos nicaragüenses. (Nicaraguan essays.)
See item no. 274.

Imperialismo y dictadura. Crisis de una formación social. (Imperialism
and dictatorship. The crisis of a social structure.)
See item no. 300.

Influencia de la crisis del 29 en Nicaragua. (Influence of the 1929
depression on Nicaragua.)
See item no. 301.

Economics

Interpretación del desarrollo social centroamericano, procesos y estructuras de una sociedad dependiente. (Interpretation of Central American social development, processes and structures of a dependent society.)
See item no. 302.

Development and dictatorship in Nicaragua, 1950-1960.
See item no. 323.

Nicaragua.
See item no. 326.

Defending the revolution.
See item no. 369.

Autonomy or dependence as regional integration outcomes: Central America.
See item no. 381.

Central American regional integration.
See item no. 382.

Regional integration in Central America.
See item no. 388.

The rise and fall of the Central American Common Market.
See item no. 390.

Fiscal intervention in Nicaragua.
See item no. 403.

Tax reform in Nicaragua.
See item no. 446.

Anuario Estadístico. (Statistical annual.)
See item no. 447.

Anuario Estadístico Centroamericano de Comercio Exterior. (Central American statistical annual of external trade.)
See item no. 448.

Compendio Estadístico Centroamericano. (Central American statistical compendium.)
See item no. 449.

Aspectos históricos de la moneda en Nicaragua. (Historical aspects of Nicaraguan currency.)
See item no. 484.

Boletín Anual. (Annual bulletin.)
See item no. 485.

Cuentas nacionales de Nicaragua, 1960-1972. (National accounts of Nicaragua, 1960-1972.)
See item no. 489.

The determinants of direct foreign investment in the Central American Common Market, 1954-1970.
See item no. 490.

Informe Anual. (Annual report.)
See item no. 492.

Nicaragua's debt renegotiation.
See item no. 493.

The Central American Common Market: economic policies, economic growth, and choices for the future.
See item no. 496.

Economic integration in Central America, empirical investigations.
See item no. 500.

Growth and integration in Central America.
See item no. 503.

Instruments relating to the economic integration of Latin America.
See item no. 505.

Tropical agribusiness structures and adjustments - bananas.
See item no. 544.

Road user charges in Central America.
See item no. 558.

Investment, Finance, Banking and Currency

484 Aspectos históricos de la moneda en Nicaragua. (Historical aspects of Nicaraguan currency.)
Luís Cuadra Cea. Managua: Banco Central de Nicaragua, 1963. 2 vols. in 1. 150p.

A history of Nicaraguan currency. See also *The coins and paper money of Nicaragua*, listed below.

485 Boletín Anual. (Annual bulletin.)
Departamento de Estudios Económicos, Banco Central de Nicaragua. Managua: Banco Central de Nicaragua, 1977- . annual.

Preceded by *Boletín Semestral* (Biennial bulletin), vols. 1-6 (1971-76); *Boletín Trimestral* (Quarterly bulletin), vols. 1-10 (1961-70); *Revista Trimestral* (Quarterly review), vols. 1-5 (1961-65); and the *Revista* (Review), vols. 1-23 (1936-60). These regular publications of the Banco Central contain data on finance and the economy, including many statistical tables. The Department of Economic Studies has also published a *Carta Quincenal* (Fortnightly newsletter) from June 1974 forward.

486 Business Latin America.
New York: Business International Corporation, 1966- . weekly.

The best weekly report on Latin American business. Well-researched and objective coverage, with considerable attention to Nicaragua.

134

487 **Central American currency and finance.**
John Parke Young. Princeton, New Jersey: Princeton
University Press, 1925. 258p.

This work is too old to be of great use in terms of contemporary currency and
finance, but it does help to explain many Central American financial difficulties
of the past. It is especially useful for its account of the relation between the
foreign bankers and Nicaragua in the early 20th century.

488 **The coins and paper money of Nicaragua.**
Brian Stickney, Alcedo F. Almanzar. USA, 1974. 63p.
bibliog.

A catalogue of Nicaraguan coinage and paper money with photos and market
values. Also contains considerable historical commentary on the money. See also
the first item in this chapter, and Guillermo de la Rocha, *Breve ensayo sobre la
numismática nicaragüense* (Brief essay on Nicaraguan numismatics), Managua:
Editorial Universitaria, Universidad Autónoma de Nicaragua, 1976. 116p.

489 **Cuentas nacionales de Nicaragua, 1960-1972.** (National
accounts of Nicaragua, 1960-1972.)
Departamento de Estudios Económicos, Banco Central de
Nicaragua. Managua: Banco Central, 1973. unpaginated.

Provides annual statistical tables on government expenditures, receipts, etc.

490 **The determinants of direct foreign investment in the Central
American Common Market, 1954-1970.**
Carmine R. Torrisi. PhD dissertation, Syracuse University,
1976. 222p. bibliog. (Available from University Microfilms,
Ann Arbor, Michigan, order no. 77-24413).

A useful study of the common market, 1954-70, and its relations to foreign
investment.

491 **Industrial finance in Nicaragua: a study of financial practice
in an underdeveloped economy.**
José Nicolas Marín X. Unpublished Harvard University
PhD thesis, 1971. 175p. bibliog. (Not available from
University Microfilms).

492 **Informe Anual.** (Annual report.)
Banco Central de Nicaragua. Managua: Banco Central de
Nicaragua, 1961- . annual.

Provides a review of the Nicaraguan and world economy and banking, followed
by detailed statistical tables on currency, banking, finance and economic indicators.

493 Nicaragua's debt renegotiation.
R. S. Weinert. *Cambridge Journal of Economics*, vol. 5 (June 1981), p. 187-94.

Describes the background to and the terms of settlement stemming from a year of negotiations and restructuring of about US$580 million of debt contracted by the Somoza government. Weinert also discusses the precedent set in these settlements and its relation to the international financial system.

494 Principal investment laws in Nicaragua.
Managua: Banco Central de Nicaragua, 1976. 52p.

An informative guide to the prospective investor, but the Sandinista revolution has probably made much of its contents obsolete. Prospective investors should secure current information from Nicaraguan consulates.

Dollars and dictators, a guide to Central America.
See item no. 9.

Principales leyes económicas y sociales: leyes bancarias y financieras.
(Principal economic and social laws: banking and financial laws.)
See item no. 442.

Anuario Estadístico. (Statistical annual.)
See item no. 447.

Nicaragua.
See item no. 468.

Trade and Commerce

495 **A case study of an international development project: the
Instituto Nacional de Comercio Exterior y Interior in Ciudad
Sandino, Nicaragua.**
R. G. Kirschenheiter. PhD dissertation, Michigan State
University, 1980. 336p. bibliog. (Available from University
Microfilms, Ann Arbor, Michigan, order no. 81-12104).
Evaluates an international development grain drying and storage project using a
wide variety of methods, including interviews with peasants and other partici-
pants. Concludes that the INCEI failed to meet the needs of the farmers over a
six-year period and had no significant impact on the lives of the rural population.
The stabilization of the market price for corn and beans in Nicaragua, the
primary objective of the INCEI programme, never became a reality.

496 **The Central American Common Market: economic policies,
economic growth, and choices for the future.**
Donald H. McClelland. New York: Praeger, 1972. 243p.
(Praeger Special Studies in International Economic
Development).
Contains a useful survey of the common market as well as policy assessments.
See also Browning's *The rise and fall of the Central American Common Market*
(q.v.).

497 **Código de comercio de Nicaragua, concordado y anotado.**
(Commercial code of Nicaragua, with concordat and
annotations.)
Edited by Aníbal Solórzano. Managua: Tipografía Ansel,
1969. 287p.
A guide to commercial law in Nicaragua.

498 **Comercio Exterior de Nicaragua.** (Foreign trade of
Nicaragua.)
Managua: Banco Central de Nicaragua, 1967-79. annual
(title varies slightly).
Annual report on Nicaraguan foreign trade with detailed statistical tables. There
has been no issue since 1979, although the series has not been formally disconti-
nued.

499 **Directorio de exportadores - Export directory, 1977-78.**
Centro Nicaragüense de Promoción de
Exportaciones. Managua: EDIPSA, 1978. 174p.
A directory, in English and Spanish, of Nicaraguan exporters and commercial
agents, with an alphabetical index of export products, a list of offices and agencies connected with Nicaragua's foreign trade, economic indicators, and laws
relating to foreign investment in Nicaragua. Although the Sandinista revolution
will have made some of the data in this useful guide obsolete, it continues to have
some value until a more up-to-date guide is published.

500 **Economic integration in Central America, empirical
investigations.**
Jeffrey B. Nugent. Baltimore, Maryland: Johns Hopkins
University Press, 1974. 209p. bibliog.
A quantitative study of the Central American Common Market experience, highly
technical, providing a theoretical analysis of customs unions and testing the Central American experience against it. Concludes that benefits from the CACM
have been substantial. Bibliography contains extensive listing of theoretical literature on customs unions.

501 **FAO Trade Yearbook.**
Food and Agriculture Organization. Rome: FAO, 1947- .
annual.
Annual statistics on the volume and value of trade in agricultural products,
agricultural equipment and materials.

502 **Free trade in manufactures: the Central American experience.**
L. Willmore. *Economic Development and Cultural Change,*
vol. 20 (July 1972), p. 659-70.
Demonstrates that most of the inter-regional trade in Central America is com-
posed of manufactured goods and points to the Common Market's role in
encouraging industry. Especially useful for its analysis of Central American
manufacturing as export-oriented industries.

503 **Growth and integration in Central America.**
Carlos M. Castillo. New York: Praeger, 1966. 188p.
bibliog. (Praeger Special Studies in International Economics
and Development).
An important study of the Common Market experience by a US-trained Costa
Rican economist. Describes in clear terms the goals and operations of the CACM

through 1965, and looks optimistically toward economic integration as a means toward more satisfactory political development in Central America.

504 **A guide to market data in Central America.**
Lawrence C. Lockley. Tegucigalpa, Honduras: Central American Bank for Economic Integration, 1964. 162p. bibliog.

Although now badly dated, this is a handy guide to basic marketing data for Central America, providing information on a wide variety of economic topics including resources, energy, transportation, communications, banking, manufacturing, trade, laws regarding business, labour laws, social security, industrial sites, organization, investment opportunities and procedures, warehousing, advertising, etc. Many statistical tables accompany the text.

505 **Instruments relating to the economic integration of Latin America.**
Inter-American Institute of International Legal Studies. Dobbs Ferry, New York: Oceana Publications, 1968. 452p. bibliog.

A valuable reference work, since it contains the principal treaties, protocols, resolutions, agreements, etc. relating to the Central American Common Market, as well as a very extensive bibliography.

506 **Tropical enterprise: the Standard Fruit and Steamship Company in Latin America.**
Thomas L. Karnes. Baton Rouge, Louisiana: Louisiana State University Press, 1978. 332p. bibliog.

A careful and enlightening history of the Standard Fruit Company in Central America, revealing considerable difference from the behaviour of the more powerful United Fruit Company. See also Karnes' 'La Standard Fruit y Steamship Company en Nicaragua (los primeros años)' (The Standard Fruit and Steamship Company in Nicaragua, the first years), *Anuario de Estudios Centroamericanos*, vol. 3 (1977), p. 175-213.

507 **Yearbook of International Trade Statistics.**
United Nations Department of International Economic and Social Affairs, Statistical Office. New York: United Nations, 1951- . annual.

Annual compilation of international trade statistics by countries and by commodities. Shows what Nicaragua imported and exported and to and from which countries.

Area handbook for Nicaragua.
See item no. 2.

Central American commerce and maritime activity in the 19th century: sources for a quantitative approach.
See item no. 185.

Estructuras socioeconómicas, poder y estado en Nicaragua, de 1821 a 1875. (Socio-economic structures, power and the state in Nicaragua,

1821-1875.)
See item no. 189.

Anuario Estadístico. (Statistical annual.)
See item no. 447.

Central America: regional integration and economic development.
See item no. 456.

Central American economic integration, the politics of unequal benefits.
See item no. 457.

Economic integration in Central America.
See item no. 461.

Family and other business groups in economic development: the case of Nicaragua.
See item no. 464.

La integración de Centroamérica. (Central American integration.)
See item no. 466.

The determinants of direct foreign investment in the Central American Common Market, 1954-1970.
See item no. 490.

Regional industrial development in Central America. A case study of the integration industries scheme.
See item no. 513.

Agriculture and trade of Nicaragua.
See item no. 521.

State and private marketing arrangements in the agricultural export industries: the case of Nicaragua's coffee and cotton.
See item no. 541.

Tropical agribusiness structures and adjustments - bananas.
See item no. 544.

Business directory of Nicaragua.
See item no. 671.

Industry and Mining

508 **Catálogo de dulces típicos nicaragüenses.** (Catalogue of
typical Nicaraguan sweets.)
Managua: Laboratorio de Tecnología de Alimentos, Banco
Central de Nicaragua, 1978. 83p.
Describes sixty-five Nicaraguan desserts and sweets, with detailed information
regarding ingredients, place of manufacture and nutritional content, with a colour
photo of each.

509 **Directorio Industrial 1977.** (Industrial directory 1977.)
Managua: Oficina Ejecutiva de Encuestas y Censos, 1978.
191p.
Lists industrial establishments in Nicaragua and their addresses. The list is organ-
ized in categories of industrial production, with a separate list for each product.
This is the last of these guides published to date.

510 **Gold mining in the Nicaraguan rain forest.**
J. J. Parsons. *Yearbook of the Association of Pacific
Coast Geographers*, vol. 17 (1955), p. 49-55. map.
A brief but informative article on Nicaraguan gold mining, highly important to
both the regional and national economy.

511 **La industria en Nicaragua.** (Industry in Nicaragua.)
Biblioteca y Servicios de Información, Banco Central de
Nicaragua. Managua: Banco Central de Nicaragua, Feb.
1978. 12p. bibliog. (Mini-bibliografía no. 3).
A bibliographical guide to industrial development in Nicaragua just before the
fall of the Somoza dynasty.

Industry and Mining

512 Informe sobre la industria de materiales para la construcción en Centroamérica. (Report on the construction materials industry in Central America.)
Instituto Centroamericano de Investigación y Tecnología Industrial. Guatemala City: INCAITI, 1965. 5 vols.
Contains a great deal of detail on construction companies and materials available in Central America.

513 Regional industrial development in Central America. A case study of the integration industries scheme.
David E. Ramsett. New York: Praeger, 1969. 136p.
A pessimistic report on the effectiveness of this programme for stimulating industrial development.

Area handbook for Nicaragua.
See item no. 2.

Anuario Estadístico. (Statistical annual.)
See item no. 447.

Industrial finance in Nicaragua: a study of financial practice in an underdeveloped economy.
See item no. 491.

Free trade in manufactures: the Central American experience.
See item no. 502.

Forestry

514 **An appraisal of the wood characteristics and potential uses of some Nicaraguan timbers.**
Gerd Behrendt, J. D. Brazier, G. L. Franklin. Rome: Food and Agriculture Organization, 1967. 86p. bibliog.
This handy reference work identifies the trees of Nicaragua, describes their wood, and classifies their possible uses. A Spanish translation was published in Managua by the Banco Central de Nicaragua in 1968.

515 **Mahogany of tropical America: its ecology and management.**
F. Bruce Lamb. Ann Arbor, Michigan: University of Michigan Press, 1966. 220p. maps. bibliog.
A careful study of the mahogany industry, describing the characteristics and management of mahogany logging throughout tropical America. The work includes discussion of the history of the industry as well as its practices, ecology and management. See also Lamb's excellent bibliography, 'A selected, annotated bibliography on mahogany', *Caribbean Forester*, vol. 20, no. 1-2 (1959), p. 17-37.

516 **The mahogany tree: its botanical characters, qualities and uses, with practical suggestions for selecting and cutting it in the region of its growth, in the West Indies and Central America, with notices of the projected interoceanic communications of Panama, Nicaragua, and Tehuantepec, in relation to their productions, and the supply of fine timber for shipbuilding and all other purposes.**
Chaloner and Fleming. Liverpool, England: Rockliff; London: Effingham Wilson, 1850. 117p. map.
A fascinating volume describing and promoting the mahogany industry, especially in Belize, but it also contains some information on Nicaragua.

517 **The upland pine forests of Nicaragua, a study in cultural plant geography.**
William M. Denevan. Berkeley & Los Angeles: University of California Press, 1961. 82p. maps. bibliog. (University of California Publications in Geography, vol. 12, no. 4, p. 251-320, plates 21-32).
Describes the Nicaraguan pine forests and their relation to human activities. Concludes that this forest is a man-made formation resulting from the clearing of broad-leaf forests and repeated burning. The pines occur only in areas of long-continued, permanent settlement. Considers geographic and economic implications of these conclusions.

518 **Yearbook of Forest Products Statistics.**
Food and Agriculture Organization, Forestry Division. Rome: FAO, 1946- . annual.
Statistics on forest production and exports.

Agriculture

519 **Agricultural land use and farming practice in the Managua region of Nicaragua.**
George Phillip Patten. PhD dissertation, Northwestern University, 1955. 288p. bibliog. (Available from University Microfilms, Ann Arbor, Michigan, order no. 00-13125).
Describes agricultural potential, activity and production in the Managua region, and recommends means of improvement.

520 **Agricultural settlement and development in eastern Nicaragua.**
James R. Taylor, Jr. PhD dissertation, University of Wisconsin, 1968. 205p. bibliog. (Available from University Microfilms, Ann Arbor, Michigan, order no. 69-1010).
Evaluates government-sponsored and spontaneous colonization of public lands in eastern Nicaragua under the 1963 agrarian reform law. Looks specifically at the Rigoberto Cabezas project in the township of Rama in the Department of Zelaya. Notes the dual nature of agriculture there, export-oriented and subsistence, and the problems connected with its development.

521 **Agriculture and trade of Nicaragua.**
Mary Susan Conyer. Washington, DC: Foreign Agricultural Service, US Department of Agriculture, 1960. 20p.
One of a series of such pamphlets published by the US Department of Agriculture on foreign agriculture and trade, this one contains considerable information. It is now, of course, rather dated.

Agriculture

522 **Analysis of objectives of the development of the agricultural frontier of Nicaragua.**
Harry E. Brautigam. PhD dissertation, University of Illinois, 1980. 240p. bibliog. (Available from University Microfilms, Ann Arbor, Michigan, order no. 80-26458).
Studies productive organization that would result in maximizing economic and social benefits on the Nicaraguan agricultural frontier, a region encompassing a third of the country's underdeveloped agricultural land and about 10 per cent of its population.

523 **Aspectos fundamentales de la reforma agraria en Nicaragua: ensayo político-económico social.** (Fundamental aspects of agrarian reform in Nicaragua: an essay in socio-political economy.)
José Córdoba Boniche. Mexico City: Costa-Amic, 1963. 190p. bibliog.
Includes the text of the Nicaraguan agrarian reform law of 1963.

524 **Breve historia de la tenencia de tierra en Nicaragua.** (Brief history of land tenure in Nicaragua.)
Francisco Pérez Estrada. *Nicaragua Indígena*, no. 47 (1969), p. 13-34.
A survey of land tenure in Nicaragua, noting major land laws and practices through the mid-20th century. A useful introduction to a topic that needs further research.

525 **Dairying in Nicaragua.**
George F. Patten. *Annals of the American Association of Geographers*, vol. 61, no. 2 (1971), p. 303-15.
Illustrated with plates and tables, this is a scholarly investigation of the Nicaraguan dairy industry with analyses of its development.

526 **Diagnóstica socio-económico del sector agropecuario.**
(Socio-economic diagnosis of the agricultural and grazing sector.)
Centro de Investigaciones y Estudios Para la Reforma Agraria. Managua: Ministerio de Desarrollo Agropecuario y Reforma Agraria, Dec. 1980. 16 vols.
A detailed research report on the agricultural situation in each Nicaraguan department (county), compiled to assist the government in implementing the agrarian reform programme. These volumes are full of statistical data on each department's production, area, population, etc. The Agrarian Reform Research and Study Centre (CIERA), located in Las Colinas, Managua, continues to publish informative bulletins on the agrarian situation.

527 **Dictionary of tropical American crops and their diseases.**
Frederick Lovejoy Wellman. Metuchen, New Jersey:
Scarecrow Press, 1977. 495p.
An important reference work.

528 **FAO Production Yearbook.**
Food and Agriculture Organization. Rome: Basic Data
Unit, Statistical Division, FAO, 1947- . annual.
Statistics on agricultural and livestock production, land use, population, means of
production and prices. Formerly part 1 of the *Yearbook of Food and Agricultural
Statistics*.

529 **Indigenous tropical agriculture in Central America: land use,
systems, and problems.**
Craig L. Dozier. Washington, DC: National Academy of
Sciences, National Research Council, 1958. 134p. map.
This survey of Central American agriculture and land use is intended only as an
introduction to the subject and it is now dated, but it is still a useful overview.

530 **An inquiry concerning the growth of cotton farming in
Nicaragua.**
Pedro Belli. PhD dissertation, University of California,
Berkeley, 1968. 140p. (Available from University
Microfilms, Ann Arbor, Michigan, order no. 69-14842).
Very useful not only for its discussion of the growth of the cotton industry in
Nicaragua, but also as a general economic history of Nicaragua in the 20th
century.

531 **Land tenure in Nicaragua.**
Alfonso Blandón. Unpublished MS thesis, University of
Florida, Gainesville, 1962. 111p. map. bibliog. (Not
available from University Microfilms).
Describes land use patterns and calls for a comprehensive agrarian reform programme that would encompass improvements in the educational system, public
health, technical assistance to farmers, agricultural credit and the marketing
system. Emphasizes the need for adequate financing of any agrarian reform.
Includes extensive statistical appendixes.

532 **Man, crops and pests in Central America.**
G. Ordish. Oxford, England: Pergamon Press; New York:
Macmillan, 1964. 119p.
A handbook of agriculture in Central America, with particular reference to pests,
diseases and their control. A chapter on pesticides is included. Specific attention
to Nicaragua is not extensive, but much of the general material in this volume
applies to Nicaragua. This work should also be of interest to economists and
sociologists.

533 **Marketing adjustments to production modernization: the case of the Nicaraguan rice industry.**
James E. Austin. Managua: Instituto Centroamericano de Administración de Empresas (INCAE), 1972. various paginations.
The author's DBA thesis at Harvard University makes an important contribution to understanding the mechanics of the Nicaraguan agro-industry.

534 **MIDINRA, Boletín Informativo.** (MIDINRA, information bulletin.)
Instituto Nicaragüense de Reforma Agraria. Managua: Departamento de Divulgación y Prensa, Ministerio de Desarrollo Agropecuario, 1980- . monthly.
This monthly bulletin provides up-to-date news on the agrarian reform programme and on agricultural development in Nicaragua. Prior to no. 20 it was entitled *MIDA INRA, Boletín Informativo.*

535 **Migraciones rurales y estructura agraria en Nicaragua.**
(Rural migrations and agrarian structure in Nicaragua.)
Edmundo Jarquín C. *Estudios Sociales Centroamericanos*, vol. 4, no. 11 (May-Aug. 1975), p. 87-166.
A thorough examination of rural migration within Nicaragua, making a major contribution to understanding the agrarian structure of pre-revolutionary Nicaragua.

536 **Nicaraguan agricultural policy; 1979-81.**
Carmen D. Deere. *Cambridge Journal of Economics*, vol. 5 (June 1981), p. 195-200. bibliog.
Describes the Sandinista efforts to redistribute agricultural income in favour of rural workers and peasants, detailing the organization of co-operatives and other agricultural restructuring. Deere is impressed by the first eighteen months of the Sandinista policies.

537 **Nicaragua's agrarian reform.**
David Kaimowitz. *Land Tenure Center Newsletter*, no. 60 (Jan.-March 1980), p. 1-3.
A brief overview of Nicaragua's agrarian reform plans in their early stages, useful for its identification of the problems and reporting of the Sandinista government's approach.

538 **Programs of agricultural colonization and settlement in Central America.**
Clarence W. Minkel. *Revista Geográfica* (Comisión de Geografía, Instituto Panamericano de Geografía e Historia), vol. 66 (June 1967), p. 19-53.
A very useful survey of land reform in Central America. Dealing with Nicaragua on p. 34-38, Minkel notes the relative lack of either land reform or rural colonization in Nicaragua in the 1960s, but describes the several projects that were under way.

539 **Reforma agraria.** (Agrarian reform.)
Managua: Biblioteca y Servicios de Información, Banco Central de Nicaragua, Aug.-Oct. 1979. 9p. (Bibliografía Corta no. 15).
Organized in five sections: Nicaragua, Central America, Latin America, general works, and a list of journals that often deal with agrarian reform. The Nicaraguan section includes books, articles and theses.

540 **Research on agricultural development in Central America.**
Heraclio A. Lombardo. New York: Agricultural Development Council, 1969. 71p. bibliog.
Discusses Central American agricultural problems and makes suggestions for needed research. See also E. T. York and H. Popenoe, *Agricultural development in Nicaragua* (Washington, DC: US Department of Agriculture, 1965).

541 **State and private marketing arrangements in the agricultural export industries: the case of Nicaragua's coffee and cotton.**
Carlos Guillermo Sequeira. DBA dissertation, Harvard University, 1981. 327p. bibliog. (Available from University Microfilms, Ann Arbor, Michigan, order no. 82-2824).
Concludes that private marketing produced higher producers' prices in these Nicaraguan industries.

542 **Technology versus tradition: the modernization of Nicaraguan agriculture, 1900-1940.**
Larry K. Laird. PhD dissertation, University of Kansas, 1974. 275p. (Available from University Microfilms, Ann Arbor, Michigan, order no. 75-6216).
Focuses on the 'agricultural revolution' that occurred in Nicaragua in the 1940s and the background to it, 1900-1940. Emphasizes the ecological history of the country in the modernization process, and Nicaragua's successful achievement of agricultural self-sufficiency.

Agriculture

543 **Tenencia de la tierra y desarrollo rural en Centroamérica.**
(Land tenure and rural development in Central America.)
Comité Interamericana de Desarrollo Agrícolo
(CIDA). Tegucigalpa, Honduras: Instituto Nacional
Agrario, 1975. 342p.
This report contains many statistical tables and analyses of the landholding
systems of all of the Central American states.

544 **Tropical agribusiness structures and adjustments - bananas.**
Henry B. Arthur, James P. Houck, George L.
Beckford. Boston, Massachusetts: Division of Research,
Harvard Business School, 1968. 210p. bibliog.
Modern methods of production and marketing of bananas.

545 **What difference could a revolution make? Food and farming
in the new Nicaragua.**
Joseph Collins, Frances Moore Lappe, Nick Allen. San
Francisco, California: Institute for Food and Development
Policy, 1982. 160p.
A sympathetic treatment of the Sandinista efforts to overcome the shortages of
food in Nicaragua. Surveys the first three years of the revolution, emphasizing
the transition from export to subsistence crops and the development of an agricultural system that meets the basic needs of the poor majority.

Area handbook for Nicaragua.
See item no. 2.

Calendario de frutas y vegetales disponibles en el mercado local. (List of
fruits and vegetables available in the local market.)
See item no. 107.

A sociological study of the relations of man to the land in Nicaragua.
See item no. 298.

Nicaragua in revolution.
See item no. 352.

Anuario Estadístico. (Statistical annual.)
See item no. 447.

**Supply and demand for Nicaraguan milk and dairy products: 1958-1977
period. An econometric analysis.**
See item no. 480.

**A case study of an international development project: the Instituto
Nacional de Comercio Exterior y Interior in Ciudad Sandino, Nicaragua.**
See item no. 495.

FAO Trade Yearbook.
See item no. 501.

**Tropical enterprise: the Standard Fruit and Steamship Company in Latin
America.**
See item no. 506.

Yearbook of Forest Products Statistics.
See item no. 518.

Labor earnings and supply of off-farm labor of rural Nicaraguan households.
See item no. 563.

Transport and Communications

546 **Cadiz to Cathay, the story of the long struggle for a waterway across the American isthmus.**
Miles P. DuVal.   Stanford, California: Stanford University Press; London: Oxford University Press, 1940. 554p. maps. bibliog.

This work is especially useful because it treats the efforts in both Panama and Nicaragua to build a canal and puts these efforts in perspective to each other.

547 **Central American transportation study, 1964-1965. Report prepared for the Central American Bank for Economic Integration.**
Transportation Consultants Inc., Wilbur Smith & Associates, Consultécnica Ltda.   Washington, DC: TSC Consortium [1965?]. 2 vols. maps.

This major, detailed report on Central American transport facilities describes the highways, railways, ports and navigable waterways, and air transport facilities of all the Central American states. Photographs and drawings enhance the descriptions. It also includes a transportation plan for development and a discussion of rates, costs, laws and regulations. The text is contained in volume 1 (656p.), with volume 2 (536p.) containing statistical appendixes. A more recent report by the Central American Bank for Economic Integration, *Estudio centroamericano de transporte, 1974-76* (Central American transportation study, 1974-76), 8 vols., is available only in Spanish.

548 **El futuro de los transportes en Nicaragua.** (The future of transportation in Nicaragua.)
Armel E. González. Managua: Ministerio de Obras Públicas, 1977. 70p.

Analysis and description of a transportation plan for Nicaragua by the Somoza government. This study is useful for understanding existing transportation facilities and problems. Other government publications provide additional detail.

549 **Interest in a Nicaraguan canal, 1903-1931.**
Thomas A. Bailey. *Hispanic American Historical Review*, vol. 16 (Feb. 1936), p. 2-28.

An excellent review of efforts during the first third of the 20th century to develop a canal through Nicaragua after the United States acquired rights to construct a canal through Panama. For earlier Nicaraguan canal efforts see the article below by Roscoe Hill, *The Nicaragua canal idea to 1913.*

550 **The key to the Pacific: the Nicaragua canal.**
Archibald Ross Colquhon. Westminster, Maryland: A. Constable, 1895. 445p. New York: Longman, Green, 1898. 448p. maps.

In addition to discussion of the engineering, history and advantages of the canal project, this illustrated volume contains a great deal of description of the social and political scene, the people and customs, descriptions of the principal towns, races, languages, ruins and geography of Nicaragua at the end of the 19th century.

551 **The land divided: a history of the Panama Canal and other isthmian projects.**
Gerstle Mack. New York: Alfred A. Knopf, 1944. 650p. bibliog.

Although primarily concerned with the Panama route, Mack does a good job of presenting the Nicaraguan efforts to get a canal in perspective. This work is also valuable for its very extensive (52p.) bibliography.

552 **List of books and articles in periodicals relating to interoceanic canal and railway routes: Nicaragua; Panama; Darien and the Valley of Atrato; Tehuantepec and Honduras; Suez Canal.**
H. A. Morrison. Washington, DC: US Government Printing Office, 1900. 174p.

A very extensive list, important because it covers the very large volume of contemporary materials published on these projects. Prepared by the Library of Congress. The Nicaragua route is covered on p. 21-51.

553 **The Nicaragua canal and the Monroe Doctrine, a political history of the isthmus transit, with special reference to the Nicaragua canal project and the attitude of the United States government thereto.**
Lindley M. Keasbey. New York: G. P. Putnam's Sons, 1896. 622p. 4 maps.

A detailed history of interest in and development of an interoceanic canal in Nicaragua. Keasbey is especially concerned with US efforts to secure rights there, and emphasizes the need for the canal and the importance of US control of such a waterway. This is essentially Keasbey's PhD dissertation (Columbia University, 1890), the first US dissertation written on Nicaragua.

554 **The Nicaragua canal idea to 1913.**
Roscoe R. Hill. *Hispanic American Historical Review*, vol. 28 (May 1948), p. 197-211.

An excellent survey of interest in and efforts to develop a canal through Nicaragua through 1913. See also Thomas A. Bailey's article above which continues this story, *Interest in a Nicaraguan canal, 1903-1931.*

555 **Nicaragua: plan nacional de transportes. Reporte de la fase I.** (Nicaragua: national transportation plan. Report on phase I.)
Richard E. Miller. Managua: Wilbur Smith & Associates, with Cisneros y Conrado Cía., 1976. 286p. bibliog. tables. charts.

A very detailed description and analysis of existing transportation facilities, analysis of the demand and proposals for new projects. A copy of this report is in the library of the Banco Central de Nicaragua.

556 **Railways of Central America and the West Indies.**
William Rodney Long. Washington, DC: US Government Printing Office, 1925. 376p. (Department of Commerce, Trade Promotion Series, no. 5).

Although this guide is now very old, the railroads were largely completed in Central America by 1925. Service has deteriorated considerably since that time and there is no modern guide to the railways of Nicaragua.

557 **Report of the Nicaraguan Canal Commission, 1897-1899.**
John G. Walker (and others). Baltimore, Maryland: Friedenwald Co., 1899. 502p. plus atlas with 7 maps in portfolio. maps. plans. tables.

This major study carried out under the direction of Rear-Admiral John G. Walker, United States Navy, for the United States Congress, provides great detail on the engineering and geological problems confronting the construction of an interoceanic canal in Nicaragua, but it also includes much other information on Nicaragua in general, especially in the area of the proposed route.

558 **Road user charges in Central America.**
Anthony Churchill (and others). Baltimore, Maryland;
London: Johns Hopkins University Press, for the
International Bank for Reconstruction and Development,
1972. 176p. maps. bibliog. (World Bank Staff Occasional
Papers no. 15).

A thorough study of road financing and road use in the Central American states,
with considerable information on data collection and statistical method in Nicaragua.

559 **A study of the trans-isthmian canal problems with emphasis
on the Nicaragua route.**
Arden William Ohl. PhD dissertation, University of
Michigan, 1965. 196p. bibliog. (Available from University
Microfilms, Ann Arbor, Michigan, order no. 66-6669.).

Concerned with contemporary problems, Ohl compares Panama and Nicaragua as
sites for an alternative canal, concluding that a future Nicaragua canal is
unlikely. A major argument for this conclusion is his assumption that nuclear
power will probably be used to excavate a future canal, necessitating construction
in an unpopulated part of Panama or Colombia.

560 **Transporte.** (Transportation.)
Managua: Biblioteca y Servicios de Información, Banco
Central de Nicaragua, Sept. 1980. 6p. (Bibliografía Corta
no. 22).

Lists items on transportation to be found in the Banco Central library, including
a substantial section dealing with Nicaragua on p. 3-6. This includes a great
many items in Spanish on railroads, highways, lake and river transportation and
urban transit, as well as government publications on transportation policy.

Nicaragua.
See item no. 51.

Red vial de Nicaragua. (Highway network of Nicaragua.)
See item no. 54.

A travers l'Amérique Centrale, le Nicaragua et le canal interocéanique.
(Across Central America, Nicaragua and the interoceanic canal.)
See item no. 86.

The Nicaragua canal.
See item no. 91.

Historia de el Realejo. (History of Realejo.)
See item no. 172.

Realejo: forgotten colonial port and shipbuilding center in Nicaragua.
See item no. 178.

The Nicaragua route.
See item no. 204.

Transport and Communications

United States commercial pressure for a Nicaraguan canal in the 1890's.
See item no. 425.

Breve historia de la aviación en Nicaragua. (Brief history of aviation in Nicaragua.)
See item no. 590.

Labour

561 **Código de trabajo.** (Labour code.)
Managua: Ministerio de Trabajo, 1976. 433p.
Nicaraguan law respecting labour, enacted in December 1975.

562 **Employment and the urban informal sector: the case of Managua.**
Silvio Domingo DeFranco. PhD dissertation, University of Wisconsin, 1979. 235p. (Available from University Microfilms, Ann Arbor, Michigan, order no. 80-4712).
Shows and analyses the major trends in population and labour force composition and the growth of Nicaragua and Managua before 1979, reflecting the strong migration trend toward the capital. Studies the working poor or 'informal sector', and concludes that most were poorly educated women. Discusses the characteristics of this labour sector and its relationship to the 'formal' labour force.

563 **Labor earnings and supply of off-farm labor of rural Nicaraguan households.**
Preston S. Pattie. PhD dissertation, Michigan State University, 1982. 245p. (Available from University Microfilms, Ann Arbor, Michigan, order no. 82-16578).
Based on a survey of rural households in central interior Nicaragua in mid-1978, this study reveals much about landholding and labour patterns in the region. Results of the study suggest that improvements in the well-being of the rural population can be increased by better educational services. Also recommends greater participation of the population in local decision-making.

Labour

564 **Labor law and practice in Nicaragua.**
Karol C. Kleiner. Washington, DC: United States Bureau of Labour Statistics, 1964. 100p. map. bibliog.

A useful overview of labour conditions and law in Nicaragua in the 1960s. Appendixes list labour legislation, 1945-64, and the principal labour organizations as of 1963.

565 **La legislación laboral de Nicaragua y los convenios de OIT.**
(The labour legislation of Nicaragua and the ILO agreements.)
J. A. Tijerino Medrano, Mario Palma Ibarra. San José: Lehmann, 1978. 2nd ed. 2 vols.

A detailed and careful analysis of Nicaraguan labour legislation in the light of International Labour Organization standards and agreements. This work includes the 149 Agreements of the ILO.

566 **The worker-peasant alliance in the first year of the Nicaraguan agrarian reform.**
Carmen Diana Deere, Peter Marchette. *Latin American Perspectives*, vol. 8, no. 2 (spring 1981), p. 40-73.

An informative and enthusiastic account of Sandinista organization of Nicaraguan labour during the first year of the revolution.

Area handbook for Nicaragua.
See item no. 2.

Human resources of Central America, Panama, and Mexico, 1950-1980, in relation to some aspects of economic development.
See item no. 246.

Anuario Estadístico. (Statistical annual.)
See item no. 447.

Environment

567 The impact of commercial exploitation on sawfish and shark populations in Lake Nicaragua.

Thomas B. Thorson. *Fisheries*, vol. 7, no. 2 (March-April 1982), p. 2-10. maps. bibliog.

Heavy fishing of the shark and swordfish has greatly depleted the population of these fish in the Lake Nicaragua and Río San Juan region. The Nicaraguan Institute of Fisheries has recently placed a two-year moratorium on fishing of both sharks and swordfish in the lake in an effort to save these species. Thorson describes the problem, and hopes that the moratorium may have saved one of Nicaragua's more unique resources.

568 Medio ambiente. (Environment.)

Compiled by Justo Pastor Zamora Herdocia. Managua: Ministerio de Salud Pública, Ministerio de Relaciones Exteriores, with the Secretaría de Información y Prensa de la Presidencia de la República, 1976. unpaginated. maps. bibliog.

The proceedings of a special programme on World Environmental Protection Day (5 June 1976). Includes a speech by Anastasio Somoza, relating to his government's efforts on behalf of the environment, a speech by the minister of public health, warning that more must be done, and two papers: Claudio Gutiérrez H., 'Los problemas de calidad de agua en Managua' (Water quality problems in Managua), and Jaime Incer B., 'Cuidar el medio ambiente o perecer' (Care for the environment or perish).

The prehistoric and modern subsistence patterns of the Atlantic coast of Nicaragua. A comparison.
See item no. 134.

Between land and water: the subsistence economy of the Miskito Indians, eastern Nicaragua.
See item no. 259.

A sociological study of the relations of man to the land in Nicaragua.
See item no. 298.

Environment

The ecology of malnutrition in Mexico and Central America: Mexico, Guatemala, British Honduras, Honduras, El Salvador, Nicaragua, Costa Rica and Panama.
See item no. 309.

The ecology of malnutrition in Sandy Bay, Nicaragua.
See item no. 310.

Technology versus tradition: the modernization of Nicaraguan agriculture, 1900-1940.
See item no. 542.

Diagnóstica preliminar sobre la ciencia y tecnología en Nicaragua.
(Preliminary diagnosis on science and technology in Nicaragua.)
See item no. 591.

Education

569 Chronicle of a crusade, Nicaragua's second revolution.
B. Treumann. *Christianity and Crisis*, vol. 41 (2 Nov. 1981), p. 291-300.

A descriptive review of the successful Sandinista literacy campaign. A more detailed account is given in Stansifer's *The Nicaraguan National Literacy Crusade*, listed below.

570 Educación para la modernización en Nicaragua. (Education for modernization in Nicaragua.)
Miguel de Castilla Urbina. Buenos Aires: Paidos, 1972. 162p. bibliog.

Surveys and evaluates the educational system of Nicaragua in a dispassionate way and discusses projects for its improvement. See also his *La educación primaria nicaragüense: sus males y sus remedios* (Nicaraguan primary education: its problems and their remedies) (Managua: Editorial Nicaragüense, 1968. 157p.), which provides considerable detail on the system as it actually was under the Somoza dynasty.

571 Educación y didáctica. (Education and teaching.)
Managua: Biblioteca y Servicios de Información, Banco Central de Nicaragua, Dec. 1978. 9p. (Mini-bibliografía no. 11).

Lists holdings of the library of the Banco Central on this topic, with a special section on Nicaraguan education, p. 8-9, listing seventeen items. Although brief, the list is a good guide to the limited literature on education before the Sandinista revolution.

Education

572 Education in Central America.
George R. Waggoner, Barbara Ashton
Waggoner. Lawrence, Kansas: University Press of Kansas,
1971. 180p.

A survey of educational facilities on the isthmus, emphasizing the co-operation
among the six countries. A chapter on Nicaragua, p. 88-106, gives an accurate
picture of the situation there before the Sandinista revolution. Many of the problems remain.

573 La ensañanza de la historia en Nicaragua. (The teaching of
history in Nicaragua.)
Carlos Molina Argüello. Mexico City: Instituto
Panamericano de Geografía e Historia, 1953. 222p.
(Publicación no. 165; Memorias Sobre la Enseñanza de
Historia, no. 11).

Surveys the role of history in Nicaraguan education from colonial times through
the mid-20th century. This includes considerable discussion of the structure of
Nicaraguan education from primary through elementary levels. It also includes a
section on textbooks and teaching methods of history, as well as a discussion of
the principal institutions promoting historical study in the state. The author is one
of Nicaragua's most noteworthy historical researchers. Documentary appendixes
include pertinent legislation, lesson plans for history courses at elementary, secondary and university levels, various historical programmes, tables of contents from
the principal history texts of Nicaragua, and other relevant documents.

574 Factors related to college graduation and professional status
of the Nicaraguan university graduates.
Tulio Benito Tablada. PhD dissertation, University of
Colorado, 1978. 141p. bibliog. (Available from University
Microfilms, Ann Arbor, Michigan, order no. 78-20566).

Studies 243 Nicaraguan professionals who graduated from Nicaraguan universities in 1970 and 1974, determining common characteristics, and the correlations
between their types of degrees, salaries, jobs, and vocational satisfactions.

575 Hacía una nueva educación en Nicaragua. (Toward a new
education in Nicaragua.)
Carlos Tunnermann Bernheim. Managua: Ministerio de
Educación, 1980. 187p.

The president of the National University of Nicaragua describes the Sandinista
effort to develop education. He sees it as a major step in bringing progress to the
country.

576 Historia de la Universidad de León. (History of the
University of León.)
Jorge Eduardo Arellano. León, Nicaragua: Editorial
Universitaria, 1973-74. 2 vols. bibliog.

A careful and detailed history of Nicaragua's first university, established in 1814,
by one of Nicaragua's leading historians.

577 **The literacy campaign, Nicaraguan style.**
Leonor Blum. *Caribbean Review*, vol. 10 (winter 1981), p.
18-21.

A brief overview of the Sandinista literacy campaign, with the argument that the
US should sponsor literacy programmes in other Latin American countries, which
would contain a high degree of pro-US propaganda in contrast to the pro-socialist
models of Cuba and Nicaragua.

578 **The loss of fear: education in Nicaragua before and after the
revolution.**
George Black, John Bevan. London: Nicaragua Solidarity
Committee, with the World University Service, 1980. 77p.
maps. bibliog.

An informative and sympathetic outline of educational programmes in Sandinista
Nicaragua. Chapter titles include 'Patterns of education in Latin America',
'Education under Somoza', 'The crisis of Somocismo and its effects on education',
'Education and revolution: reconstructing or creating a new system?', 'Non-formal
education', 'The meaning of literacy'. Appendixes contain basic documents regarding Sandinista educational policy, a Nicaraguan statistical profile and a chronology of Nicaraguan history.

579 **Nicaragua en la educación: una aproximación a la realidad.**
(Nicaragua in education: approaching reality.)
Juan B. Arrién, Rafael Kauffmann. Managua: Universidad
Centroamericana, 1977. 423p. bibliog.

Considerable statistical material along with an analysis and description of the
Nicaraguan educational system. Calls for major reforms, especially in the universities.

580 **Nicaragua: revolución y proyecto educativo.** (Nicaragua: the
revolution and its education project.)
Juan Bautista Arrién. Managua: Ministerio de Educación,
1980. 203p.

Detailed description of the philosophy and method of the Sandinista educational
method. The author is a Spanish immigrant to Nicaragua long recognized as a
leader in Nicaraguan educational circles and active in the Nicaraguan literacy
crusade.

581 **Nicaragua triunfa en la alfabetización: documentos y
testimonios de la cruzada nacional de alfabetización.**
(Nicaragua triumphs in literacy: documents and testimony
from the national literacy crusade.)
Edited by Hugo Assmann. San José: Ministerio de
Educación (de Nicaragua), Departamento Ecuménico de
Investigaciones, 1981. 672p.

A remarkable collection of testimonies, examples and descriptions of the method
by which the highly successful literacy campaign was accomplished in Nicaragua.

Education

582 The Nicaraguan National Literacy Crusade.
Charles L. Stansifer. Hanover, New Hampshire: Wheelock House, 1981. 14p. (American University Field Staff Reports, South America, no. 6).

An excellent description of the origins, organization and development of the successful Nicaraguan campaign against illiteracy, by a North American historian who has specialized in Nicaragua.

583 Nonformal education in Latin America, an annotated bibliography.
Susan L. Poston. Los Angeles: University of California, Los Angeles, Latin American Center, 1976. 268p. (UCLA Latin American Center Publication no. 8).

Lists and annotates eight items on Nicaragua on p. 150-51. An additional twenty-three are listed in the general section on 'Central America and the Caribbean' (p. 199-204), but few have relevance to Nicaragua.

584 Pensamiento universitario centroamericano. (Central American university thought.)
Carlos Tunnermann. San José: EDUCA (Editorial Universitaria Centroamericana), 1980. 521p.

A collection of essays by the Nicaraguan minister of education reflecting the strengths and weaknesses of Central American universities and the difficulties of effecting reform in Nicaragua. It makes a genuine contribution to the history of university development in Central America.

585 A plan for the introduction and organization of guidance services in the secondary schools of Nicaragua.
Roberto Belarmino Cardenal, SJ. PhD dissertation, Catholic University of America, 1968. 211p. (Available from University Microfilms, Ann Arbor, Michigan, order no. 69-9151).

Treating the nature and extent of guidance services for Nicaraguan secondary-school students, the dissertation notes major deficiencies and makes recommendations for their remedy. Useful for its detailed examination of the inner workings of the Nicaraguan educational system.

586 El sistema educativo en Nicaragua: situación actual y perspectivas. (The educational system in Nicaragua: present situation and possibilities for the future.)
Consejo Superior Universitario Centroamericano. San José: CSUCA, 1965. 115p. tables. (Estudios de Recursos Humanos en Centroamérica, no. 4).

A very good description of the Nicaraguan educational system and plans for development as they existed in the mid-1960s.

587 **Statistics for the analysis of the education sector: Nicaragua.**
US Agency for International Development, Bureau for Latin
America. Washington, DC: AID, 1975. 109p.

Describes the educational system and quality in Nicaragua through seventy tables
and eighteen graphs. Nineteen additional tables in the introduction summarize the
data. There is also a flow chart showing the structure of the Nicaraguan educational system as of 1971. This detailed statistical information covers population,
school enrolments, labour force, literacy, schools and classrooms, teachers, fund-
ing, movement of students through the system from pre-primary through university, etc.

588 **Utilization of education and planning specialists in Nicaragua
- final report.**
Elizabeth Vallely Truesdell. EdD dissertation, Harvard
University, 1978. 154p. bibliog. (Available from University
Microfilms, Ann Arbor, Michigan, order no 79-27933).

Part of the Utilization of Educational Specialists in Less Developed Countries
Project, this study examines the current state of utilization of selected educational
specialists in Nicaragua who have been trained in the US and their availability to
assist in planning and analysis, and evaluates the status of existing US information systems to determine their adequacy for supporting such investigations.

Area handbook for Nicaragua.
See item no. 2.

**Progressive drug involvement: marihuana use careers among Nicaraguan
private secondary school students.**
See item no. 304.

Nicaragua in revolution.
See item no. 352.

Anuario Estadístico. (Statistical annual.)
See item no. 447.

**Labor earnings and supply of off-farm labor of rural Nicaraguan
households.**
See item no. 563.

Cultural policy in the old and the new Nicaragua.
See item no. 593.

**American dissertations on foreign education: a bibliography with
abstracts. Volume X, Central America, West Indies, Caribbean and Latin
America, general.**
See item no. 693.

Science and Technology

589 **The adaption of technology in Nicaragua.**
Nancy Beth Jackson. PhD dissertation, University of
Miami, 1973. 269p. bibliog. (Available from University
Microfilms, Ann Arbor, Michigan, order no. 73-25912).

In spite of the close connection between the US and Nicaragua during the
Somoza years, Nicaragua did not become a model for the adaption of technology
in developing countries. This dissertation examines the reasons for this and is
highly critical of the nature of US-Nicaraguan relations.

590 **Breve historia de la aviación en Nicaragua.** (Brief history of
aviation in Nicaragua.)
Ana Lorena Medrana. Licenciatura thesis, Universidad
Centroamericana, Managua, 1976. unpaginated. bibliog.

An episodic account, narrating the pioneers of Nicaraguan aviation and commercial aviation. This does an adequate job of describing the organization and development of aviation in Nicaragua and is the only thing available.

591 **Diagnóstica preliminar sobre la ciencia y tecnología en
Nicaragua.** (Preliminary diagnosis on science and technology
in Nicaragua.)
Managua: Banco Central de Nicaragua, Departamento de
Investigaciones Tecnológicas, Dirección de Planificación
Nacional, 1977. 67p.

Although fairly brief, this publication outlines the scientific projects under way in
Nicaragua in 1977 in both the public and private sectors. Describes the existing
infrastructure for scientific and technological research in Nicaragua, based on a
survey carried out. It concluded that there was little basic research going on and
that the infrastructure was weak. Appendixes include fourteen statistical tables, a
list of the principal research projects under way in the scientific and technical

institutions in the country, questionnaires used in the survey, and a list of the seventeen institutions that were undertaking scientific research and development in Nicaragua as of November 1976.

The Nicaragua canal and the Monroe Doctrine, a political history of the isthmus transit, with special reference to the Nicaragua canal project and the attitude of the United States government thereto.
See item no. 553.

Literature

Anthologies and general guides

592 **El cuento nicaragüense. Antología.** (The Nicaraguan short
story. Anthology.)
Edited by Sergio Ramírez. Managua: Ediciones El Pez y la
Serpiente, 1976. 267p.
A fine collection of thirty-four Nicaraguan short stories with an introduction and
brief discussion of each by the editor. Sixteen Nicaraguan authors are represented
in addition to five anonymous pieces.

593 **Cultural policy in the old and the new Nicaragua.**
Charles L. Stansifer. Hanover, New Hampshire: Wheelock
House, 1981. 17p. map. (American University Field Staff
Reports, South America, no. 41).
Stansifer describes cultural policy under the Somozas and Sandinistas. He also
traces the principal literary currents in the country since the 1930s. Includes a list
of the principal 20th-century Nicaraguan poets, artists and intellectuals (p. 6) and
a detailed discussion of Nicaraguan literary publications. Emphasizes the role of
the Conservative élite of Granada in preserving Nicaragua's cultural heritage
during the Somoza years and the recent Sandinista cultural promotion.

594 **Diccionario de la literatura latinoamericana: América
Central.** (Dictionary of Latin American literature: Central
America.)
Pan American Union, Division of Philosophy and
Letters. Washington, DC: Pan American Union, 1963. 2
vols. bibliog.
Volume 2 of this very important contribution to the field of literature and biblio-
graphy includes an ample section on Nicaragua.

595 **Literatura nicaragüense.** (Nicaraguan literature.)
Managua: Biblioteca y Servicios de Información, Banco
Central de Nicaragua, Aug. 1981. 20p. (Bibliografía Corta
no. 26).
Nicaragua has a rich literary tradition for so small a nation, but few works have
been translated into English. Based on holdings in the library of the Banco
Central, this is an excellent introductory bibliographical guide to Nicaraguan
literature. It is organized topically, with substantial sections listing anthologies,
biography, criticism and interpretation, travel accounts, history of literature,
novels and short stories, poetry, theatre and miscellaneous.

596 **Nicaragua in revolution: the poets speak/Nicaragua en
revolución: los poetas hablan.**
Edited by Bridget Aldaraca, Edward Baker, Ileana
Rodríguez, Marc Zimmerman. Minneapolis, Minnesota:
Marxist Educational Press, 1980. 301p. bibliog.
A bilingual collection of poems focusing on the Sandinista revolution.

597 **Panorama de la literatura nicaragüense.** (Panorama of
Nicaraguan literature.)
Jorge Eduardo Arellano. Managua: Ediciones Nacionales,
1977. 3rd ed. 195p. bibliog.
A well-done history and critique of Nicaraguan literature from the conquest to
the present, with bio-bibliographical sketches of thirty late 19th- and early 20th-
century Nicaraguan authors.

598 **El Pez y la Serpiente.** (The fish and the snake.)
Edited by Pablo Antonio Cuadra. Managua: El Pez y la
Serpiente, 1961- . somewhat irregular.
One of the finest literary magazines in Central America. Emphasizes poetry, in
the Nicaraguan tradition.

599 **Poets of Nicaragua: a bilingual anthology, 1918-1979.**
Selected and translated by Steven F. White. Greensboro,
North Carolina: Unicorn Press, 1982. 209p. bibliog.
An excellent selection of Nicaraguan poetry, including the work of Alfonso
Cortés, Salomón de la Selva, José Coronel Urtecho, Pablo Antonio Cuadra,
Joaquín Pasos, Juan Francisco Gutiérrez, Ernesto Mejía Sánchez, Carlos
Martínez Rivas, Ernesto Cardenal, Ernesto Gutiérrez, Francisco Valle, Anna Ilce,
and Alvaro Urtecho. The poems are given here in English and Spanish.

600 **La Prensa Literaria.** (The literary press.)
Edited by Pablo Antonio Cuadra. Managua: La Prensa,
1952- . weekly.
This weekly supplement to *La Prensa* is a very important medium for a broad
range of literary efforts, including not only poetry and literary prose, but also art,
science, bibliography, history and other topics. This has been one of the principal

Literature. Anthologies and general guides

transmitters of Nicaraguan culture since it began publication. An *Indice selectivo de La Prensa Literaria: mayo 1972-agosoto 1978*, prepared by René Rodríguez Masís and Antonio Acevedo E., was published in Managua by the Biblioteca y Servicios de Información of the Banco Central de Nicaragua in November 1981 (85p.). Although reduced in size in 1978, *La Prensa Literaria* remains the leading independent critic of the arts in Nicaragua.

601 **Sucinta reseña de las letras nicaragüenses en 50 años, 1900-1950.** (Succinct survey of fifty years of Nicaraguan letters, 1900-1950.)
Juan Felipe Toruno. In: *Panorama das literaturas das Américas de 1900 a la actualidade* (Panorama of the literature of the Americas from 1900 to the present). Edited by Joaquím de Montezuma de Carvalho. Nova Lisboa, Angola: Edicão do Municipio de Nova Lisboa, 1958-63, 4 vols., vol. 3, p. 1,093-202.
An extensive essay, with excerpts and commentary. An excellent guide to principal literary figures during the first half of the 20th century in Nicaragua.

602 **El teatro como creación literaria en Nicaragua: obras e intentos teatrales de autores nicaragüenses.** (The theatre as a literary creation in Nicaragua: works and theatrical efforts of Nicaraguan authors.)
Jorge Eduardo Arellano. *Boletín Nicaragüense de Bibliografía y Documentación*, no. 41 (May-June 1981), p. 1-18, 130-32.
This entire issue of the *BNBD* is devoted to Nicaraguan theatre. Arellano's succinct survey of Nicaraguan theatre from pre-Columbian times to the present introduces a selection of Nicaraguan dramatic literature, p. 9-129. See also *3 obras de teatro vanguardia nicaragüense* (Managua: Ediciones El Pez y la Serpiente, 1975. 180p.), an anthology including *Chinfonia, Petenera*, and *Por los caminos...*, three plays that were part of an attempt to create a popular theatre in the 1930s.

Handbook of Middle American Indians.
See item no. 266.

El folklore en la literatura de Centro América. (Folklore in Central American literature.)
See item no. 276.

Nicarauac. (Nicarauac.)
See item no. 657.

Enciclopedia nicaragüense: cultura literaria y científica. (Nicaraguan encyclopaedia: scientific and literary culture.)
See item no. 674.

Autores nicaragüenses del sigo XX. (20th-century Nicaraguan authors.)
See item no. 695.

Rubén Darío

603 An analytical index of the complete poetical works of Rubén Darío.
Compiled by Helene Westbrook Harrison. Washington, DC: Microcard Editions, 1970. 104p.

Alphabetical indexes of subject matter, proper names, Darío's titles, and other titles, based on Darío's *Poesías completas* (Complete poetry), edited by Alfonso Méndez Plancarte (Madrid: Aguilar, 1952).

604 Autobiografía. (Autobiography.)
Rubén Darío. Madrid: Mundo Latino, 1918. 217p. (several later editions).

The personal reminiscences of Nicaragua's most famous poet.

605 A bibliography of Rubén Darío, 1867-1916.
Henry Grattan Doyle. Cambridge, Massachusetts: Harvard University Press, 1935. 27p.

A useful list of the writings of Nicaragua's most celebrated poet.

606 Breve antología de Rubén Darío. (Brief anthology of Rubén Darío.)
Alberto M. Vásquez. New Orleans, Louisiana; Mexico City: El Colibri, 1971. 137p.

A carefully chosen collection of the stories, essays and poems of Darío, accompanied by a biographical sketch.

607 Critical approaches to Rubén Darío.
Keith Ellis. Toronto: University of Toronto Press, 1974. 170p. bibliog.

A series of perceptive essays on Darío's career and work. Successive chapters review Darío's biography, socio-political considerations, literary history, philosophy, themes, motifs, language and structural analysis. An appendix discusses 'Rubén Darío as a literary critic'. The work is a major scholarly effort to understand Darío and his work.

608 La dramática vida de Rubén Darío. (The dramatic life of Rubén Darío.)
Edelberto Torres. Barcelona, Spain: Ediciones Frijalbo, 1966. 4th ed. 537p.

One of the most complete and popular of the many biographies of Darío.

609 **Homenaje a Rubén Darío, 1867-1967: memoria del XIII Congreso Internacional de Literatura Iberoamericana.**
(Homage to Rubén Darío, 1867-1967: proceedings of the 13th International Congress of Ibero-American Literature.)
Edited by Aníbal Sánchez-Reulet. Los Angeles: University of California Press, 1970. 298p.
A collection of twenty-six scholarly papers dealing with Darío, his work and his influence.

610 **Poesía.** (Poetry.)
Rubén Darío, selected and introduced by Jorge Campos. Madrid: Alianza Editorial, 1977. 143p. bibliog.
(El Libro de Bosilla no. 66, Sección Literaria).
A representative selection of Darío's poems with an introduction reviewing his life and writings.

611 **Poet-errant: a biography of Rubén Darío.**
C. D. Watland. New York: Philosophical Library, 1965. 266p.
A biography of Nicaragua's most famous poet.

612 **Repertorio bibliográfico del mundo de Rubén Darío.**
(Bibliographical repertoire of the world of Rubén Darío.)
Arnold Armand del Greco. New York: Las Américas, 1969. 666p. bibliog.
A massive collection of 3,179 entries on books, articles and other works by and about Rubén Darío. Includes brief critiques and commentary on many of the works. A detailed index adds to the utility of this major work. It lists sixty-four separate bibliographies on Darío.

613 **[Rubén Darío].**
Inter-American Review of Bibliography, vol. 17 (April-June 1967), p. 145-221.
This entire issue is devoted to the Nicaraguan poet, Rubén Darío, on the 100th anniversary of his birth. It includes an extensive bibliography of his works, p. 202-21, including some items not found in Doyle's 1935 bibliography listed above.

614 **Rubén Darío: centennial studies.**
Edited by Miguel González-Gerth, George D. Schade. Austin, Texas: Institute of Latin American Studies, Department of Spanish and Portuguese, University of Texas, 1970. 120p. bibliog.
Five scholarly studies in English of Darío's work: Miguel Enguidaños, 'Inner tensions in the work of Rubén Darío'; Eugenio Florit, 'The modernist prefigurement in the early work of Rubén Darío'; Allen W. Phillips, 'Rubén Darío and Valle Inclán: the story of a literary friendship'; Arturo Torres-Ríoseco, 'Rubén

Darío: classic poet'; and Enrique Anderson-Imbert, 'Rubén Darío and the fantastic element in literature'.

615 **Rubén Darío: a critical bibliography.**
Hensley C. Woodbridge. *Hispania*, vol. 50 (1967), p.
982-95; vol. 51 (1968), p. 95-110.

One of the best efforts to present an annotated and critical bibliography of works dealing with the Nicaraguan poet. Woodbridge quotes liberally from the reviews and critiques of Darío's works. A Spanish translation of this work is available: *Rubén Darío: bibliografía selectiva, clasificada y anotada* (León, Nicaragua: UNAN, 1975. 146p.).

Pablo Antonio Cuadra

616 **El nicaragüense.** (The Nicaraguan.)
Pablo Antonio Cuadra. Managua: Distribuidora Cultural
Nicaragüense, 1968. 2nd ed. 172p. (several subsequent
editions).

Chiefly articles published in *La Prensa Literaria* in 1959 under the title 'Apuntes sobre el nicaragüense' (Notes on the Nicaraguan), subsequently in the *Revista Conservadora*, no. 14 (Nov. 1961). They contain much insight into the nature of Nicaraguan society and its individuals. This edition also includes José Coronel Urtecho's 'Sobre la universalidad nicaragüense' (On Nicaraguan universality), p. 153-72.

617 **Songs of Cifar and the sweet sea. Selections in English and Spanish.**
Pablo Antonio Cuadra, translated and edited by Grace
Schulman, Ann McCarthy Zavala. New York: Columbia
University Press, 1979. 120p.

A careful and sensitive translation of Cuadra's lyrical poems about the mythical Cifar, who travels about Lake Nicaragua in an Odyssean voyage. Schulman and McCarthy effectively present Cuadra's work to English-reading audiences.

618 **Homenaje a Pablo Antonio Cuadra.** (Tribute to Pablo
Antonio Cuadra.)
Edited by Xavier Zavala Cuadra. *Revista del Pensamiento
Centroamericano*, vol. 37, no. 177 (Oct.-Dec. 1982), p.
8-200. bibliog.

Critical commentary on the work of the Nicaraguan poet and essayist, Pablo Antonio Cuadra, by Melchor Fernández Almagro, Antonio Tovar, Stefán Baciu, Gloria Guardia de Alfaro, Emilio del Río, Rodolfo O. Floripe, Franco Cerutti, Ramón Xirau, Carlos Tunnermann Bernheim, Jean Louis Feiz, Félix Grande, Guillermo Yepes Boscán, Guisepe Bellini, Juana Rosa Pita, José Emiliano Balladares, Fernando Quiñónez, Francisco Valle, Jose Ma. Caballero, Luis Jiménez

Martos, Sergio Ramírez, Jorge Eduardo Arellano, Alberto Ordóñez Argüello, José Ma. Valverde, Eduardo Cote Lemus, Guillermo Rothschuh Tablada, Jacinto Herrero Esteban, John Battle, Eduardo Zepeda, Raúl Gustavo Aguirre, César Brañas, and Luis Wainerman. Also includes a collection of Cuadra's poems, written in 1934-35 but previously unpublished, entitled 'Cuaderno del sur: poemas viajeros' (p. 9-24), an extensive bibliography of Cuadra's work by Jorge Eduardo Arellano (p. 189-200), and many photos of Cuadra at various points in his career.

Ernesto Cardenal

619 **An annotated bibliography of and about Ernesto Cardenal.**
Janet L. Smith.   Tempe, Arizona: Center for Latin
American Studies, Arizona State University, 1979. 61p.
(Special Studies).
Partially annotated, this extensive bibliography lists works in English, Spanish and German by and about Cardenal, in seven categories: critical articles or essays; book-length works of Cardenal; poetry of Cardenal; articles and essays of Cardenal; works edited or compiled by Cardenal; translations into English of Cardenal's works; and translations by Cardenal of others' works into Spanish and English.

620 **Apocalypse and other poems.**
Ernesto Cardenal, edited by Robert Pring-Mill, Donald D.
Walsh.   New York: New Directions Publishing, 1977. 78p.
A collection of translated poems of the Nicaraguan Sandinista priest and minister of culture.

621 **Homage to the American Indians.**
Ernesto Cardenal, translated by Monique Altschul, Carlos
Altschul.   Baltimore, Maryland: Johns Hopkins University
Press, 1973. 116p.
Poetry on the Indians.

622 **The poetry of Ernesto Cardenal.**
Paul W. Borgeson, Jr.   PhD dissertation, Vanderbilt
University, 1977. 258p. (Available from University
Microfilms, Ann Arbor, Michigan, order no. 77-19364).
An excellent description of Cardenal's career and analysis of his poetry.

623 **To live is to love.**
Ernesto Cardenal, translated by Kurt Reinhardt.   New
York: Image Books, 1974. 156p.
Translation of *Vida en el amor.*

624 **Zero hour and other documentary poems.**
Ernesto Cardenal, selected and edited by Donald D. Walsh,
translated by Paul W. Borgeson (and others). New York:
New Directions, 1980. 106p.
More of Cardenal's revolutionary poetry.

Love in practice - the Gospel in Solentiname.
See item no. 286.

Revolution and peace: the Nicaraguan road.
See item no. 360.

Other Nicaraguan literary figures

625 **Crucified Nicaragua of Pedro Joaquín Chamorro.**
G. J. Conliffe, Thomas W. Walker. *Latin American
Research Review*, vol. 13, no. 3 (1978), p. 183-88.
A review article of two important essay novels by Pedro Joaquín Chamorro, *Jesús
Marchena* (Managua, 1975), and *Richter 7* (Managua, 1976). These novels are
firmly rooted in Nicaraguan history, culture, folklore and socio-political
experience, and reveal the extraordinary talents of the editor of *La Prensa*, whose
assassination in 1978 precipitated the downfall of Somoza.

626 **Omnibus.**
Julio Cabrales. León, Nicaragua: Universidad Nacional
Autónoma de Nicaragua, 1975. 78p. (Colección Poesía, no.
9).
An anthology of Cabrales' poems (in Spanish).

627 **Te dió miedo la sangre?** (Did the blood frighten you?)
Sergio Ramírez. Caracas: Monte Avila Editores, 1977.
281p. (Colección Continentes).
A fictional, but seemingly accurate, description of the world of political exiles in
Central America and of the corruption and repression of the Somoza dynasty. A
bitter denunciation of the Somozas and their North American allies by a member
of the Sandinista junta.

628 **Trágame tierra.** (Bring me land.)
Lizandro Chávez Alfaro. Mexico City: Editorial Diógenes,
1979. 2nd ed. 282p.
Set on the Nicaraguan Caribbean coast, this novel reveals important ideological
conflicts in Somoza's Nicaragua, as well as generational differences, as a father is
committed to United States development plans for Nicaragua while his son joins
the guerrillas. First published in 1969.

629 **Versos y versiones nobles y sentimentales.** (Noble and
sentimental verses and versions.)
Salomón de la Selva. Managua: Fondo de Promoción
Cultural, Banco de América, 1975. 181p. (Colección
Cultural, Serie Literaria, no. 2).
A new collection of hitherto unpublished poems by Selva, inspired by the classics.

Language

630 **Bibliografía fundamental del español en Nicaragua.** (Basic
bibliography of Nicaraguan Spanish.)
Jorge Eduardo Arellano. *Boletín Nicaragüense de
Bibliografía y Documentación*, no. 19 (Sept.-Oct. 1977), p.
92-124.
Reviews sixty works on Nicaraguan Spanish. This issue of the *BNBD* contains
several articles on Nicaraguan Spanish and the origins of Nicaraguan colloquialisms.

631 **Como pronuncian el español en Nicaragua.** (How Spanish is
pronounced in Nicaragua.)
Herberto Lacayo. Mexico City: Universidad
Iberoamericana, 1962. 33p.
Best guide to Nicaraguan pronunciation. This pamphlet was essentially reprinted
in Lacayo's 'Pronunciación y entonación del español en Nicaragua' (Pronunciation
and intonation of Spanish in Nicaragua), *Boletín Nicaragüense de Bibliografía y
Documentación*, no. 19 (Sept.-Oct. 1977), p. 1-12.

632 **The creole English of Nicaragua's Miskito Coast; its
socio-linguistic history and a comparative history of its
lexicon and syntax.**
John A. Holm. PhD dissertation, University of London,
University College, 1978. 639p. bibliog. (Available from
University Microfilms, Ann Arbor, Michigan, order no.
82-08490.
A thorough study of creole English on Nicaragua's Caribbean coast and the
social and political changes that shaped the language's development. Shows the
relation of the language to African languages, 18th-century English and Black
English of the United States.

Language

633 Diccionario del habla nicaragüense. (Dictionary of spoken Nicaraguan.)
Alfonoso Valle.   Managua: Editorial Unión, 1972. 2nd ed. 322p.

An extensive dictionary of Nicaraguan Spanish, including the many colloquialisms and local definitions found in this country.

634 Diccionario trilingüe Miskito-Español-Inglés. (Trilingual Miskito-Spanish-English dictionary.)
Adolfo I. Vaughan Warman.   Managua: Misión Católica de Waspán, Río Coco, Nicaragua, 1959. 790p.

Containing 12,660 Miskito words, this is the major dictionary for the most important Indian people of eastern Nicaragua. The author died in 1958 and the work was edited and revised by Friar Carlos Repole, a Capuchin missionary among the Miskitos in Río Coco. The dictionary provides definitions for Miskito into Spanish and English, Spanish into Miskito, and English into Miskito. This work eclipses earlier, smaller Miskito dictionaries such as H. Berkenhagen, *English-Miskito-Spanish phrase book* (Bethlehem, Pennsylvania: Moravian Mission in Bluefields, Nicaragua, 1905. 75p.).

635 El habla nicaragüense, estudio morfológico y semántico.
(Spoken Nicaraguan, a morphologic and semantic study.)
Carlos Mantica.   San José: EDUCA (Editorial Universitaria Centroamericana), 1973. 429p. bibliog.

One of the most thorough studies of Nicaraguan Spanish. Includes a dictionary of Nicaraguan Nahualisms, p. 89-273, and a comparative dictionary of Spanish with the pre-Columbian languages of Nicaragua: Uluaska, Tawaska, Miskito, Nahuatl, Mangue, Sumu and Subtiaba, p. 275-423. Most of this important work has been reprinted in the *Revista del Pensamiento Centroamericano*, vol. 37, no. 174 (Jan.-March 1982), p. 11-129. This issue of the *Revista* also published a collection of Nicaraguan linguistic usages in César A. Ramírez Fajardo's 'Lengua madre' (Mother tongue), p. 130-65.

Handbook of Middle American Indians.
See item no. 266.

The Gueguence: a comedy ballet in the Nahuatl-Spanish dialect of Nicaragua.
See item no. 278.

Visual Arts

636 **Art as a source for the study of Central America.**
Vera Blinn Reber. *Latin American Research Review*, vol.
13, no. 1 (1978), p. 39-64. bibliog.
A very useful study showing how art in each of the Central American states
represents a unique and collaborating source for understanding history. Reber's
extensive bibliography especially enhances this work.

637 **Breve bibliografía de la arquitectura en Nicaragua.** (Brief
bibliography of architecture in Nicaragua.)
Boletín Nicaragüense de Bibliografía y Documentación, no.
28 (March-April 1979), p. 124.
Lists ten works from the period 1947-78.

638 **Catálogo - provisional - del patrimonio histórico-artístico de
Nicaragua.** (Provisional catalogue of the historical and
artistic patrimony of Nicaragua.)
Ernesto la Orden Miracle. Managua: Ministerio de
Educación Pública, 1971. 157p bibliog.
Brief descriptions and photographs of principal historic and architectural treasures
of Nicaragua.

639 **De Guatemala a Nicaragua, diario del viaje de un estudiante
de arte.** (From Guatemala to Nicaragua, travel diary of an
art student.)
Manuel González Galván. Mexico City: Instituto de
Investigaciones Estéticas, Universidad Nacional Autónoma
de México, 1968. 148p.+plates.
A study of architectural styles, based on a trip through Central America in 1958.
Richly illustrated with photos and drawings, including seventeen plates on Nicar-

179

agua, from León, Granada and Managua. Additional drawings are found within the text, discussing Nicaraguan architecture on p. 107-36.

640 **A journey to Nicaragua: paintings by Milford Zornes.**
Milford Zornes. Norman, Oklahoma: International Training Program, University of Oklahoma, 1977. 60p.

A collection of watercolours painted in 1974, mostly on the Caribbean coast of Nicaragua. A brief text by the painter accompanies each of these colourful views.

641 **Pintura y escultura en Nicaragua.** (Painting and sculpture in Nicaragua.)
Jorge Eduardo Arellano. Managua: Banco Central de Nicaragua, 1978. 214p. bibliog.

The most complete published guide to Nicaraguan painters and sculptors. It originally appeared in the *Boletín Nicaragüense de Bibliografía y Documentación*, no. 20 (Nov.-Dec. 1977). It is heavily illustrated, and, like all of Arellano's work, includes an extensive bibliography. A revised edition of the sculpture section appeared in no. 34 (March-April 1980) of the same journal, while a revised version of the painting section comprised no. 39 (Jan.-Feb. 1981).

642 **Sandino en la plástica de América.** (Sandino in the art of America.)
Selected by Jorge Eduardo Arellano. León, Nicaragua: Editorial Universitaria, 1981. unpaginated.

Twenty-one reproductions of paintings, sketches, and sculpture which portray Augusto C. Sandino, with notes on the authors, titles, dates and locations of the works.

Area handbook for Nicaragua.
See item no. 2.

Nicaragua, tierra de maravillas. (Nicaragua, land of marvels.)
See item no. 14.

Introducción al arte precolombino de Nicaragua. (Introduction to the pre-Columbian art of Nicaragua.)
See item no. 127.

The art and archaeology of pre-Columbian Middle America: annotated bibliography of works in English.
See item no. 694.

Performing Arts

643 **Apuntes sobre la música en Nicaragua.** (Notes on music in Nicaragua.)
Salvador Cardenal Argüello. *Boletín Nicaragüense de Bibliografía y Documentación*, no. 8 (Nov.-Dec. 1975), p. 23-31.

A rather brief overview of Nicaraguan music, overlooking a great deal. This issue of the *Boletín* is dedicated to Nicaraguan music and contains a few other short articles on the subject.

644 **Romances y corridos nicaragüenses.** (Nicaraguan ballads and songs.)
Ernesto Mejía Sánchez. Mexico City: Imprenta Universitaria, 1946. 122p.

A nice collection of Nicaraguan ballads and songs, including the music, with bibliographical footnotes.

Folklore de Nicaragua. (Nicaraguan folklore.)
See item no. 275.

The Güegüence: a comedy ballet in the Nahuatl-Spanish dialect of Nicaragua.
See item no. 278.

El teatro como creación literaria en Nicaragua: obras e intentos teatrales de autores nicaragüenses. (The theatre as a literary creation in Nicaragua: works and theatrical efforts of Nicaraguan authors.)
See item no. 602.

Sports and Recreation, Leisure Time

645 **Deportes.** (Sports.)
Managua, 1981- . weekly.
A weekly sports newspaper discussing both Nicaraguan and international sports events.

South American Handbook.
See item no. 17.

Fodor's Central America.
See item no. 56.

A cruising guide to the Caribbean and the Bahamas, including the north coast of South America, Central America, and Yucatan.
See item no. 59.

Libraries and Archives

646 **Archivo histórico de la República de Nicaragua, tomo I: 1821-1826.** (Historical archives of the Republic of Nicaragua, volume I: 1821-1826.)
Edited by José Dolores Gámez. Managua: Tipografía Nacional, 1896. 373p.

Covering the first five years of independence, this collection of published documents is especially important owing to the destruction by fire of the Nicaraguan national archives in 1931. Unfortunately, this is the only volume published.

647 **Boletín del Archivo General de la Nación.** (Bulletin of the General Archives of the Nation.)
Managua: Archivo General de la Nación, 1979- . irregular.

Contains useful articles as well as inventories of documents in the AGN. An earlier *Revista del Archivo General de la Nación* (Review of the General Archives of the Nation), vol. 1, no. 1 (Jan.-March 1964), did not survive, but under the capable editorship of the indefatigable Jorge Eduardo Arellano nos. 1-7 of this new venture have been very useful in their publication of historical articles, documentation and information about the national archives. Arellano is no longer directing the national archives nor the *Boletín*, but the publication is scheduled to continue.

648 **Guide to libraries and archives in Central America and the West Indies, Panama, Bermuda, and British Guiana, supplemented with information on private libraries, bookbinding, bookselling, and printing.**
Compiled by Arthur E. Gropp. New Orleans, Louisiana: Middle American Research Institute, Tulane University, 1941. 721p. (Publication no. 10).

Nicaragua is dealt with on p. 511-34. Although much of the information provided is now outdated, some of it is still applicable and is not easily obtained elsewhere.

649 **Research guide to Central America and the Caribbean.**
Edited by Kenneth Grieb. Madison, Wisconsin: University of Wisconsin Press. in press.

A work promoted by the Caribe-Centroamérica Committee of the Conference on Latin American History, the Central American section is edited by R. L. Woodward, Jr., and consists of two parts: 1. a series of articles by distinguished historians of Central America on research needs for the region, including articles on modern Nicaragua by Charles Stansifer and Richard Millett. Articles on the colonial period by Murdo MacLeod and Mario Rodríguez, and topical articles by Neill Macaulay (military history and guerrilla warfare), Miles Wortman (quantitative history), and Kenneth Grieb (international relations), also touch upon Nicaragua; and 2. descriptive articles on archives and libraries containing Central American materials in Central America, Mexico, the United States, Great Britain and Europe. The description of Nicaraguan archives and libraries is written by Charles Stansifer. This volume is intended primarily for historians but will also be useful for other social scientists.

La costa atlántica de Nicaragua. (The Nicaraguan Atlantic coast.)
See item no. 35.

Ciencias políticas y temas afines. (Political science and related topics.)
See item no. 318.

A. C. Sandino y el FSLN. (A. C. Sandino and the FSLN.)
See item no. 335.

Bibliografía económica selectiva de Nicaragua. (Selective economic bibliography of Nicaragua.)
See item no. 454.

Seguros. (Insurance.)
See item no. 478.

Reforma agraria. (Agrarian reform.)
See item no. 539.

Transporte. (Transportation.)
See item no. 560.

Cultural policy in the old and the new Nicaragua.
See item no. 593.

Literatura nicaragüense. (Nicaraguan literature.)
See item no. 595.

A bibliography of books and pamphlets published in Nicaragua, in 1942 or before, according to their date of publication, which are found in some

private libraries of Nicaragua.
See item no. 678.

Boletín Bibliográfico. (Bibliographic bulletin.)
See item no. 680.

Mini-bibliografías (nos. 1-12)/Bibliografías Cortas (nos. 13-).
(Mini-bibliographies/Short bibliographies.)
See item no. 692.

Catálogo colectivo de publicaciones periódicas y fuentes de referencias técnicas: principales bibliotecas de Nicaragua. (Collective catalogue of periodicals and technical reference sources in the principal libraries of Nicaragua.)
See item no. 698.

Selección de la obra *La costa atlántica de Nicaragua*. (Selection from the work *The Atlantic coast of Nicaragua*.)
See item no. 702.

Books and Publishing

650 **Los 'incunables' de Nicaragua: 1829-1859.** (The 'incunabula' of Nicaragua: 1829-1859.)
Jorge Eduardo Arellano. *Boletín Nicaragüense de Bibliografía y Documentación*, no. 24 (July-Aug. 1978), p. 92-103.
Lists eighty-eight of the first publications in Nicaragua following independence, providing an idea of the cultural life of the state in those years.

Guide to libraries and archives in Central America and the West Indies, Panama, Bermuda, and British Guiana, supplemented with information on private libraries, bookbinding, bookselling, and printing.
See item no. 648.

Mass Media

651 **Barricada.** (Barricade.)
Edited by Carlos F. Chamorro B. Managua: Frente
Sandinista de Liberación Nacional, 25 July 1979-. daily.
The official daily of the FSLN, this paper has wide circulation in Nicaragua and
is useful for the 'party line'. Indexes for *Barricada* for 1979 and 1980 were
published by the Biblioteca y Servicios de Información of the Banco Central de
Nicaragua in 1981: *Indice selectivo y temático 'Barricada' 1979* and *'Barricada',
índice temático y onomástico 1980*.

652 **Breves apuntes para la historia del periodismo nicaragüense.**
(Brief notes for the history of Nicaraguan journalism.)
José H. Montalván. León, Nicaragua: Universidad
Nacional de Nicaragua, 1958. 89p.
Reviews both technical and journalistic developments in the Nicaraguan press
since independence, with emphasis on describing contributions by individual jour-
nalists.

653 **Covering the Sandinistas, the foregone conclusions of the
fourth estate.**
Shirley Christian. *Washington Journalism Review*, vol. 4,
no. 2 (March 1982), p. 32-38.
Reviews US press coverage of the Sandinista revolution against Somoza. Highly
critical of the failure of the US press to cover the Soviet and Cuban role in the
revolution and of its tendency to present biased views of the Nicaraguan news.
Christian says that US reporters ignored the rise of Tomás Borge and Marxist
power in the Sandinista organization, charging that the 'American media, like
most of the United States, went on a guilt trip in Nicaragua'.

654 **Editoriales de** *La Prensa.* (Editorials from *La Prensa.*)
Enrique Guzmán Selva, edited by Franco
Cerutti. Managua: Fondo de Promoción Cultural, Banco de
América, 1977. 459p. bibliog. (Colección Cultural, Serie
Literaria, no. 8).

Guzmán Selva, a leading Liberal of 19th-century Nicaragua, founded *La Prensa*
in 1878. These editorials reveal much of Nicaraguan political and social thought
during this period, especially from the point of view of the Liberal Party, out of
power then. Other works by Guzmán, also edited by Cerutti and published by the
Banco de América's Fondo de Promoción Cultural, included *Escritos biográficos
de Enrique Guzmán* (Biographical writings of Enrique Guzmán) (1976), *Las
gacetillas, 1878-1894* (The pamphlets, 1878-1894) (1975), and *Las pequeñeces
cuiscomeñas de Antón Colorado* (The Cuiscomeñan fragments of Antón Colorado) (1974), a series of newspaper columns written under the pseudonym Antón
Colorado and consisting mostly of political satire aimed at the Zelaya administration.

655 **La Gaceta, Diario Oficial.** (The gazette, official daily.)
Managua: Nicaraguan government, 1860- . daily.

The official publication of the Nicaraguan government, where laws, decrees, official proclamations, etc. are published. An *Indice cronológico y temático* of *La
Gaceta* has been published for the period July 1979-Dec. 1980 (Managua:
Biblioteca, Banco Central de Nicaragua, 1981. 88p). This is an especially important period, since it records the substantial revolutionary legislation of the Sandinista government.

656 **Letter from Nicaragua; the junta and the press: a family
affair.**
J. E. Maslow. *Columbia Journalism Review,* vol. 19
(March-April 1981), p. 46-77.

An informative description of the Nicaraguan press, emphasizing the domination
by the Chamorro family of all three of Nicaragua's daily newspapers. Even
though serious ideological differences separate the Chamorros, they remain,
according to this article, socially cohesive.

657 **Nicarauac.** (Nicarauac.)
Managua: Ministerio de Cultura, 1980- . bimonthly.

A literary publication, featuring works by both Nicaraguan and other Latin
American writers and interviews with literary figures. Emphasizes Nicaraguan
revolution.

658 **Novedades.** (News.)
Managua, 1937-79. daily.

The official organ of the Somoza Partido Liberal Nacional (National Liberal
Party), published daily until Somoza's overthrow in 1979. It was second only to
La Prensa in circulation during the Somoza years, and was replaced by the
Sandinista *Barricada* following the 1979 revolution.

659 **El Nuevo Diario.** (The new daily.)
Directed by Xavier Chamorro C. Managua, 1980- . daily.
A morning daily, with a circulation of about 40,000. It developed as an offshoot of *La Prensa*, among workers supporting the Sandinistas. It is vehemently pro-government and anti-American, even more than *Barricada* (q.v.). It is especially favourable to the interests of the minister of the interior, Tomás Borge.

660 **Patria Libre.** (Free fatherland.)
Managua: Ministerio del Interior, 1980- . monthly.
A news and features illustrated magazine supporting the position of the Nicaraguan government. Strongly hostile toward the United States.

661 **El periodismo en Centroamérica.** (Journalism in Central America.)
Alfonso Orantes. *Cultura, Revista del Ministerio de Educación de El Salvador*, vol. 38 (Oct.-Dec. 1965 [1966]), p. 11-25.
A useful survey of major newspapers in Honduras, Nicaragua and Costa Rica in the mid-60s.

662 **La Prensa.** (The press.)
Directed by Pablo Antonio Cuadra, edited by Pedro Joaquín Chamorro, Jr. Managua, 1926- . daily.
La Prensa, an independent evening daily, has by far the largest circulation of any Nicaraguan newspaper, and generally reflects the views of the Conservative Party. It was the principal opposition press to the Somoza dynasty and it is now the focus of press opposition to the Sandinistas. Often censored, it has resumed a practice formerly used under the Somozas, which is to distribute clandestinely the censored portions.

663 **Publicaciones periódicas de Granada.** (Periodical publications of Granada.)
Jimmy Aviles. *Boletín Nicaragüense de Bibliografía y Documentación*, no. 8 (Nov.-Dec. 1975), p. 14-18.
Lists thirty periodicals published in Granada, Nicaragua, 1907-75.

664 **Soberanía.** (Sovereignty.)
Edited by Fredy Balzán. Managua: Tribunal Antimperialista Centroamericano y del Caribe, 1982- . monthly.
A monthly, published in English and Spanish, containing vitriolic anti-American articles. Edited by Fredy Balzán, with an editorial board that includes leftist intellectuals from Nicaragua, the other Central American states, Cuba and elsewhere.

Envio. (Mailing.)
See item no. 20.

Mass Media

Religión, iglesia, cristianismo y revolución en el diario *Barricada*.
(Religion, Church, Christianity and revolution in the daily *Barricada*.)
See item no. 291.

La Prensa Literaria. (The literary press.)
See item no. 600.

Deportes. (Sports.)
See item no. 645.

Professional Periodicals and Cultural Reviews

665 Cuadernos Universitarios. (University notebooks.)
León, Nicaragua: Universidad Nacional, 1954- . somewhat
irregular.

Although published somewhat irregularly, this is a major publication of Nicaraguan letters, history, social sciences, etc. Essentially, it is the principal publishing
outlet for faculty members at the National University of Nicaragua.

666 Encuentro, Revista de la Universidad Centroamericana.
(Encounter, review of the Central American University.)
Managua, 1968-79. somewhat irregular.

Encuentro was an important journal of literature, philosophy, law and sociology,
emanating from the Universidad Centroamericana and reflecting the growing
intellectual ferment there. It was first edited, in 1968, by Julio Ycaza Tigerino,
then by Romano García until 1972, and later by Horacio Peña. An *Indice
analítico de la revista 'Encuentro', años 1968-1978* was published by the
Biblioteca of the Banco Central de Nicaragua in 1980 (159p.).

667 Estudios Sociales Centroamericanos. (Central American
social studies.)
San José: Consejo Superior Universitario de Centroamérica,
1971- . quarterly.

A major academic journal, containing articles on a broad range of social science
topics by both Central American and foreign academics.

Professional Periodicals and Cultural Reviews

668 **A guide to current Latin American periodicals: humanities and social sciences.**
Irene Zimmerman. Gainesville, Florida: Kallman Publishing, 1961. 357p.

The brief section on Nicaragua, p. 163-65, reveals the paucity of Nicaraguan periodical publishing, although Zimmerman has overlooked a few.

669 **Revista del Pensamiento Centroamericano.** (Journal of Central American thought.)
Edited by Xavier Zavala Cuadra. Managua: Centro de Investigaciones y Actividades Culturales, 1960- . quarterly (title varies).

The most important publication in Nicaragua in the past quarter-century for the social sciences and humanities. Carries a wide variety of scholarly articles, literary pieces, poetry and photographs of Nicaraguan art. Also reprints important older publications now out of print. The journal began as a monthly in 1960 under Joaquín Zavala Urtecho with strong ties to the Nicaraguan Conservative Party and the élite of Granada. It published under the title *Revista Conservadora* (Conservative review) (nos. 1-45) until 1965 when it became the *Revista Conservadora del Pensamiento Centroamericano* (Conservative journal of Central American thought) (nos. 46-140). In 1972 the title was shortened to its present name, reflecting a desire to appeal to a wider audience and to shed its close ties with the Conservative Party. Publication was interrupted by the disastrous earthquake of that year, but resumed under the direction of Zavala's son, Xavier Zavala Cuadra, as a quarterly with no. 146 in 1975. The journal has continued to publish, although sometimes irregularly, through the difficult civil war and Sandinista revolution. It is a mine of serious study and commentary on Nicaraguan history and only a few of its articles can be noted in this bibliography. An index for the first 161 numbers appeared in vol. 34, nos. 162-65 (1979), prepared by Lily Soto. A separate index, *Indice temático de la Revista del Pensamiento Centroamericano, no. 1, agosto 1960-no. 161, diciembre 1978* (Topical index to the Journal of Central American Thought, no. 1, Aug. 1960-no. 161, Dec. 1978), prepared by Antonio Acevedo Espinosa, was published in 1980 by the Biblioteca y Servicios de Información of the Banco Central de Nicaragua (110p.).

670 **Revista Feminina Ilustrada.** (Illustrated feminist journal.)
Edited by Josefa T. de Aguerri. Managua: Tipografía Pérez, 1918-193?. monthly.

Contains articles and stories of interest to women, including many on women's rights. Edited by the female activist Nicaraguan intellectual Josefa T. de Aguerri, the *Revista* is one of the earliest Latin American feminist publications. Copies are rare and a complete set may not exist. See also *Enciclopedia nicaragüense* (q.v.).

El Pez y la Serpiente.
See item no. 598.

La Prensa Literaria. (The literary press.)
See item no. 600.

Catálogo colectivo de publicaciones periódicas y fuentes de referencias técnicas: principales bibliotecas de Nicaragua. (Collective catalogue of periodicals and technical reference sources in the principal libraries of Nicaragua.)
See item no. 698.

Encyclopaedias and Directories

671 **Business directory of Nicaragua.**
Guillermo Lang, Rudolph Mayorga Rivas.   New York: Stag
Printers and Stationers, 1957-58. 238p.
Issued by the consul-general of Nicaragua in New York, Guillermo Lang, this is
a most useful guide. Unfortunately, a more recent guide has not appeared. This
one now has more historical than current value.

672 **Diccionario de siglas e inicialismos nicaragüenses.**
(Dictionary of Nicaraguan acronyms and initial
abbreviations.)
Orlando Gómez.   Managua: Banco Central de Nicaragua,
1980. 68p. bibliog.
An extensive list of nearly a thousand acronyms and initials used in Nicaragua
for government agencies, business and financial institutions, private and public
associations, foundations, educational and cultural institutions, etc. A very handy
reference work.

673 **Directorio comercial y de servicios, Departamento de
Managua, Nicaragua, 69-70.** (Commercial and service
directory, Department of Managua, Nicaragua, 69-70.)
Comité Nacional de Ferias.   Managua: Editora Mundial,
1970. 222p.
Alphabetical listings, with addresses and telephone numbers, of commercial and
service establishments in the Department of Managua. More recent commercial
directories may have been published, but were not located by the compiler.

674 **Enciclopedia nicaragüense: cultura literaria y científica.**
(Nicaraguan encyclopaedia: scientific and literary culture.)
Edited by Josefa T. de Aguerri. Managua: Imprenta
Nacional, vol. 2, 1932. 422p.

This remarkable volume was issued as a supplement to the *Revista Feminina Ilustrada* (q.v.). It contains a variety of articles on Nicaraguan culture, life, etc.

Nuevo diccionario de jurisprudencia nicaragüense. (New dictionary of
Nicaraguan jurisprudence.)
See item no. 441.

Directorio Industrial 1977. (Industrial directory 1977.)
See item no. 509.

Bibliographies

General

675 **Bibliografía de las publicaciones del Banco Central.**
(Bibliography of the publications of the Central Bank.)
René Rodríguez M., Antonio Acevedo E. Managua:
Biblioteca y Servicios de Información, Banco Central de
Nicaragua, Aug.-Sept. 1978. 25p. (Mini-bibliografía no. 8).
The Banco Central de Nicaragua is one of the leading publishers in Nicaragua. It
publishes not only a wide range of series on finance and the economy, but also
items of cultural and practical use ranging from science and technology through
the social sciences and humanities. This compilation, listing alphabetically by
titles all of the publications of the Banco Central since its inception in 1961,
constitutes a major bibliography of Nicaraguan publishing during the past
quarter-century. It includes works published by the bank for other government
agencies or ministries.

676 **Bibliografía general de Nicaragua, 1674-1972.** (General
bibliography of Nicaragua, 1674-1972.)
Jorge Eduardo Arellano, Noël Lacayo Barreto. Managua:
El Latinoamericano, 1972. 3 vols. (typescript). Now being
published in *Cuadernos de Bibliografía Nicaragüense.*
This is a very substantial, but not completely comprehensive, bibliography of
books published in and about Nicaragua. The original typescript is in the
Biblioteca of the Banco Central de Nicaragua, but a few other copies exist.
According to George Elmendorf, of Libros Latinos, UNESCO published a *Bibliografía general nicaragüense* in this year (1972), containing 3,975 entries, which
appears to be the same work, but I have been unable to locate a copy for
annotation. More importantly, as indicated above, it is now being published in the
Cuadernos de Bibliografía Nicaragüense, with no. 1 (Jan.-June 1981) including
the portion covering the period 1674-1900. The work includes an introductory
essay on 'Bibliografía en Nicaragua' (Bibliography in Nicaragua) and 'La bibliografía nicaragüense en el extranjero' (Nicaraguan bibliography abroad). The
entries are listed alphabetically within the following categories: colonial authors,

general bibliography (comprising by far the majority of the three volumes - most of vol. 2 and half of vol. 3), theses, and works on Nicaragua by foreign authors published abroad. The latter section overlooks a very large quantity of foreign works on Nicaragua, thus the principal utility of this work is the section on native authors. The bibliography does not include periodical articles nor official government publications. It is not annotated.

677 **Bibliographic Guide to Latin American Studies.**
Boston, Massachusetts: G. K. Hall, 1978- . annual. 3 vols.
This major bibliographic aid lists publications catalogued during the past year by the Latin American Collection of the University of Texas at Austin, supplemented by Latin American publications catalogued by the Library of Congress. Books as well as non-book materials are included, although in general serial publications are not included.

678 **A bibliography of books and pamphlets published in Nicaragua, in 1942 or before, according to their date of publication, which are found in some private libraries of Nicaragua.**
Managua: Editorial Neuvos Horizontes, 1945. 157p.
(Bibliographical Series of the American Library, no. 4).
For works published before 1943 this is a very important bibliography, the first attempt at a comprehensive Nicaraguan bibliography. Other publications in this series (nos. 1-3 and 5-9) published by the American Library of Nicaragua, 1944-48, list works published in Nicaragua in each year 1944-47.

679 **A bibliography of Latin American bibliographies.**
Compiled by Arthur E. Gropp. Metuchen, New Jersey: Scarecrow Press, for Pan American Union, 1968. 515p.
This edition updates through 1964 the first edition (1942) prepared by G. K. Jones and J. A. Granier. About 4,000 additional references have been added to the 1942 edition. The bibliography is arranged by seventy subject divisions, with geographical country subdivisions.

680 **Boletín Bibliográfico.** (Bibliographic bulletin.)
Managua: Biblioteca y Servicios de Información, Banco Central de Nicaragua, 1977- . somewhat irregular.
An important guide to current Nicaraguan bibliography, with individual issues dedicated to specific bibliographical topics or problems. Each issue lists the works recently processed in the Banco Central library. This publication succeeds a *Boletín de Adquisiciones* (Acquisitions bulletin). Eighteen issues had been published through June 1982.

681 **Boletín Nicaragüense de Bibliografía y Documentación.**
(Nicaraguan bulletin of bibliography and documentation.)
Biblioteca, Banco Central de Nicaragua. Managua: Banco Central de Nicaragua, 1974- . bimonthly.
A very competent journal containing a great many articles on a wide spectrum of Nicaraguan bibliographical topics. Issue no. 21 (Jan.-Feb. 1978), prepared by

Antonio Acevedo Espinoza, contains an index for the first twenty issues (1974-78), as well as a brief history of this important bibliographic tool. Only the more general of these bibliographical articles have been listed separately in this volume, so the serious researcher should consult the *BNBD*. Forty-six issues had been published before the end of 1982.

682 **A Central American bibliography of works available at the University of Kansas.**
Herman D. Luján. Lawrence, Kansas: Program Coordination Office, Ford Cooperative Research Grant (University of Kansas), 1970. 157p.

The University of Kansas Library holds one of the better collections of Nicaraguan materials in the world.

683 **Cuadernos de Bibliografía Nicaragüense.** (Nicaraguan bibliography notebooks.)
Edited by Jorge Eduardo Arellano. Managua: Dirección General de Bibliotecas y Archivos, Ministerio de Cultura, 1981- .

The first issue of yet another bibliographic labour by Jorge Eduardo Arellano was entirely dedicated to publication of Arellano's *Bibliografía general de Nicaragua* (q.v.). Subsequent issues will complete publication of that work and publish other bibliographies.

684 **Current national bibliographies of Latin America; a state of the art.**
Irene Zimmerman. Gainesville, Florida: University of Florida Center for Latin American Studies, 1971. 139p.

Emphasizes the scarcity of bibliographies of Nicaragua.

685 **Guía de recursos básicos contemporáneos para estudios de desarrollo en Nicaragua.** (Guide to basic contemporary resources for the study of Nicaraguan development.)
Managua: Instituto Geográfico Nacional de Nicaragua, with the Instituto Panamericano de Geografía e Historia, 1977. 86p. maps. bibliog.

A very useful guide to existing maps and published works dealing with Nicaraguan resources and development in the broadest sense. Part 1 describes maps and part 2 contains a series of useful bibliographies on Nicaraguan cartography, agriculture and livestock, meteorology, electric energy, communications, transportation, health, education, social studies, legal studies, economics and statistics, urban affairs, offical reports, geography and history, and seismic research. The earlier OAS study, *Annotated index of aerial photographic coverage and mapping of topography and natural resources* (Washington, DC: Pan American Union, 1965), has an index of geological maps of Nicaragua.

686 **A guide for the study of culture in Central America (humanities and social sciences).**
Mario Rodríguez, Vincent C. Peloso. Washington, DC: Pan American Union, 1968. 95p. (Basic Bibliographies, no. 5).
A carefully selected list of basic works on Central America, now somewhat dated.

687 **Handbook of Latin American Studies.**
Cambridge, Massachusetts: Harvard University Press, 1935-51; Gainesville, Florida: University of Florida Press, 1952- . annual.
The most important single source for current bibliography in Latin American studies, the *Handbook* is issued annually (since 1965 with alternate years devoted respectively to the humanities and the social sciences). Annotated entries are organized by regions within disciplines. Author and subject indexes allow the researcher to quickly locate entries dealing with Nicaragua. The *Handbook* is not completely comprehensive, but it attempts to include significant books and articles published throughout the world. Each section is edited by a leading scholar in the subject and area for which he is responsible.

688 **Indice bibliográfico de Costa Rica.** (Bibliographic index of Costa Rica.)
Luis Dobles Segreda. San José: Lehmann, 1927-68. 11 vols.
This massive bibliographical series contains a great many references to Nicaraguan works and Central American works in general. No comparable work exists for Nicaragua, although the Sandinista government has commissioned George Elmendorf to compile a union catalogue of publications in and about Nicaragua. Dobles Segreda's compendium, although dated, is still a magnificent guide to the bibliography on many topics, and most of the entries are annotated. Section 1: agriculture and veterinary science; 2: physical and natural sciences; 3: philosophy and grammar; 4: geography and geology; 5: education; 6: philosophy and religion; 7: hygiene and medicine; 8: mathematics and engineering; 9: history; 10: military; 11: police and law; 12: literature: 13: psychology; 14: sociology and demography; 15: theatre; 16: poetry. A final volume contains an author index.

689 **Inter-American Review of Bibliography.**
Washington, DC: Organization of American States, 1951- . quarterly.
A quarterly, with articles on Latin American bibliography and letters, and an extensive book review section.

690 **Latin America and the Caribbean, bibliographical guide to works in English.**
S. A. Bayitch. Coral Gables, Florida: University of Miami Press, 1967. 943p.
An extensive bibliography on the region, with topical listings. Nicaragua is covered on p. 704-18.

691 **A list of books, magazine articles and maps relating to**
Central America, including the republics of Costa Rica,
Guatemala, Honduras, Nicaragua and Salvador, 1800-1900.
P. Lee Phillips, International Bureau of the American
Republics. Washington, DC: US Government Printing
Office, 1902. 109p.
Excellent bibliography for 19th-century materials.

692 **Mini-bibliografías (nos. 1-12)/Bibliografías Cortas (nos. 13-).**
(Mini-bibliographies/Short bibliographies.)
Banco Central de Nicaragua, Biblioteca y Servicios de
Información, René Rodríguez Masís. Managua: Banco
Central, 1977- .
A very useful ongoing series, each volume listing the works on a particular
subject, including periodical articles, to be found in the Banco Central library.
Topics so far covered are: 1. administration; 2. inflation; 3. industry; 4. Harvard
Business Administration Library; 5. budgets; 6. employment and unemployment;
7. dictionaries, glossaries, etc. 8. Banco Central publications; 9. abstracts; 10.
architecture and construction; 11. education and teaching; 12. political science;
13. insurance; 14. Sandino and the FSLN; 15. agrarian reform; 16. Sandino and
Sandinism; 17. bank nationalization; 18. Caribbean coast; 19. co-operativism and
agricultural credit; 20. Grijalba collection on Marxism and revolution; 21. public
and business administration; 22. transport; 23. economy; 24. communications; 25.
socialism; 26. housing; 27. not yet published; 28. literature. Those items dealing
solely with Nicaragua are listed in their respective sections in this bibliography.
The series succeeds the earlier *Boletín Informativo de Publicaciones Periódicas.*

Central America, a nation divided.
See item no. 139.

Handbook of Middle American Indians.
See item no. 266.

Topical

693 **American dissertations on foreign education: a bibliography**
with abstracts. Volume X, Central America, West Indies,
Caribbean and Latin America, general.
Edited by Franklin D. Parker, Betty June Parker. Troy,
New York: Whitson Publishing, 1979. 620p.
Abstracts of 220 doctoral dissertations on all aspects of education in the region,
which includes Mexico. The bibliography is organized alphabetically by author,
with a subject and geographical index appended. Thirteen of the dissertations deal
specifically with Nicaragua.

694 **The art and archaeology of pre-Columbian Middle America: annotated bibliography of works in English.**
Aubyn Kendall. Boston: G. K. Hall, 1977. 324p.
Containing 2,147 annotated entries, this compilation represents one of the most important bibliographical tools on pre-Columbian Middle America. The bibliography is organized alphabetically by authors, including both books and periodical articles. An ample subject index reveals only nineteen items specifically on Nicaragua.

695 **Autores nicaragüenses del sigo XX.** (20th-century Nicaraguan authors.)
Jorge Eduardo Arellano. *Boletín Nicaragüense de Bibliografía y Documentación*, no. 13 (Sept.-Oct. 1976), p. 1-72.
Lists 1,500 works by 273 20th-century Nicaraguan authors.

696 **A bio-bibliography of Franciscan authors in colonial Central America.**
Eleanor B. Adams. Washington, DC: Academy of American Franciscan History, 1953. 118p.
An important study of colonial writing in Central America, with several references to Nicaraguans.

697 **Boletín de Referencias, Centro de Documentación.** (Reference Bulletin, Documentation Centre.)
Managua: Instituto de Estudio del Sandinismo, 1981- . bimonthly.
A bimonthly publication of the new Institute of Sandinista Studies, directed by Jorge Eduardo Arellano. Each issue, beginning in Sept.-Oct. 1981, publishes detailed bibliographies based on research on specific journals, newspapers, etc., on topics dealing with Sandino, the revolution, and modern Nicaraguan history in general. Some important documents and out-of-print publications are also published in this series.

698 **Catálogo colectivo de publicaciones periódicas y fuentes de referencias técnicas: principales bibliotecas de Nicaragua.** (Collective catalogue of periodicals and technical reference sources in the principal libraries of Nicaragua.)
Centro Nicaragüense de Información Tecnológica, Departamento de Investigaciones Tecnológicas, División Industrial. Managua: Banco Central de Nicaragua, 1976. 125p. (Bibliografía y Documentación, no. 1).
A bibliography of technical journals and reference works in eight government and university libraries in Nicaragua.

699 **Celebrating the demise of Somocismo, fifty recent Spanish sources on the Nicaraguan revolution.**
John A. Booth. *Latin American Research Review*, vol. 17, no. 1 (1982), p. 173-89. bibliog.
A bibliographical essay discussing fifty recent titles published in Spanish on the Nicaraguan revolution. Not entirely comprehensive, but very useful.

700 **The memorias of the republics of Central America and of the Antilles.**
James B. Childs. Washington, DC: US Government Printing Office, 1932. 170p.
A guide to government publications, indicating which are in the Library of Congress in Washington. Useful especially for late 19th- and early 20th-century study.

701 **Middle American anthropology: directory, bibliography and guide to the UCLA library collections.**
Eileen A. McGlynn. Los Angeles: University of California, Los Angeles, Latin American Center and University Library, 1975. 131p. map.
A reference guide to the library of the University of California, Los Angeles, but also useful as a guide to Mesoamerica in general.

702 **Selección de la obra *La costa atlántica de Nicaragua.***
(Selection from the work *The Atlantic coast of Nicaragua.*)
René Rodríguez Masís. *Boletín Nicaragüense de Bibliografía y Documentación*, no. 26 (Nov.-Dec. 1978), p. 112-244.
Lists 163 articles on Nicaragua's Caribbean coastal region, mostly from *La Prensa* and *Novedades*. Arranged by subject. See also *La costa atlántica de Nicaragua* (q.v.).

703 **A tentative bibliography of the belles-lettres of the republics of Central America.**
Henry Grattan Doyle. Cambridge, Massachusetts: Harvard University Press, 1935. 136p.
Valuable for 19th- and early 20th-century works. Unfortunately there is not a more current work of this type.

La costa atlántica de Nicaragua. (The Nicaraguan Atlantic coast.)
See item no. 35.

Central America early maps up to 1860.
See item no. 48.

Mesoamerican archaeology, a guide to the literature and other information sources.
See item no. 129.

Bibliographies. Topical

The historiography of Central America since 1830.
See item no. 141.

Bibliografía historiográfica de Nicaragua. (Historiographical bibliography of Nicaragua.)
See item no. 148.

Anthropological bibliography of aboriginal Nicaragua.
See item no. 257.

El folklore en la literatura de Centro América. (Folklore in Central American literature.)
See item no. 276.

Religión, iglesia, cristianismo y revolución en el diario *Barricada*.
(Religion, Church, Christianity and revolution in the daily *Barricada*.)
See item no. 291.

A. C. Sandino y el FSLN. (A. C. Sandino and the FSLN.)
See item no. 335.

The rise and fall of the Central American Common Market.
See item no. 390.

A bibliography of United States-Latin American relations since 1810; a selected list of eleven thousand published references.
See item no. 397.

Bibliografía económica selectiva de Nicaragua. (Selective economic bibliography of Nicaragua.)
See item no. 454.

Seguros. (Insurance.)
See item no. 478.

La industria en Nicaragua. (Industry in Nicaragua.)
See item no. 511.

Mahogany of tropical America: its ecology and management.
See item no. 515.

Reforma agraria. (Agrarian reform.)
See item no. 539.

List of books and articles in periodicals relating to interoceanic canal and railway routes: Nicaragua; Panama; Darien and the Valley of Atrato; Tehuantepec and Honduras; Suez Canal.
See item no. 552.

Transporte. (Transportation.)
See item no. 560.

Educación y didáctica. (Education and teaching.)
See item no. 571.

Nonformal education in Latin America, an annotated bibliography.
See item no. 583.

Diccionario de la literatura latinoamericana: América Central. (Dictionary of Latin American literature: Central America.)
See item no. 594.

Literatura nicaragüense. (Nicaraguan literature.)
See item no. 595.

A bibliography of Rubén Darío, 1867-1916.
See item no. 605.

Repertorio bibliográfico del mundo de Rubén Darío. (Bibliographical repertoire of the world of Rubén Darío.)
See item no. 612.

[Rubén Darío].
See item no. 613.

Rubén Darío: a critical bibliography.
See item no. 615.

An annotated bibliography of and about Ernesto Cardenal.
See item no. 619.

Bibliografía fundamental del español en Nicaragua. (Basic bibliography of Nicaraguan Spanish.)
See item no. 630.

Breve bibliografía de la arquitectura en Nicaragua. (Brief bibliography of architecture in Nicaragua.)
See item no. 637.

Publicaciones periódicas de Granada. (Periodical publications of Granada.)
See item no. 663.

A guide to current Latin American periodicals: humanities and social sciences.
See item no. 668.

Index

The index is a single alphabetical sequence of authors (personal and corporate), titles of publications and subjects. Index entries refer both to the main items and to other works mentioned in the notes to each item. Title entries are in italics. Numeration refers to the items as numbered.

209

221

229

Lainez, F. 45
Laird, L. K. 430, 542
Lake Nicaragua
  19th-century accounts 71
  fish conservation 567
Lakes 560
  fish 111-112
Lalley, J. M. 413
Lamb, F. B. 515
*Land divided: a history of the Panama
  Canal and other isthmian
  projects* 551
Land ownership 274, 298, 520, 524,
  531, 563
  law 444, 524
  maps 53
  reform 16, 538
  statistics 543
Land tenure in Nicaragua 531
Land use 41, 519, 524, 529
  statistics 528
Landívar, R. 149
Lang, G. 671
Langan, J. 314
Langley, L. D. 420
Language 266, 275, 550, 692
  ancient 124
  bibliographies 688
  colloquialisms 630, 633
  creole English 632
  Miskito-Spanish-English
    dictionary 634
  Nahuatl 124, 278
  pre-Columbian 635
  Spanish 278, 635
  Spanish, bibliographies 630
  Spanish, dictionaries 633
  Spanish, pronunciation 631
Lanuza Matamoros, A. 189
Lappe, Frances Moore 15, 545
Larreynaga, M. 149
*Last night of General August C.
  Sandino* 221
Latin America 22-24
*Latin America and the Caribbean,
  bibliographical guide to works in
  English* 690
Latin America Economic Report 24
Latin America Political Report 24
*Latin America Regional Reports:
  Caribbean* 24
Latin America Weekly Report 24
Latin American Mission 282

Latin American Perspectives 10
Latin American Research Review 6
Laviana, Gaspar García
  biography 239
Law 439, 441-444
  16th century 166
  agricultural 444, 520, 523
  bibliographies 685, 688
  commercial 442, 444, 494, 497, 499,
    504
  copyright 444
  court cases 440
  courts 435-436
  education 573
  family 444
  La Gaceta 655
  human rights 313
  Indians 269
  labour 444, 504, 561, 564-565
  land 16, 524
  Liberal Reform 437
  mining 444
  municipal 445
  periodicals 435-436, 666
  post-revolutionary 655
  social 442, 444
  Statute of Rights 357
  taxation 444, 481
  transport 547
Lawyers 14
*La legislación laboral de Nicaragua y
  los convenios de OIT* 565
Lejarza, Emilio Alvarez 438
Lemus, Eduardo Cote 618
LeoGrande, W. M. 361
León 37
  19th-century accounts 71
  geography 36-37
  history 36-37
  illustrations 639
  León Viejo, history 170
  maps 51
  university 576
León-Portilla, M. 290
Lethander, R. W. O. 462
Levy, P. 32
Liberal Party 137
  19th century 196, 200, 209
  Novedades newspaper 658
  La Prensa editorials 654
  Zelaya period 187, 198, 207

232

M

234

241

242

V

W

Map of Nicaragua

This map shows the more important towns and other features.

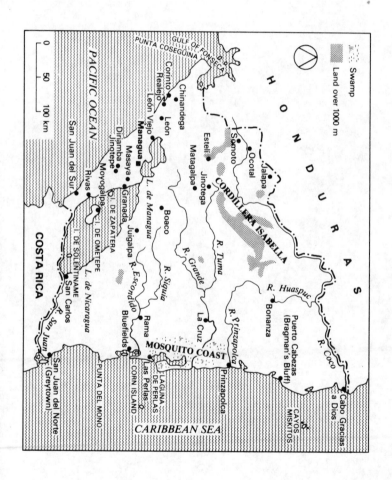